*U*nfolding Covenant History

An Exposition of the Old Testament

a series by Homer C. Hoeksema and David J. Engelsma

WRITTEN BY HOMER C. HOEKSEMA

Volume 1: From Creation to the Flood

Volume 2: From the Flood to Isaac

Volume 3: From Jacob to the Exodus

Volume 4: Through the Wilderness into Canaan

WRITTEN BY DAVID J. ENGELSMA

Volume 5: Judges and Ruth

*U*nfolding Covenant History

An Exposition of the Old Testament

Volume 6
FROM SAMUEL TO SOLOMON

written by David J. Engelsma

series editor Mark H. Hoeksema

REFORMED
FREE PUBLISHING
ASSOCIATION
Jenison, Michigan

Reformed Free Publishing Association
1894 Georgetown Center Drive
Jenison MI 49428
616-457-5970
www.rfpa.org
mail@rfpa.org

Cover design by Jeff Steenholdt
Interior design by Katherine Lloyd/theDESKonline.com

ISBN: 978-1-944555-63-4 (hardcover)
ISBN: 978-1-9444555-64-1 (ebook)
LCCN: 00133970

To the special friends—
they know who they are

And the Lord came, and stood, and called as
at other times, Samuel, Samuel.
Then Samuel answered, Speak; for thy servant heareth.

I SAMUEL 3:10

And Samuel grew, and the Lord was with him,
and did let none of his words fall to the ground.
And all Israel from Dan even to Beersheba knew that
Samuel was established to be a prophet of the Lord.

I SAMUEL 3:19–20

And he [Kish] had a son, whose name was Saul,
a choice young man, and a goodly:
and there was not among the children of Israel
a goodlier person than he:
from his shoulders and upward he was higher
than any of the people.

I SAMUEL 9:2

And Samuel said, Hath the Lord as great delight
in burnt offerings and sacrifices,
as in obeying the voice of the Lord?
Behold, to obey is better than sacrifice,
and to hearken than the fat of rams.

I SAMUEL 15:22

Then Saul said to David, Blessed be thou, my son David:
thou shalt both do great things, and also shalt still prevail.
So David went on his way, and Saul returned to his place.

1 SAMUEL 26:25

And when he [God] had removed him [Saul],
he raised up unto them David to be their king; to whom
also he gave their testimony, and said,
I have found David the son of Jesse,
a man after mine own heart,
which shall fulfil all my will. Of this man's seed hath
God according to his promise raised unto Israel a Saviour, Jesus.

ACTS 13:22–23

And Solomon's wisdom excelled the wisdom of
all the children of the east country, and all the wisdom of Egypt.
For he was wiser than all men…
and his fame was in all nations round about.
And there came of all people to hear the wisdom of Solomon,
from all kings of the earth, which had heard of his wisdom.

1 KINGS 4:30–31, 34

Contents

Editor's Preface

Following a hiatus of fifteen years since the publication of volume 5, the Reformed Free Publishing Association is pleased to present volume 6 of *Unfolding Covenant History.*

As in volume 5, the author is Professor David J. Engelsma, professor emeritus of Dogmatics and Old Testament at the Theological Seminary of the Protestant Reformed Churches. An ordained minister, he holds a B.A. degree from Calvin College (1960), a B.D. from the Theological Seminary of the Protestant Reformed Churches (1963), and a Th.M. from Calvin Seminary (1994). He is the author of numerous books and was former editor of the *Standard Bearer* magazine.

It will be beneficial to remind the reader of the general structure of Old Testament history, which is divided into seven major eras or epochs, as explained in the introduction to this series. Within each epoch rages the battle of the antithesis. Thus there are variations—cycles and sub-cycles—within each epoch.

This is true of the fifth main period of Old Testament history: from the judges through Saul to the victory of the seed of the woman in David and Solomon, the high point of the Old Testament.

Because this major era is so large, it has been treated in two volumes: *Judges and Ruth* in volume 5, and now in volume 6, *From Samuel to Solomon.*

Although Prof. Engelsma by no means treats every detail of the prophet and the three kings, he draws from the history its salient points, always from the viewpoint of the covenant.

Blessed be those who read and understand!

Mark H. Hoeksema

Series Editor

Introduction to Volume 6

*O*ld Testament history is not merely a collection of more or less interesting and more or less important events concerning Israel. It is not even merely a collection of events the record of which is inspired by God the Holy Ghost. Neither is it only a remembrance of events, some or all of which are instruction for the New Testament believers.

It is certainly all the above. What needs emphasis and defense in our day is that the history is inspired by God, as 2 Peter 1:20–21 affirms:

20. Knowing this first, that no prophecy of the scripture is of any private interpretation.
21. For the prophecy came not in old time by the will of man: but holy men of God spake as they were moved by the Holy Ghost.

Much of Old Testament scholarship is unbelieving concerning the inspiration of especially this section of the Bible. As a result, almost nothing is regarded as historical. All is redaction, the borrowing of religion from the heathen, and fiction. Jehovah himself is the creation of Israelite imagination. All of the Old Testament is of private interpretation, because the prophecy came by the will of man. Therefore, almost nothing is authoritatively instructive for the New Testament believer.

But Old Testament history is the inspired record of events that really took place in the special providence of God. Therefore, it is instructive for the church, instructive especially for the right knowledge of God, whose only relation to the deities of the heathen is that of hatred of these false gods and whose relation to the heathen and their worship is that of wrath. However, Old Testament history is instructive for the church as the inspired record of these events *with their meaning*. And this meaning is the coming of the Messiah, who is Jesus. Unifying all the events was the divine promise of the seed of Abraham. This seed is Christ (Gal. 3:14–29). More precisely, Old Testament history was the revelation and development of the one covenant of grace in Jesus Christ, the head of the covenant. This covenant would find its fulfillment in the coming and ministry of Jesus Christ (vv. 17–29).

This is the truth of the history that is explored and explained in this volume in the series Unfolding Covenant History. The previous volume treated the history of the judges and Ruth. The history of the judges demonstrated that the covenantal people of God in the old dispensation needed the king. The history of Ruth began the account of God's giving the king to Israel from the family of Ruth the Moabitess and Boaz.

This volume concludes with God's gift of the king, typically, in the person of David, from whose descendants the real king will come, and in the person of Solomon, ruler of the kingdom of peace and glory and builder of the temple of God. God's gift of David overrules the efforts of the citizens of the kingdom to accomplish the necessary kingship on their own and according to their own liking. This was Saul. For the coming of the king after the heart of God and his reception by Israel, the office of the prophet was necessary, both to announce the king and his coming and to prepare the people for his godly kingship. This was Samuel, certainly one of the most important figures in all the history of the old covenant. In Samuel was embodied and inaugurated the fundamental office of the prophet in the kingdom of God. In anointing the king, which Samuel might do in his secondary office as Levitical priest, installing the king into his office, and calling the nation to honor and obey the king, Samuel performed outstanding service in the history of the covenant and kingdom of God.

Mention of the "kingdom of God" warrants calling to the reader's attention that in this volume effort is made to do justice to the importance of the kingdom of God in the history of the old dispensation and to suggest the close, indeed inseparable, relation between covenant and kingdom. In a series of volumes whose title emphasizes the covenant of God, there is the danger of minimizing, even overlooking, the prominence and importance of the messianic kingdom of God. This is a danger regarding even that section of the Old Testament that has the formation of the kingdom and the election of the king as its main message. Covenant and kingdom are not rivals. They are two aspects of one and the same saving relationship of God in Christ with his elect people. The covenant is a royal covenant; the kingdom is a covenantal kingdom. Jesus the Christ is both a sovereign friend and a friendly sovereign. Work remains in dogmatics to develop this truth. Such work will find a goodly amount of its biblical material in the history covered in this volume.

Since the covenant/kingdom of God is one in all ages, there is much in this history that is of immediate practical application to the church and to the individual believer. Most immediate and most practical is the honoring of him who is the real David, a greater than Solomon, and as the Heidelberg Catechism identifies him, "our chief Prophet," Jesus Christ.[1] The church and the believer do this by believing on him, confessing him, and obeying him.

The title of the volume is *From Samuel to Solomon*.

It might more accurately be *Jesus the Messiah in the Shadowy History of the Old Covenant/Kingdom*.

David J. Engelsma

December 2019

---

1 Heidelberg Catechism A 31, in Philip Schaff, ed., *The Creeds of Christendom with a History and Critical Notes*, 6th ed., 3 vols. (New York: Harper and Row, 1931; repr., Grand Rapids, MI: Baker Books, 2007), 3:317.

Samuel:
Voice of God

Chapter One

———

Introduction
to the Ministry of Samuel

*I*n the original Hebrew Old Testament, 1 and 2 Samuel were one undivided book. It was the Septuagint (or LXX), the Greek translation of the Hebrew Old Testament, that divided the book into two books. The Septuagint calls 1 and 2 Samuel "the books of the kingdoms."

The Hebrew title is Samuel, after the chief figure in the beginning of what is now 1 Samuel and the one who anointed both the other leading figures, Saul and David. According to Keil, the title Samuel also points out that the soul of the true kingdom in Israel was the Spirit who lived in the prophet.[1]

Jewish tradition holds that the human author of 1 Samuel was Samuel himself. Although Samuel did write a book concerning "the manner of the kingdom" (1 Sam. 10:25), the author is in fact unknown. The book was written after the division of the kingdom and therefore after the death of Samuel: "Ziklag pertaineth unto the kings of Judah unto this day" (27:6).

The exact time of the history covered by the book is disputed. On the reckoning of Keil, 1 and 2 Samuel cover about 125 years, from about 1140 BC to about 1015 BC.[2] Leon Wood has Samuel born about

---

1   See C. F. Keil and F. Delitzsch, *Biblical Commentary on the Books of Samuel*, tr. James Martin (Grand Rapids, MI: William B. Eerdmans, 1950), 1–2.
2   Keil and Delitzsch, *Biblical Commentary on Samuel*, 2.

1100 BC.[3] What is important about the time of the history of 1 Samuel is that it covers the period of the unfolding of the covenant from the end of the judges to the end of the reign of King Saul, at his death, and therefore to the beginning of the reign of King David.

Regarding the nature and purpose of this history, modern higher-critical scholarship severely criticizes it as nothing more than a compilation of stories without unity. Unbelief is blind to every aspect of the word of God. In reality the history is unified as to its content by the main theme of all scripture, the covenant of grace, here in its royal form as the kingdom of God. The covenant of grace, which is the communion of God with his elect people, is ordered by the reign of God over this people, and God reigns by the messianic king, Jesus Christ. On their part the people live with God by submitting to his rule. Covenant and kingdom therefore are essentially one. Kingdom is the order or structure of the life of the covenant, and covenantal communion is the purpose and nature of the kingship of God in Christ over the people. For the people of God, whether kingdom and church in the Old Testament or church and kingdom in the New Testament, their life is fellowship in submission, or obedient communion. God is to them their friendly king, or their royal friend. This truth about covenant and kingship renders void the controversy whether covenant or kingship is the fundamental reality in scripture.

First Samuel is the history of the kingdom/covenant during and immediately following upon the chaotic period of the judges. This history centers around God's institution of the kingship in Israel, which kingship will be realized in David, who is both type and father of the messianic king, Jesus. The book of Judges prepared for this kingship by demonstrating Israel's urgent need. The coming of the king and his kingship was the prophecy of the book of Ruth. The corruption of the priesthood in Israel in the house of the high priest Eli, in the beginning of 1 Samuel, points up the need of a strong and faithful king.

---

3 Leon Wood, *A Survey of Israel's History* (Grand Rapids, MI: Zondervan Publishing House, 1970), 229. Regarding the dates of Samuel's life and ministry, Wood places Samuel's birth "just prior to…the birth of Samson" (229).

That the significance of Samuel himself is that he serves to bring about the kingship in Israel is indicated in his mother Hannah's prayer. Her prayer concludes with the prophecy, "The LORD shall judge the ends of the earth; and he shall give strength unto his king, and exalt the horn of his anointed" (1 Sam. 2:10). Her entire prayer celebrates Jehovah's victory for his oppressed people (of whom Hannah is an instance) over their enemies. Verse 10 is a climax that explains all that precedes: the victory of the saints will be accomplished by Jehovah's anointed king. Hannah's prayer is messianic. The Old Testament type of Messiah is David, for whom Hannah's son will prepare the way, indeed whom he will anoint. This prayer has its New Testament echoes and counterparts in the song of Mary (Luke 1:46–55) and in the song of Zacharias (vv. 67–79), which likewise celebrate the victory of the people of God over their enemies by God's king.

Samuel therefore brings the age of the judges to a close. He was himself a judge, although this was not his main office. He began judging Israel at Mizpeh, on the occasion of his deliverance of Israel from the Philistines: "There he judged Israel" (1 Sam. 7:17). This completed the deliverance that was begun by Samson, who had died only shortly before this. Samuel continued to judge Israel after his deliverance of them at Mizpeh (vv. 15–17). He publicly announced the termination of his own judgeship and thus the end of the office of judge itself, on the renewal of the kingdom (11:14–15; chap. 12). The office of king in Israel renders the office of judge obsolete. The kingship now must do what the judgeship did much less effectively, as Israel recognized when they requested a king (8:5–6, 20).

In the words of Edward J. Young, the purpose of the two books of Samuel is "to relate the account of the establishment of the monarchy, and Samuel's part therein."[4]

With its revelation of the appearance of the office of king in Israel, 1 Samuel also makes known the rise of the prophetic office. There were

---

4   Edward J. Young, *An Introduction to the Old Testament* (Grand Rapids, MI: William B. Eerdmans, 1973), 179.

prophets prior to Samuel, but their ministry was sporadic. With Samuel the office of prophet comes to be a permanent, powerful reality in Israel. By this office, the Holy Spirit both strengthens and corrects the king. In addition, the prophet teaches the people. By this teaching, the prophet often brings the sinful people to repentance. Characteristic of the prophetic teaching was Samuel's instruction in 1 Samuel 7:3:

> And Samuel spake unto all the house of Israel, saying, If ye do return unto the LORD with all your hearts, then put away the strange gods and Ashtaroth from among you, and prepare your hearts unto the LORD, and serve him only: and he will deliver you out of the hand of the Philistines.

The Holy Spirit established the office of prophet in Israel in the person of Samuel. Although he functioned as a Levitical priest, as a judge, and as a prophet, his dominant office was that of prophet. That the office of Samuel was preeminently that of prophet is the testimony of 1 Samuel 3:19–4:1. Verse 19 speaks of Samuel's words and of their not failing. Verse 20 calls him a prophet of the Lord. First Samuel 3:21 and 4:1 declare that Jehovah revealed himself unto Samuel in the word of the Lord and that Samuel then gave the word to all Israel, which perfectly describes the reality of the office of a prophet, as defined by the prophet Amos: "Surely the Lord GOD will do nothing, but he revealeth his secret unto his servants the prophets. The lion hath roared, who will not fear? The Lord GOD hath spoken, who can but prophesy?" (Amos 3:7–8).

At the same time, and in connection with the establishment of the office of prophet in Samuel, there appeared in Israel the company of prophets (1 Sam. 10:5, 10–12; 19:20). This was a school of prophets under the headship and tutelage of Samuel, a kind of Old Testament seminary.

Franz Delitzsch is correct in estimating Samuel thus highly: "As Abraham is the father of believers, and Moses is the mediator of the law, so Samuel is the father of the kingdom and the prophetic office, and through the medium of the prophetic schools, father of the literature of the royal and prophetic period which now follows."[5]

By no means, therefore, may 1 Samuel be viewed merely as biography of Samuel, Saul, and David, much less as stories, doubtful regarding their historical authenticity and haphazardly thrown together, as the modern, unbelieving scholars charge. But the history must be viewed and explained as covenantal/royal history along the lines thus proposed.

Ultimately, the reality of this history is neither Samuel, nor Saul, nor even King David. But the reality is the one whom all this history foreshadows. This one is Jesus the Messiah. He is the king and the prophet. He is also the priest, whose office certain of the persons recorded in this history debased. First Samuel contains the revelation of the apostasy of the priesthood and of the ruin of the public worship of Jehovah by this apostasy. The public worship at Shiloh is destroyed, spiritually by Eli's sons and physically by the Philistines at the time of the battle at Aphek. The Levitical priesthood fails with the direst consequences in that the worship of Jehovah ceases.

Against this background, there is prophecy of a better priesthood: "And I will raise me up a faithful priest, that shall do according to that which is in mine heart and in my mind: and I will build him a sure house; and he shall walk before mine anointed for ever" (1 Sam. 2:35).

By the faithful exercise of his threefold office, namely prophet, priest, and king, Messiah will perfect the covenant/kingdom of God and give to the Israel of God the blessings that inhere in and flow from the office.

---

5 Franz Delitzsch, *An Old Testament History of Redemption* (Winona Lake, IN: Alpha Publications, 1980), 82–83.

Chapter Two

The Gift of Samuel

(1 Samuel 1–7)

The prominence and importance of this man in the history of the Old Testament covenant/kingdom of God are indicated in Jeremiah 15:1: "Then said the LORD unto me, Though Moses and Samuel stood before me, yet my mind could not be toward this people: cast them out of my sight, and let them go forth." Not only is Samuel ranked with Moses as one of two outstanding persons in the Old Testament, but also he with Moses is one who could conceivably intercede with God for the preservation of the nation of Israel. Higher commendation of Samuel and his office in Israel it would be difficult to conceive.

Regarding tribal descent, Samuel was a Levite, born into a family that had lived in Ephraim but was now living in Ramathaim-zophim, or Ramah, in Benjamin (see Josh. 18:25). His father, Elkanah, was an "Ephrathite," that is, an Ephraimite, by civil reckoning. The family's living in the territory of Benjamin (the city of Ramah) is to be explained from the fact that the mountains of Ephraim extended into the precincts of Benjamin. Here Samuel was born, lived, worked, died, and was buried (see 1 Sam. 7:17; 15:34; 16:13; 19:18–19, 22–23; 25:1; 28:3).

Samuel was a Levite. A comparison of the genealogy in 1 Chronicles 6:33–38 with the genealogy of Samuel's father in 1 Samuel 1:1 shows that the Elkanahs mentioned in the two passages are one and the same.

According to the genealogy in 1 Chronicles 6, Elkanah and therefore Samuel were in the family of Levi, specifically in the line of Levi's son Kohath (see vv. 1, 22). Shemuel, in verse 33, is the name of Samuel in its original Hebrew form. Also verses 27–28 place Samuel in the family of Levi through Kohath. A member of the tribe of Levi is found in the tribe of Ephraim because the Levites had been given no tribal territory of their own but had their dwelling in cities in the territories of the other tribes (see Num. 35:1–8). Elkanah, the name of Samuel's father, means "the man whom God has bought," with reference to the redemption of the Levites for the special service of God in lieu of the firstborn of Israel (see Num. 3:11–51). It is interesting to note that Heman, the singer and the director of music in the tabernacle under David, was the grandson of Samuel, by Samuel's son Joel (see 1 Chron. 6:33).

Because Samuel was a Levite, it was right that he sacrificed, as he did more than once in his ministry. In addition, it belonged to his priestly office that he functioned as a mediator between Israel and God (see 1 Sam. 7:5–10).

A WONDER-CHILD

In view of his multifaceted work of salvation on behalf of God's people, it was appropriate that Samuel was a wonder-child. Hannah was a barren woman who conceived Samuel only by a miracle of God in gracious answer to her prayer. This was acknowledged by Samuel's mother in her naming of him. The name Samuel means "heard of God," deriving from the Hebrew verb "to hear." "Hannah…called his name Samuel, saying, Because I have asked him of the LORD" (1 Sam. 1:20). God heard her when she asked of him a son, performing the wonder of conception by a barren woman.

The history of Hannah's request of Jehovah for Samuel is rich salvation history. Hannah was one of the two wives of Elkanah; the other was Peninnah. Peninnah had children, whereas Hannah had none, for "the LORD had shut up her womb" (1 Sam. 1:5). Elkanah favored Hannah: "he loved Hannah" (v. 5). This was the occasion of the jealousy and strife that plagued polygamy in the Old Testament. The marital and familial strife that attended polygamy was God's judgment upon that deviation from his law of marriage and the manifestation of his will for marriage from the beginning, that it be the union of one man and one woman. It is a mistake to suppose that God simply tolerated polygamy in the Old Testament. On the contrary, he judged that corruption of the institution of marriage by the miseries that he inflicted upon the corruption, thus also teaching the truth of marriage. "From the beginning it was not so," that a man should have a plurality of wives (Matt. 19:8; see also Gen. 2:18–25).

But there was more to the strife between Hannah and Peninnah than merely the natural jealousy of two females married to the same man. Peninnah persecuted Hannah. The persecution was hatred of a godly woman by one who was ungodly. It was real persecution. It was persecution for God's sake. This was evident in Hannah's inspired song, or prayer (1 Sam. 2:1–10). Hannah regarded her adversary as "the wicked," as one of the "adversaries of the LORD" (vv. 9–10). Therefore, in herself Hannah can see affliction of God's people by Jehovah's and their own foes, and in her own deliverance the salvation of God's people: "My heart rejoiceth in the LORD, mine horn is exalted in the LORD: my mouth is enlarged over mine enemies; because I rejoice in thy salvation" (v. 1).

Peninnah "provoked" Hannah at the time of the yearly trek to Shiloh to worship God at the feast of passover (1 Sam. 1:7). Her provocation took the form of charging that Hannah's barrenness was God's punishment of her in his wrath for her sins. It was therefore severe persecution. This is stated: "provoked her sore" (v. 6). The severity was evident in Hannah's grief (vv. 7, 10). Hannah gave expression to the severity of the persecution and to the intensity of her grief in her prayer: her deliverance was a real salvation and a resurrection of one who was as good as dead (2:6).

GOD'S MAN FROM BIRTH

At Shiloh, in the tabernacle, Hannah prayed for a son, vowing to give him to Jehovah as a devoted, special servant of God (1 Sam. 1:9–11). High priest Eli supposed that Hannah was a drunken woman, which indicates the sad state of Israel and the corrupt behavior at the tabernacle at that time. There was more, *much* more, to Hannah's prayer than only her personal desire for a child: by devoting the child to Jehovah as a Nazarite, Hannah sought the kingdom of God with her request. Jehovah answered Hannah's petition and gave her the son she requested (vv. 19–20). As a reward for Hannah's gift of Samuel to Jehovah and as the effect of Eli's blessing of Hannah, Jehovah gave Hannah five more children, three sons and two daughters (2:21).

Samuel, however, was special. In reality, he did not belong to Elkanah and Hannah at all. As a Nazarite, he belonged solely to Jehovah God. Samuel was not "lent" to the Lord as the Authorized Version (AV) translates in 1 Samuel 1:28, but given to the Lord, as was the vow of Hannah in her prayer (see v. 11). The Hebrew verb twice translated "lent" in verse 28 expresses that Hannah *granted*, or *made over*, Samuel to Jehovah, so that the child is no longer Hannah's but Jehovah's. The same applies to chapter 2:20. The verb does not have the sense of our loaning, as though Samuel remained Hannah's but was temporarily merely placed in the service of God. That Samuel was given to God so that he is God's child, not Elkanah's and Hannah's, is the implication of verse 21: Samuel developed before Jehovah, as a child develops before his father, whose child he is.

That the gift of Samuel to God included his being a Nazarite is indicated by Hannah's statement in her prayer that "there shall no razor come upon his head" (1 Sam. 1:11). A Nazarite in Israel was one who was consecrated to God in a special way for special service of God. Consecration or devotion is the meaning of the word itself. One of the signs of this consecration was that his hair remained uncut, which Hannah mentioned in her vow devoting her son to God. There were Nazarites for life and Nazarites for only a time. Samuel was one of the former, as Hannah stipulated in her vow: "I will give him unto the LORD all the days of his life" (v. 11).

SON OF A GODLY MOTHER

Although she gave him away to God, spiritually Samuel is the child of his mother. His mother, a deeply spiritual woman, took the initiative in all aspects of Samuel's birth, rearing, and consecration to God. The spirituality of the woman is apparent from her prayer (1 Sam. 2:1–10). It is also evident in her vow (1:11). It is obviously evident in her keeping of the vow, and promptly, although she had no other child nor at that time the promise of any other. But her spirituality is evident in her making the vow. There was nothing selfish about the vow, as though by it she could satisfy her own personal, motherly desire for a child, for the child would be God's, not her own. Hers was a vow that intensely sought the glory of God.

The vow of Hannah was extraordinary. It belonged to an era of the miraculous and was an aspect of God's providing his people a wonderful deliverer in a time of great need. Barren women may not take Hannah as their model, asking God for a child whom they promise to dedicate to God as a minister or a missionary. Nevertheless, there is in Hannah and her vow instruction of New Testament saints concerning their ordinary, holy lives. New Testament believers live out their holy lives as those who are under willing vows, for example, the rearing of our children in the fear of God; living in godliness; faithfulness in marriage and the home; membership in a church that displays the marks of a true church; and more. These vows the New Testament Christian keeps at loss to himself, even as Hannah gave up her firstborn, and at the time her only, son.

Surely Hannah is an example for godly mothers in New Testament Israel, and her actions with their outcome—great deliverances for Israel—are an example of the influence they have for good in the covenant/kingdom of God. Glorious things in the kingdom/covenant of God happen still today through the prayers and wonderful deeds of godly mothers.

Here, then, it is beneficial to examine more closely Hannah's prayer in 1 Samuel 2:1–10. Generally, the prayer is prophetic. Its message is the gospel of God's mighty, gracious salvation of his lowly people, accompanied by his destruction of the wicked, who are foes of both Jehovah and his people. Hannah rightly views her own personal deliverance as representative of God's dealings with all his people ("his saints," v. 9) always, as well as with all the wicked always. Her salvation, as is the salvation of all the people of God, is by means of Jehovah's "king," who is his "anointed" (v. 10). The song of Mary in Luke 1:46–55 and to a lesser extent the song of Zacharias in verses 67–79 are modeled after and based on Hannah's prayer or song. The similarity of the prayer of Hannah and the song of Mary is remarkable. Both rejoice in God and his salvation. Both celebrate God's saving goodness to the lowly. Both declare God's destruction of his proud enemies. And obviously both are occasioned by the birth of a messianic child.

Specifically regarding the prayer of Hannah, it is exuberant joy in salvation, which salvation is deliverance from enemies (1 Sam. 2:1). This salvation is gracious: the deed of the holy, faithful, almighty God ("rock," v. 2). In this history of the birth of Samuel appears for the first time in scripture the naming of God as "LORD of hosts" (v. 11). Such is the strength of God to establish his covenant, to realize his kingdom, and to save his oppressed people that every creature, willingly or unwillingly, is a soldier in his army. With a negative that runs throughout the scriptures, as it runs also throughout the history of the New Testament church, Hannah denies that salvation is by human "strength" (v. 9). The salvation of God is always deliverance of the lowly, accompanied by the destruction of the proud (vv. 3–8). Significantly concerning salvation, it is accomplished by God's king, who will eventually establish a worldwide kingdom: "The LORD shall judge the ends of the earth; and he shall give strength unto his king, and exalt the horn of his anointed" (v. 10). This messianic climax of Hannah's prayer prophesies the Davidic kingship, culminating in Jesus the Christ. This messianic note is sounded because Hannah's son will anoint King David.

CORRUPTION OF THE PRIESTLY OFFICE

Hannah's consecration of her son must be validated by Jehovah's call of the lad (1 Sam. 3). This call occurred against the backdrop of and indeed at the very heart and center of the apostasy and corruption of Israel: the perversion of the worship of Jehovah at the tabernacle in Shiloh by a wicked priesthood in Israel.

The public worship at Shiloh and the officiating priesthood do not appear in the book of Judges except in Judges 20:26–28, which records history early in the period of the judges. At that time Phineas, the son of Eleazar, was high priest. Israel inquired of Jehovah at the tabernacle, which had removed near Gibeah, in Benjamin, whether they should fight Benjamin because of the Levite's concubine. Judges 17–18 indicates neglect of the worship at the tabernacle in the behavior of Micah and the Danites, who engaged in private worship.

At the end of the period of the judges, in addition to all the other miseries of Israel, a corrupt priesthood has destroyed the public worship of Jehovah at Shiloh. The priests, Hophni and Phinehas, the sons of the high priest, Eli, were profane, worthless men, children of the devil, "sons of Belial" as they are described in 1 Samuel 2:12. The spiritual root of their evil deeds was that they did not know Jehovah (v. 12). Deliberately they violated their priestly office in hatred for Jehovah, even as knowing Jehovah is love for him that honors him by worshiping him as he prescribes.

The seriousness of the sin of these two reprobates was that it caused Israel to despise the offering of Jehovah: "Wherefore the sin of the young men was very great before the LORD: for men abhorred the offering of the LORD" (1 Sam. 2:17). Effectively, they put an end to the public worship of God in Israel. They did this especially by two vile deeds. One was that they robbed Jehovah by taking the best of the sacrifices for their own benefit. The rule governing the priest's portion of the offerings had been prescribed in Leviticus 7:28–38. Disregarding the rule governing the portions of the sacrificial beasts that were allotted to the priests, Hophni and Phinehas took the best parts of the animals for themselves—the parts that were required to be sacrificed to God. And they took these parts by force (1 Sam. 2:12–17). In the words of God himself, they made themselves "fat with the chiefest of all the offerings of Israel, my people." Thus they kicked "at my sacrifice and at mine offering, which I have commanded in my habitation" (v. 29). The second vile deed that brought the tabernacle and its services into disrepute was that Eli's sons fornicated "with the women that assembled at the door of the tabernacle of the congregation" (v. 22).

The same sins especially of ministers shame the public worship of God today. Ministers seduce women of the congregation. They also obviously take the oversight of the church "for filthy lucre," that is, for money and luxuries, in the words of 1 Peter 5:2. Because of these sins on the part of officebearers, the world mocks the church's worship of God and the zeal of the godly is weakened.

Eli himself was not guilty of these abominations. Personally, he was a God-fearing man. He served God as a high priest and a judge for forty years. The misbehavior of his sons grieved him, especially that they made "the Lord's people to transgress" (1 Sam. 2:24). In fact, he rebuked them, however mildly, for their sinful conduct. Nevertheless, God held him responsible for the wickedness of his sons and the consequent ruinous effects upon the public worship of Israel. Not only did Eli not discipline his sons as a father, but also he failed to discipline them as an officebearer. The latter would likely have been Eli's seeing to the sentencing of them to death by stoning, the Old Testament equivalent of New Testament excommunication. Eli warned his sons, but he *did* nothing. "His sons made themselves vile, and he restrained them not" (3:13).

The discipline that Eli failed to execute, God himself would carry out (see 1 Sam. 4:11). In fact, the reason why his sons did not heed Eli's belated admonitions was that God hardened their hearts in his determination to slay them (see 2:25). So grave a sin is the corruption of the public worship of God.

The history of Eli and his sons speaks powerfully to our day, when, similarly, there is the destruction of God's worship by worthless officebearers (contemporary "sons of Belial") and when other, truly good men do nothing about it except to wring their hands and say weakly, "Why do ye such things? Nay, my colleagues; for it is no good report that I hear: ye make God's people to transgress." Men honor their colleagues and friends above God. The gravity of the failure to exercise discipline is that the worship of God, centering on the proclamation of the cross, is abhorred by the members of the church.

This history of Israel makes plain that there was no help for Israel from the one, regular, instituted office in Israel at the time: the priesthood. The priestly office was the source of the evil, rather than the correction of the evil. The priesthood had degenerated into the very opposite of the spiritual power that it was instituted and called to be. Rather than holiness unto the Lord, it had itself become ungodliness and immorality. Rather than leading the people of God in pure worship, it had made the public worship an abhorrence. Thus the account of the decline of the priesthood reinforces the need for the king in Israel.

Chapter Three

Samuel the Prophet

(1 Samuel 3)

*T*his history also points out the need for the prophetic office in Israel, which office came into being with the call of Samuel. To the office of prophet belongs the free, living, unbound word of God, spoken fearlessly by a man called of God and faithful. The prophet subjects the institution of the church and the official worship of the Lord to scrutiny. When the institution and its worship fall away, the prophet exposes the apostasy and calls the faithful element in the church to reformation. The prophet of God, like Samuel, is the means by which God renews his covenant and saves his covenantal people.

Prophetic preaching and teaching are of essential importance to the church throughout her history. Such proclamation does not stand in absolute opposition to the institutional forms and worship of the church. But it is a distinct aspect of the institutional life of the church. All preachers are called of God to address the rise of false doctrine in the church, as also to speak out boldly against the tolerance of wickedness of life in the institute. But when the majority of preachers fall silent and connive, so that the assemblies of the churches approve heresy and unholiness, invariably God raises up a prophetic preacher in whom the Spirit of prophecy shows himself especially courageous to expose the falling away of the church and to call the church back to the old paths. Such was the ministry of Samuel.

That savior of Israel arose out of the cesspool of official, priestly corruption. God brought life out of death and light out of darkness, as he does time and again, not only in the time of the Old Testament, but also in the time of the New Testament. Indeed, he does the same to the present day. The man who will be the instrument of Israel's renewal in so many ways comes out of the sphere of Eli, Hophni, and Phinehas.

Jehovah himself called Samuel to the office of prophet in Israel: he "came, and stood, and called…Samuel, Samuel" (1 Sam. 3:10). The call was objective: God appeared in some form and addressed Samuel through his ears. Early in the morning, before the light of the candlestick went out, God called Samuel three times before Eli concluded that Jehovah was calling the lad. At Eli's suggestion, Samuel responded appropriately to the fourth issuance of the call: "Speak Lord; for thy servant heareth" (v. 9). Whereas Jehovah had not before revealed his word to Samuel in the manner suitable to the office of prophet (v. 7), now he does.

The revelation is judgment on Eli and his house (1 Sam. 3:11–14). God confirmed that he will carry out the judgments that he had earlier pronounced by a man of God against Eli and his family (2:27–36). The judgments will be severe. Even though in the case of Eli God's judgments are not punishment but chastisement, the misery and its suffering are grievous. This was God's own analysis: "Behold, I will do a thing in Israel, at which both the ears of every one that heareth it shall tingle" (3:11). An especially severe aspect of the judgment upon Eli was that it fell upon his "house." Not only would his family be stripped of the office of the priesthood, but also God would damn them: "The iniquity of Eli's house shall not be purged with sacrifice nor offering for ever" (3:14). Covenantal blessing is generational. So also is covenantal curse: it runs from father to son.

It is noteworthy that at the time of his call to the office of prophet Samuel was merely a "child" (1 Sam. 3:1). The Hebrew word for child refers to a boy, although the lexicographer Gesenius states that the word can refer to a young man as old as twenty. The commentator Leon Wood puts Samuel's age at the time of his call at ten.[1] The Hebrew original

---

1 Wood, *A Survey*, 230.

simply conveys the thought that Samuel was young at the time of his call. First Samuel 3:19 acknowledges his youth: "And Samuel grew."

The call went out from the temple, where was the ark of God, upon which was Jehovah's throne. Jehovah honored his covenantal dwelling place, corrupted as it was by the wickedness of the priesthood, and began to bring deliverance for Israel from the mercy seat. God remembered his covenant with Israel.

The call of Samuel was the call to the office of prophet. From that time, and by virtue of that call, "all Israel from Dan even to Beersheba knew that Samuel was established to be a prophet of the LORD" (1 Sam. 3:20). What a prophet was, the great Old Testament prophecy of the prophet makes plain: "I will raise them up a Prophet from among their brethren, like unto thee [Moses], and will put my words in his mouth; and he shall speak unto them all that I shall command him" (Deut. 18:18). The evidence that a man is a genuine prophet, sent from God, is that his prophecy "come[s] to pass" (vv. 21–22). This was true of Samuel's prophetic words (1 Sam. 3:19).

Fundamentally then, the prophet is one in whose mouth Jehovah places his words. These words the prophet then speaks to the people of God as God commands. He does not speak his own words, but only the words that God has revealed to him. Samuel himself expressed the nature of the prophetic office in his response to God's call, as Eli instructed him to do: "Speak: for thy servant heareth" (1 Sam. 3:10). The prophet hears Jehovah speaking, and hears as a servant. Then the prophet speaks— speaks what he has heard.

Essential to the prophetic task is that the man has been placed in the office by Jehovah himself. "Established" in 1 Samuel 3:20 is virtually "ordained." Jehovah himself conducted the ordination ceremony, just as he would do in calling the real prophet of whom Samuel was the type, Jesus the Christ (see Mark 1:9–11). The prophet therefore speaks the word of Jehovah in Jehovah's name. He speaks the word also on behalf of Jehovah. The Hebrew original of 1 Samuel 3:20 suggests this aspect of the nature of the prophetic office more strongly than does the English translation. The Hebrew has "a prophet *unto* Jehovah." The Hebrew word for the prophet is in keeping with this nature of the prophetic office. The Hebrew word translated "prophet" in 1 Samuel 3:20 derives from the verb that means "cause to bubble up, pour forth [the word of God]." This does not refer only to prediction, but simply to the proclamation of the word of God.

Whereas formerly the word of Jehovah was "precious" or rare in Israel (1 Sam. 3:1), from the time of the call of Samuel as prophet "the word of Samuel came to all Israel" (4:1). Even when the word of Samuel took the form of rebuke and judgment, it was a word of salvation, especially in bringing the people to repentance and in preparing them for the kingship of David. By the office of prophet Jehovah saved his people, as he saves still today by the prophetic office of Christ, which office Christ exercises especially by the preaching of the word in his church.

THE PROPHETIC WORD OF JUDGMENT

Samuel at once proved the genuineness of his call by faithfully declaring the word of Jehovah to Eli concerning the judgment of God upon the old priest and his house (1 Sam. 3:11–18). This announcement of judgment was of importance first because it demonstrated the reality of severe judgment upon sin within the sphere of the covenant, and second because it was a splendid prophecy of the coming Messiah as a "faithful priest."

The severe judgment, as announced earlier to Eli by a "man of God" (1 Sam. 2:27–36), consisted of God's stripping of the high priesthood from the family of Eli and giving it to another family in the tribe of Levi. Also, God would weaken the strength of the men in Eli's family, so that they would die young. Those who would survive to old age would be poor, wretched, and insignificant. In general, Eli and his descendants would see distress: "enemy" in verse 32 should here be translated distress. Seeing the distress in the habitation of God, resulting in the destruction of the public worship, is the reason for the consuming of the eyes and grief of the heart of Eli and whoever of his descendants survive and fear God (v. 33).

The sign of this dreadful judgment would be the death of Eli's two sons in one day. Eli would see the sign and know that all the rest of the judgment would also follow. The event of the death of Eli's two sons would also be for Eli the seeing of distress in God's habitation, for the ark will have been captured.

The transfer of the high priesthood from Eli's family to another Levitical family will take place when King Solomon deposes Abiathar and installs Zadok as high priest. "So Solomon thrust out Abiathar from being priest unto the LORD; that he might fulfil the word of the LORD, which he spake concerning the house of Eli in Shiloh" (1 Kings 2:27). Eli was in the family of Aaron's son Ithamar. Somehow the high priesthood had passed from the family of Eleazar to that of Ithamar. Solomon will transfer it back to Eleazar's family.

The judicial ground of this heavy judgment upon Eli and his house was the profaning of God's worship, chiefly involving the sacrifice, *which typified the cross*! Hophni and Phinehas, with the connivance of Eli, had "trodden under foot the Son of God" and had "counted the blood of the covenant…an unholy thing," in the language of Hebrews 10:29. What made the sin heinous was that it was sin against the covenant. In the language of the announcement of the judgment to Eli, the sin was a kicking "at my sacrifice and at mine offering" (1 Sam. 2:29). Within the sphere of the covenant, there is place for severe judgment. Jehovah himself warns of this reality: "I said indeed that thy house, and the house of thy father, should walk before me for ever: but now the LORD saith, Be it far from me; for them that honour me I will honour, and they that despise me shall be lightly esteemed" (v. 30). It is not that God goes back on his word of promise: "I said indeed." This stands. The priesthood remains in the house of Levi. But with this promise, and by this promise, God honors those who honor him and abases those who despise him.

The prophetic word of Samuel to Eli was not only judgment. It was also the promise of the coming Messiah as the faithful priest of God. "And I will raise me up a faithful priest, that shall do according to that which is in mine heart and in my mind: and I will build him a sure house; and he shall walk before mine anointed for ever" (1 Sam. 2:35). Typically, this faithful priest is Samuel himself, who will walk before King David and High Priest Zadok, who will walk before King Solomon. "Mine anointed" in the text is the coming king of the people of God.

The reality of "a faithful priest" is the Christ, Jesus, in whom the office of the priesthood will cooperate with and serve the office of the king, God's "anointed."

This divine judgment upon the unfaithful priesthood—Eli and his sons—which was first declared by the unnamed man of God, was repeated to Samuel, and Samuel prophesied it to Eli. The very first prophetic message of the young prophet was dreadful judgment. Samuel faithfully announced the judgment, although the duty was extremely unpleasant to him: "Samuel feared to shew Eli the vision" (1 Sam. 3:15). The true prophet must speak judgment, death, and damnation. He must do this first because judgment is always part of Jehovah's word, and second because judgment is necessary for the salvation of the covenantal people. Any reputed prophet who refuses to preach "negatively" shows that he is no true prophet at all. Such are many contemporary preachers, whose message is all "sweetness and light." A contributing factor are many congregations that express distaste for "negative" sermons. By such congregations and preachers the covenant of God is corrupted and his kingdom is laid waste.

Miserable old Eli showed his personal godliness by receiving the judgment upon himself and his house submissively: "It is the LORD: let him do what seemeth him good" (1 Sam. 3:18). There are men who fail in the execution of an office in the kingdom who nevertheless are personally godly.

From this time on, Samuel functioned as prophet in Israel (1 Sam. 3:19, 21; 4:1). Israel recognized Samuel as a prophet of the Lord (3:20).

Chapter Four

The Ministry of Samuel

(1 Samuel 4–7)

A word of explanation is in order regarding this part of the history in general. First, I regard the dreadful judgment of God upon Israel consisting of the battle of Aphek and its consequences, recorded in 1 Samuel 4:1–7:2, as part of the ministry of Samuel in Israel, rather than as the miserable straits Israel got itself into and from which Samuel then delivered Israel. My reasons are the following. First, such is the heading over chapters 4:1–7:2, whether the first part of 1 Samuel 4:1 is found at the end of chapter 3 or, as in the AV, at the beginning of chapter 4. Second, Samuel had spoken this judgment prophetically to Eli.

Third, 1 Samuel 3:19 expressly stated that Jehovah "did let none of his [Samuel's] words fall to the ground." What Jehovah does in the history of the covenant he first announces through the prophet (see Amos 3:7). This word of the prophet then, as the very word of Jehovah, is a living, effectual word that brings to pass the event that it announces or threatens, as the case may be. The prophetic word is not "in word only," to quote the apostle Paul, but "also in power" (1 Thess. 1:5). Jehovah does not let the word fall to the ground but realizes it. It is no wonder that the hardened unbeliever hates and kills the prophet! The prophet is the agent of the miseries that God sends upon the ungodly.

I reserve for later the explanation of this judgment, particularly its saving purpose for the true Israel.

A second word of explanation, generally, of this part of the history is that the ministry of Samuel set forth in this section continues significantly with the ministry of the anointing of Saul and David as kings and thus the institution of the kingship in chapters 10 and 16.

Third, Samuel's ministry, although certainly for the benefit of Israel, is emphatically a service of Jehovah. Already before his formal appointment to office by God's call of him, Samuel "ministered unto the LORD" in the tabernacle (1 Sam. 3:1; see also 2:11, 18). Especially in this all-important aspect of his position and labor did Samuel distinguish himself from the sons of Eli, just as faithful officebearers in the New Testament distinguish themselves from their carnal, self-seeking, and invariably disobedient colleagues. Like Samuel, they devote themselves to God and his glory. By their consequent obedient carrying out of the work of their office, they minister unto the covenantal God of the church.

The consciousness of ministering unto God as his primary calling guards the faithful officebearer against disobedience in his duties. It is characteristic of the unfaithful professor, minister, elder, or deacon that he justifies his dereliction of duty (to himself and to any who call him to account) by appeal to his "love" for the congregation and desire to please and help them. Love for the church as the primary element of the ministry of contemporary officebearers accounts for the compromise of doctrinal soundness; for the loss of doctrinal preaching; for the failure to exercise discipline; and for the refusal of the assemblies to take the uncompromising decisions that are called for. What such officebearers have forgotten is that they are called to minister unto the Lord and that this is their primary calling. They are ignorant also that only a ministry that always devotes itself to the glory of God as its primary concern truly loves the people of God and serves their welfare. Love for the church and her members as the primary and all-consuming calling of her officebearers spells the ruin of churches and their members.

Samuel's ministry in Israel began with severe judgment upon the nation (1 Sam. 4:1–7:2). As I have already suggested, the judgment upon

Israel recorded in chapters 4:1–7:2 is the realization of Samuel's prophetic word to Eli in chapter 3. It is not, however, the case that Samuel commanded Israel to declare war on the Philistines, as the commentator Keil explains: "At Samuel's word, the Israelites attacked the Philistines, and were beaten."[1] The chapter division is mistaken: what is 4:1a in the AV is, in fact, the ending of chapter 3, rather than the beginning of chapter 4, as the words and thought themselves demand. It was, in fact, presumptuous of Israel to make war with the Philistines. Israel attempted its own deliverance apart from any command of Jehovah and without any deliverer appointed by God. What made Israel's assault especially presumptuous was that Israel launched the attack without any repentance on its part.

The result of the assault upon the Philistines was very severe, divine judgment upon Israel. The Philistines defeated Israel, killing some 34,000 Israelites at Aphek. Aphek was deep in the territory of Israel, in the land of the tribe of Benjamin. The Philistines were ruling Israel at this time. The book of Judges ends with Samson's *beginning* to deliver Israel from the Philistines. At the time of the battle, the Philistines referred to Israel as their servants (1 Sam. 4:9). "Ebenezer" (v. 1) is so named only later, after God's deliverance of Israel recorded in 1 Samuel 7 (see 7:12).

Another aspect of God's judgment was the death of Eli and his two sons. Thus began the execution of the judgment upon Eli that God had announced in 1 Samuel 2 and 3. Eli died at age ninety-eight. He had judged Israel for forty years.

The worst of the judgments was that the Philistines captured the ark of God. The awful symbolism of the event was that God himself was departed from Israel. As the ark of the covenant symbolized God's presence with Israel in the covenant of grace—which is salvation—so the absence of the ark symbolized the departure of God at Israel's violation of the covenant. Understanding this, however dimly in the time of the old covenant, Eli reacted to the report of the capture of the ark with such an involuntary, violent convulsion of the body as to break his neck. His daughter-in-law, a godly woman though married to a reprobate, reacted

---

1 Keil and Delitzsch, *Biblical Commentary on Samuel*, 52.

similarly. She gave birth prematurely and named the child Ichabod, "the glory is departed from Israel: because the ark of God was taken" (1 Sam. 4:12–22). Whereupon this godly woman married to an ungodly husband in the church died (v. 20).

The capture of the ark was further iniquity on the part of Israel. God does not depart, even symbolically, from the visible, nominal church and kingdom without gross, grievous sin against the covenant on the part of the people. Israel took the ark into the camp of war in order to guarantee God's help in their battle against the Philistines. This was presumption upon the covenantal promise that God would be the God of Israel, defending Israel from their foes. It was presumption upon the covenantal presence of God with his people, rather than trust in this promise and presence. The trust that is born of true faith manifests itself by repentance and by reliance not upon the symbol of the covenantal presence but on the reality of that presence, namely, Jehovah himself.

Presumption is a danger to the church always. Rome is guilty of this presumption by its trust in the elements of the Lord's supper and in the eating of the bread with the physical mouth of the celebrant. This is the meaning of its "*ex opere operato*" ("by the [external] work being accomplished"). Like Israel at Aphek, Rome identifies God and his salvation with the symbol of his saving presence and puts its trust in the symbol, rather than in the reality who is signified. This is superstition. As Rome misunderstands Christ's word of institution of the sacrament, "This is my body," Israel very likely misunderstood Moses' word in the wilderness when the ark began to travel: "Rise up, LORD, and let thine enemies be scattered; and let them that hate thee flee before thee" (Num. 10:35).

In addition to its sin of presumption, and closely related to it, Israel's trust in the ark for salvation was the evil of antinomianism. This is the sin of rejecting the law of God as the authoritative guide of the thankful life of the redeemed. Antinomianism supposes that God will save even though the sinner goes on impenitently in his sin. This aspect of Israel's sin at Aphek is suggested by the observation that the ark of the covenant was in the camp of Israel in the care of Eli's two wicked sons (1 Sam. 4:4). Salvation is expected even though the holy presence of God, who is to give this salvation, is in subjection to the unholy and vile. For this, the nation is responsible.

Jeremiah 7 explicitly charges Israel with antinomianism at this time. The prophet asked the Judah of his day,

> 9. Will ye steal, murder, and commit adultery, and swear falsely, and burn incense unto Baal, and walk after other gods whom ye know not;
> 10. And come and stand before me in this house, which is called by my name, and say, We are delivered to do all these abominations? (vv. 9–10)

The charge of sin in this rhetorical question is that of textbook antinomianism: grace permits, if it does not require, a wicked life. In Jeremiah's day, Judah was trusting in the temple, as earlier Israel had trusted in the ark, not to forgive but to excuse and even justify their wickedness. By his prophet, God refutes this abominable theology in verse 12: "But go ye now unto my place which was in Shiloh, where I set my name at the first, and see what I did to it for the wickedness of my people Israel." The reference is to the history of 1 Samuel 4. God judged the antinomianism of Israel by removing the ark and his dwelling place in Israel from Shiloh, where it had been previously. The Philistines' capture of the ark meant the end of the public worship at Shiloh.

Psalm 78:60–72 recalls this event. God "forsook the tabernacle of Shiloh, the tent which he placed among men; and delivered his strength [the ark] into captivity, and his glory into the enemy's hand. He gave his people over also unto the sword; and was wroth with his inheritance" (vv. 60–62). Verse 64 remembers the death of Hophni and Phinehas and the striking response to her husband's death of Phinehas' widow: "Their priests fell by the sword; and their widows made no lamentation."

From Shiloh, the tabernacle and public worship of God removed to Nob (1 Sam. 21:1; 22:19). King David would bring the ark to Jerusalem, although the tabernacle would remain in Gibeon until King Solomon built the temple in Jerusalem (see 2 Sam. 6; 2 Chron. 2).

The significance of the removal of the ark from Shiloh, in light of the explanation of Psalm 78, is that the tabernacle/temple with the ark of the covenant moves from the tribe of Ephraim to the tribe of Judah, eventually to be located in Jerusalem, the city of David. Thus God over-ruled the wickedness of Israel at Aphek to accomplish his purpose that his covenantal presence be closely associated with the coming messianic king in Jerusalem in Judah: "He refused the tabernacle of Joseph, and chose not the tribe of Ephraim [where the ark and tabernacle had been before the capture of the ark by the Philistines]: but chose the tribe of Judah, the mount Zion which he loved" (Ps. 78:67–68).

ICABOD

For Israel, the capture of the ark of the covenant can only have been regarded as the departure of Jehovah from them, which departure they well deserved. The departure of the ark was a shocking warning of future reality. The day will come for national Israel that its "house is left unto you desolate" (Matt. 23:38). Since the presence of God, which is both symbol-ized by the ark and sacramentally and instrumentally realized by the ark, is Israel's glory, the judgment of the removal of the ark means "Ichabod" for Israel, literally "not glory." This was the inspired testimony of Eli's daughter-in-law in the naming of her son: "The glory is departed from Israel: for the ark of God is taken" (1 Sam. 4:22). If the glory is departed, Israel is shameful. The same is true of the churches today from whom God has departed, in judgment upon their unbelief and unfaithfulness, so that they are without the ark of the preaching of the pure doctrine of the gospel and the pure administration of the sacraments as instituted by Christ.[2]

What cannot be overlooked is that glory had also departed from God, in its manifestation in Israel in that day. This is the psalmist's inspired analysis of the capture of the ark in Psalm 78:61: "And delivered...his glory into the enemy's hand." The reference is to the ark. But the ark was the visible token of the glory of God. The transfer of the ark from Israel to Philistia, in the circumstances of the wickedness of Israel and their

---

2 Belgic Confession 29, in Schaff, *Creeds of Christendom*, 419–21.

defeat by their enemy, was a besmirching of the glory of God as though he could not save his people and as though he was helpless before the might of the gods of the Philistines, indeed as though he were unable to save his people from the wickedness that made the capture of the ark necessary. God's intimate covenantal fellowship with his sinful people means the endurance of shame for him.

He himself is sovereign in taking this shame upon himself. No one, whether Philistia or the devil, brings shame upon him apart from his will. According to Psalm 78:61, God himself delivered his glory into the enemy's hand. But his covenant with his people is costly for God himself. The Philistines mocked him as they carted the ark ignominiously into the temple of their god Dagon. The fulfillment of this deliverance of God's glory into the enemy's hand will be the crucifixion of God in the flesh, Jesus. The cross is the reality of Ichabod.

As the Israelites superstitiously put their trust in the box that was the ark, so the Philistines superstitiously were afraid of the box that was now in the camp of Israel (1 Sam. 4:5–9). They supposed that God himself, a kind of captive of the box, as Rome holds him a captive of a piece of consecrated bread, was in the camp fighting for Israel. The Philistines were afraid of the God of Israel. With the other nations, they had heard of his deliverance of Israel from Egypt by the ten plagues, which plagues virtually destroyed Egypt. "Woe unto us!" they cried in dread, "who shall deliver us out of the hand of these mighty Gods?" (1 Sam. 4:8; see Ex. 15:14–15). As heathens, they attributed a plurality of gods to the nation of Israel: "these mighty *Gods*." But they had heard of his mighty deeds on behalf of his people, and they trembled. So also today, regardless that the modern heathens in North America and Europe ridicule Christianity, they have heard of the mighty acts of the God of Christianity and are afraid of him, as well they might be.

Even though God's name is dishonored by the Philistines' capture of the ark, a thing necessary for the chastisement of God's people, God will impress upon those heathen idolaters in due time that he is God—God *alone*—holy and mighty, and that the Philistines do well to be afraid of him. His presence among them will be destructive.

God's judgment upon his people at that time did not end with the defeat at Aphek, the death of Eli and his sons, and the loss of the ark. It continued upon the ark's return to Israel in the killing of the men of Bethshemesh for looking into, or upon, the ark (1 Sam. 6:19–21). Israel still did not reverence God as the Holy One. The lament of Bethshemesh after their irreverence was punished was, "Who is able to stand before this holy LORD God?" (v. 20). Jehovah defends his glory among his people. The covenant never allows for carelessness on the part of those who confess to be his covenantal people.

It is possible that the number fifty thousand in verse 19 of 1 Samuel 6 is an insertion into the text and that the number of Bethshemites who were killed on that occasion was seventy.[3] Nor was it necessary that those men lifted the lid of the ark to peer into the golden box. It would have been sufficient that they looked upon it with profane and foolish staring. The men of Bethshemesh were aware of Jehovah's law concerning the ark, that it was to be set apart from all that was common, including the common people, as the mention of the Levites in verse 15 indicates. Only the high priest was to look upon the ark, and he only once in the year, at the appointed time.

The significance of the judgment upon the men of Bethshemesh is that the return of Jehovah is the return of the Holy One, before whom unholy sinners cannot stand. Bethshemesh understood this, as their response to the death of their fellows indicated: "Who is able to stand before this holy LORD God?" (1 Sam. 6:20). The words that they added, "to whom shall he go up from us?" will be echoed by Peter, "Depart from me; for I am a sinful man, O Lord" (Luke 5:8).

The judgment upon Israel of the loss of the ark, however severe it may have been, intended and accomplished the repentance of Israel, that is, the true Israel of God (see Rom. 9:6–8). This saving purpose and effect of the judgment are evident, first, in old Eli's trembling

---

3 Keil and Delitzsch, *Biblical Commentary on Samuel*, 68. The text here is suspect, and the number is impossibly high for the city. There are other reasons also to conclude that the number fifty thousand is a later insertion into the text, so that the number of persons killed at Bethshemesh was three score and ten.

for the ark (1 Sam. 4:13) and in the grief of the wife of Phinehas (vv. 19–22). These were among the remnant according to the election of grace (Rom. 11:5). Second, the severe judgment resulted in "all the house of Israel lament[ing] after the LORD" (1 Sam. 7:2). Following the judgment at Aphek, there was a definite, widespread, and steadily developing movement of repentance in Israel. The movement culminated in Israel's repentance and their doing the works worthy of repentance (vv. 1–6). Israel confessed, "We have sinned against the LORD" (v. 6). They "put away Baalim and Ashtaroth, and served the LORD only" (v. 4). The purpose always of the strokes of Jehovah upon his elect people is their repentance and salvation.

There was also judgment upon the Philistines (1 Sam. 5:1–6:18). This judgment was essentially different from that upon Israel. Whereas the judgment upon Israel was sent in love with the purpose to bring that nation to repentance and thus save it, the judgment upon the Philistines was punitive. God inflicted it in hatred—*righteous* hatred, but hatred— for that reprobate, ungodly people, with the purpose of destruction. Although the Philistines have defeated Israel and captured the ark of the covenant, God immediately punishes them, so that they must acknowledge his Godhead in contrast to the vanity of their idol, and so that they are compelled to return the ark to Israel. In this judgment of the Philistines, God defends his own honor, which has been compromised by the capture of the ark. At the same time, he exposes the idol as nothing. In accomplishing the return of the ark to Israel, God reveals his covenantal faithfulness: he is, and will be, Israel's God, despite Israel's unworthiness. Nor does God permit the disruption of his presence in Israel to last long. The ark remains with the Philistines, outside Israel, for only seven months (6:1).

Were the issues not so serious, both the accomplishing of the presence of Israel's covenantal God with them and the punishment of Israel's and God's enemies, the history of the judgment upon the Philistines would be humorous. To celebrate the victory of their idol over the God of Israel— always a fatal mistake of the wicked at the moment of their apparent defeat of the church—the Philistines placed the ark in the temple of the

Philistine god Dagon in Ashdod. Dagon was the fish-god of the seafaring Philistines, located as they were on the coast of the Mediterranean Sea. It was yet another pagan fertility god, a god of the powers of nature. It had a human head and hands and the body of a fish. Placing the ark before this idol in the temple of the fish-god expressed the superiority of Dagon over the God of Israel, indeed the victory of Dagon over Jehovah. Jehovah God is made out to be subservient to the idol.

For this dishonoring of God, Israel was responsible. God therefore arises to his own defense. The very next morning after the gross sacrilege, Dagon is found prone before the ark, as though acknowledging God, who dwells above the ark, as the true God. Strikingly expressing the folly of all idolatry, the Philistines propped their god up again.

The next morning, they find their god demolished. The stump of fish again lies prone before the ark. But now the head and hands are severed from the torso of the idol. They lie on the threshold of the temple for all to walk on. God has exposed the nothingness of the gods of the nations, including the gods of the modern nations. The priests and diviners of the Philistines were right in their analysis of the remarkable happenings in the temple of Dagon. The fundamental issue was the contest between Jehovah God of Israel, the church, and the gods of the nations: "Ye shall give glory unto the God of Israel: peradventure he will lighten his hand from off you, and from off your gods" (1 Sam. 6:5).

Chapter Five

Repentance and Deliverance

(1 Samuel 4–7)

The Godhead of God is the fundamental issue of history. The meaning of history is not economic. It is not social. It is not the struggle for earthly power. The fundamental issue is spiritual: God versus the gods. In this struggle, God has tipped the Dagons over—broken, humiliated, impotent vanities, prostrate before himself. He has done this in the cross, resurrection, and exaltation at his right hand of his Son in human flesh, Jesus Christ. The demonstration of this triumph in history is the gathering and perseverance of the church by the preaching of the gospel, which preaching exposes the idols as nothings and demolishes them, as it were, before the ark of the covenant.

It is not enough that God expose the idols; he must also put to shame and suffering the heathens themselves, who not only know him as God from nature itself (Rom. 1:18–32), but also have some knowledge of his redemption of his people from Egypt (1 Sam. 4:8; see also 6:6). While his ark abode in various Philistine cities, God struck their inhabitants with large numbers of extraordinary deaths, with a painful affliction of emerods, and with a plague of mice that devastated the crops of the Philistines. Emerods were hemorrhoids—painful tumors in and around the anus. Some explain them as boils over all the body. All expositors agree that they were a very painful affliction. The words "in their secret parts" in chapter 5:9 do not occur in the Masoretic text of the Hebrew Bible, which has only "there broke out to them emerods." The Hebrew word translated "emerods" means tumor or swelling.

The plague of mice marred the land (1 Sam. 6:5). This was the destruction of the Philistines mentioned in chapter 5:6. The devouring of the crops by the mice threatened the very existence of the Philistines.

All this devastation and pain was caused by the presence of the ark, as the Philistines knew: "The ark of the God of Israel shall not abide with us: for his hand is sore upon us, and upon Dagon our god" (1 Sam. 5:7). God was present to the Philistines by the symbol of his presence, but he was present to his and his people's enemies as death and destruction, not as life and blessing. Always the truth and presence of God are antithetical: blessing and salvation to his covenantal people; curse and damnation to the reprobate ungodly.

By the same curse that destroyed the idolaters, God struck at the pretensions of Dagon, god of fertility and natural, earthly power. He made the country a desolation. He stripped the people of health and of life itself. If the emerods were indeed hemorrhoids, the idolaters lacked even the natural power to defecate easily or painlessly.

Ashdod had the ark sent on to the city of Gath, in a hurry. The plagues of emerods and mice then fell upon the inhabitants of Gath. The ark was traveling destruction among the Philistines. Gath sent the ark off to the city of Ekron. Ekron objected: Gath sends the ark to us to kill us all (1 Sam. 5:10). Ekron called for an emergency meeting of all the rulers of Philistia, to decide to return the ark to Israel. Before this could be done, the plagues fell upon Ekron. Indeed, there was increase of the severity of the judgment: "a deadly destruction"; "the hand of God was very heavy there"; "the cry of the city went up to heaven" (vv. 11–12).

God's hardening of the ungodly in their rebellion against him and their resistance to his punishments are always accompanied by his intensifying of the punishments.

At the advice of their priests and soothsayers, the Philistines decided to send the ark back to Israel. The curious manner of the return of the ark proved that the evils visited upon the Philistines while the ark resided among them were indeed inflicted by the God of Israel, who was present with his ark. By this curious manner of the ark's return, God revealed to the Philistines his providential power and thus the reality of his Godhead. The cart on which the ark was to be conveyed to Israel was pulled by two young cows that had never before been yoked and whose calves were separated from them. Contrary to the powerful instincts of the beasts, the cows left their calves, submitted to the yoking, and headed straight for Israel, lowing as they went.

With the ark, the Philistines sent a "trespass offering" of five golden emerods and five golden mice, as many of each as the number of Philistine cities affected by the divine judgments of emerods and mice. These images of the divine punishments inflicted on the Philistines were intended to atone for the sin of taking the ark. "Trespass offering" in 1 Samuel 6:3, 4, and 8 is the translation of the Hebrew word that means guilt. It comes to mean "sacrifice for transgression." The heathen knew the reality of guilt, the necessity of sacrifice to remove guilt, and the healing that is the benefit of sacrifice. "Return him [the God of Israel] a trespass offering: then ye [the Philistines] shall be healed" (v. 3).

God makes known to fallen humans, outside the sphere of special revelation, their guilt, their exposure to his wrath, and their need of redemption by sacrifice. This revelation, however, is not saving. It only serves to leave them without excuse. In this revelation is no making known of the one and only sacrifice for sin, the divinely appointed Lamb of God. The Philistines offered golden emerods and golden mice. These pitiful, offensive offerings were the attempt of the Philistines themselves to pay for their misdeed. This offering did not satisfy Jehovah. That the plagues upon Philistia came to an end was not due to the offerings of emerods and mice, but to the return of the ark to Israel.

Neither the presence of the ark among the Philistines nor the return of the ark to Israel, with the accompanying offering of emerods and mice, indicated a work of saving grace among that heathen nation. It was not God's time of salvation for the other nations. As Paul will preach at Lystra,

"In times past [God] suffered all nations to walk in their own ways" (Acts 14:16). His covenant was with Israel, and only the covenant is salvation.

Yet once again in 1 Samuel 6, having already made this known in chapter 4, scripture emphasizes that the heathen nations knew of God's deliverance of Israel from Egypt and his destruction of the enemies of his people. The religious leaders of the Philistines could ask the political lords, "Wherefore then do ye harden your hearts, as the Egyptians and Pharaoh hardened their hearts? when he had wrought wonderfully among them, did they not let the people go, and they departed?" (v. 6). Also today, the ungodly, whether in nominally Christian lands or in pagan countries, know of the wonderful works of God in Jesus Christ both for salvation and for the destruction of the church's enemies. By scripture, by missions, and by the personal testimony of Christians among all nations, even the heathen know of God's wonders of salvation in Jesus Christ. The gospel goes out into all the world. Even where there is no saving work of the Holy Ghost, there is a powerful work of the Spirit to impress the truth of God's work in Jesus Christ upon the souls of the ungodly. Although they do not bow to him and serve him, the ungodly nations are afraid of him.

Upon its return to Israel, the ark finds lodging in Kirjath-jearim, a city in Judah on the border of Benjamin. There it will remain until King David takes it to Jerusalem (see 2 Sam. 6). Bethshemesh may not have the ark because of the sin of the inhabitants of this city. Shiloh may not again be the dwelling of the holy Jehovah because of the sins of Eli and his sons (see Jer. 7:12). In Kirjath-jearim, the ark abides in the common house of one Abinadab. Such is the holiness of the symbol of the dwelling of the covenantal Jehovah with his people, as the covenantal people know, that the inhabitants of the city "sanctified Eleazar his son to keep the ark of the LORD" (1 Sam. 7:1). One must be specially set apart merely to look after the ark of the covenant. God's covenantal dwelling with his people does not compromise his awesome holiness among them.

Regarding the history of the judgment upon the Philistines for their laying profane hands on the symbol of the covenant and for their effort thus to disrupt the covenant of God with his people, there is a certain grim humor about the history, which bespeaks the folly of the enemies of God's people: poor, helpless Dagon; the Philistines' solicitous care of their helpless god; emerods; rodents everywhere; the Philistines' passing on among themselves the ark like a hot potato; Ekron's terror at the approach of the ark.

Scarcely less foolish is the explanation of the plague of emerods by Old Testament scholar R. K. Harrison. According to Harrison, the plague of emerods was bubonic plague spread by the ark as it traveled, because rat fleas infested the curtains of the ark.[1] Thus he explains the deaths at Bethshemesh also. The effect, if not the intention, of this far-fetched explanation is to deny the obviously miraculous nature of the event.

By the judgment upon the Philistines, God glorified himself among the heathen. He is the covenantal God of his chosen people, but he is also the sovereign God of heaven and earth and of all creatures and conditions, including mice and emerods. He is not a local deity. This the Philistines were compelled to acknowledge in their own heathen way: they gave "glory unto the God of Israel" (1 Sam. 6:5).

EBENEZER

Samuel's deliverance of Israel recorded in 1 Samuel 7:3–17 occurred twenty years after the return of the ark to Israel. During this time, we hear nothing of Samuel and his ministry. The Philistines' oppression of Israel continued, with deep incursions into Israel. Then Samuel called a penitent people to Mizpeh for public reconciliation to Jehovah. Mizpeh was in Benjamin, near the border with Judah. It had been the site of significant gatherings and events earlier in the history of Israel (see Judges 11:11; 20:1). The nature of the assembly called by Samuel was purely religious. It was not military. Israel had no intention of making war against the Philistines. When Israel heard that the Philistines were advancing upon them at Mizpeh, "they were afraid of the Philistines" (1 Sam. 7:7).

The Philistines made Israel's religious assembly the occasion for an attack upon the worshiping people of God. In response to Samuel's

---

1 R. K. Harrison, *Introduction to the Old Testament* (Grand Rapids, MI: William B. Eerdmans, 1969), 714–15.

intercession, Jehovah terrified the Philistines with extraordinary thunder preceded by extraordinary lightning, so that the Philistines fled. Then Israel pursued and smote the Philistines as they were fleeing to their own land.

As a memorial of this wholly gracious and decisive victory over the Philistines, Samuel reared up the monument of a stone that he called Ebenezer, that is, stone of help. Samuel explained the name thus: "Hitherto hath the LORD helped us" (1 Sam. 7:12). Thus the prophet and judge proclaimed to Israel that their deliverance from their enemy was wholly the gracious deed of their covenantal God, who is faithful to them even when they have been unfaithful to him. Of this faithfulness, the monument of stone would be a lasting reminder.

First Samuel 7:13 points out that this victory over the Philistines was decisive, regarding both the labors of Judge Samson and the work of Judge Samuel: "So the Philistines were subdued, and they came no more into the coast of Israel: and the hand of the LORD was against the Philistines all the days of Samuel." Samuel was the judge by whom God delivered Israel from the Philistines, completing the deliverance that had been begun by Judge Samson (compare Judges 13:5 and 1 Sam. 7:13). Samson began to deliver Israel from the Philistines (Judges 13:5). Samuel completed the work.

The way to this complete deliverance was Israel's repentance. It is significant that repentance occurred before the completion of Israel's deliverance from the Philistines. There was no repentance during the judgeship of Samson. Repentance was necessary for complete deliverance.

This necessity was not, even as it is not today, the condition required of Israel to render herself worthy of deliverance. The worthiness of Israel to be delivered was the sacrifice of the lamb that Samuel "offered... for a burnt offering wholly unto the LORD" (1 Sam. 7:9). Rather, the necessity of repentance was the necessity of the way in which it pleases God to deliver his people. Bringing his people to repentance is always an aspect—and not the least—of the deliverance. To represent the necessary repentance as the condition that God's people must fulfill in order to render themselves worthy of salvation is the denial of the grace of salvation. The salvation of the covenant of grace is not only deliverance from the misery of the chastisements with which God visits the sins of his people, as also from the misery of the punishment that their sin deserves. It is also, indeed mainly, deliverance from sin itself, and repentance is deliverance from sin. All of this deliverance is the gracious gift *and work* of God.

Regarding the spiritual condition of Israel during her oppression by the Philistines, the beginning of the necessary repentance was effected by the severe judgment of Aphek, including the exile from Israel of the ark and the cessation of the public worship of God at Shiloh. This is the teaching of 1 Samuel 7:2: "All the house of Israel lamented after the LORD." The Hebrew verb translated "lamented" is a strong word that conveys the thought of wailing in sorrow and suggests gatherings of Israel to lament her sins. For twenty years there is a definite, powerful, continuing, spiritual movement of genuine reformation in Israel. The root of the movement is the sorrow of true repentance: sorrow over sin; sorrow that Jehovah is far from them; sorrow over his severe judgment in the oppression by the Philistines.

After twenty years, Samuel called the nation to heartfelt, thorough repentance. He did this prior to the assembly at Mizpeh. Likely, he issued the call at the gatherings in which Israelites lamented after Jehovah. Samuel recognized these gatherings as the beginning of genuine conversion: "If ye do return unto the LORD with all your hearts" (1 Sam. 7:3). The judge emphasized that conversion must be from the heart. It includes forsaking former sins, particularly idolatry: "Then put away the strange gods and Ashtaroth from among you" (v. 3). It ends in serving Jehovah, and him only: "And prepare your hearts unto the LORD, and serve him only" (v. 3). The promise to the repentant people that encourages this repentance is that "he will deliver you out of the hand of the Philistines" (v. 3). The call of the gospel, and this is what the words of Samuel in 1 Samuel 7:3 were, opens up the way of salvation to the church that has strayed and to the penitent sinner.

Israel responded to Samuel's call with heartfelt and thoroughgoing conversion. This was Israel's response because the call was the irresistible call of God himself to his chosen, covenantal people. This repentance and turning from idols to serve Jehovah were themselves deliverance and the necessary way of the covenant to receive deliverance from the Philistines.

The great, national gathering at Mizpeh was a public, covenantal ceremony of repentance toward and reconciliation with Jehovah. Israel publicly confessed her sin: "We have sinned against the Lord" (1 Sam. 7:6). She confessed her sin and sinfulness also in symbolic acts: pouring out water before Jehovah and fasting. Fasting is always a sign of deep spiritual distress over one's sinfulness and sins. The pouring out of water expressed that Israel poured "out their heart like water in penitence before the Lord."[2] In his capacity as mediatorial priest, Samuel prayed for Israel that God would forgive on the basis of the sacrificial lamb that Samuel offered on behalf of the people. Thus Jehovah reconciled the people unto himself in the close covenantal communion that Israel had disturbed, but not broken, by her sin.

Then and there God graciously delivered the penitent and forgiven people from their tormentors, who had afflicted Israel for many years. The deliverance was a remarkable wonder of the grace of God. The actual deliverance was a terrifying thundering upon the Philistines, a heavenly act, the voice of God. Israel did nothing to bring about the deliverance. She was afraid. She trusted entirely in God "that he will save us out of the hand of the Philistines" (1 Sam. 7:8).

God delivered by means of his appointed mediator, Samuel, as Israel acknowledged. She called on Samuel, "Cease not to cry unto the Lord our God for us" (1 Sam. 7:8). "Samuel cried unto the Lord for Israel; and the Lord heard him" (v. 9). It is noteworthy regarding the reality of the salvation of God's people that Samuel was the mediatorial savior of Israel in his threefold office. As prophet he taught the people repentance and forgiveness. As priest he both offered the redemptive sacrifice and interceded for the people with God. As king he "judged the children of Israel in Mizpeh" (v. 6) and undoubtedly led the nation in battle against the Philistines. Thus, as was extremely rare in the history of the

---

2 Keil and Delitzsch, *Biblical Commentary on Samuel*, 72. (See also 2 Sam. 14:14; Ps. 22:14; 42:4; 62:8; Lam. 2:19).

old covenant, Samuel typified the coming Christ, who is Jesus, in all the fullness of his threefold office.

True servant of God that he was, Samuel gave God the glory for the deliverance by means of the commemorative stone, Ebenezer, the stone of help. The stone became the permanent recognition for Israel that "hitherto hath the LORD helped us" (1 Sam. 7:12).

The victory over the Philistines celebrated by the Ebenezer-stone was decisive: "So the Philistines were subdued, and they came no more into the coast of Israel: and the hand of the LORD was against the Philistines all the days of Samuel" (1 Sam. 7:13). Their power over Israel was broken: they made no more regular, deep incursions into Israel, although garrisons remained. Cities of Israel that had been taken by the Philistines were restored to Israel on the north/south line from Ekron to Gath. The Amorites, who had been emboldened by the Philistines' dominance and had been attacking Israel, now sued for peace. This decisive victory occurred at the very place where the Philistines had defeated Israel twenty years earlier: "Ebenezer." In chapter 4:1, the place is called by the name it would have twenty years later, when Samuel erected the monument of the stone. God graciously delivered a repentant people at the very place where earlier he had chastised them for their sins.

There are many victories of the covenantal people over their enemies. The Old Testament records many such victories. There are also victories in the age of the New Testament. One was the Reformation of the church in the sixteenth century. Other victories are similar reformations on a smaller scale. Not all are decisive as was the victory over the Philistines by Samuel at this time. This victory was typical of the decisive victory over the gates of hell by Jesus Christ in his atoning death and resurrection, which victory will be perfected in Christ's return with thousands of his hosts of angels on the world's last day.

Samuel entered fully into his office of judge on this occasion (see 1 Sam. 7:6, 15–17). As judge, he brought the people to repentance; delivered Israel from all their enemies; ordered the life of the nation in the law of God; and brought the extraordinary office of judge to its conclusion by instituting the office of the king in Israel.

Saul:
The People's Choice

Chapter Six

Saul:
The People's Choice

(1 Samuel 8–15)

INTRODUCTION

In 1 Samuel 8 begins the history of the (human) kingship in Israel: "human" because God himself was always the divine king of the nation. Samuel yields to the request of Israel and anoints Saul as king. The office of king, thus inaugurated in Israel, will be filled by God's choice, David. From this time on, the history of Israel is largely the history of the kings, both good and evil. Finally, the Davidic kingship culminates in King Jesus, the everlasting king of the kingdom of God.

This is the appropriate place therefore, in the account of the history of the Old Testament people of God and their salvation, to estimate the significance of the kingdom, specifically in comparison with the covenant. This study of Old Testament history presents the covenant as the fundamental and outstanding reality, the reality that unifies God's dealings with his people, as the title of this series expresses.

There is, however, a case to be made on behalf of the kingdom of God as the fundamental reality in the history of salvation, specifically the history of the salvation of Israel. The kingdom is the reign of God in the Messiah over his elect people, a reign or kingship that calls for and

45

realizes their submission to his authority and obedience to his will. This reign is beneficent and saving, although it also consists of discipline and chastisement. This reign of God is not direct but a reign in the Messiah (the "Anointed One") who is Jesus, prefigured in the Old Testament especially by David. This kingship delivers God's people from all their enemies, including Satan, sin, the wicked and hostile world, and death. It bestows upon the citizens of the kingdom all the blessings of salvation, including righteousness, holiness, and eternal life. The Messiah is savior of Israel.

This deliverance from evil unto good was typified in the Old Testament by salvation from earthly evils and bondage to earthly goods and freedom.

Whether or not one acknowledges the kingdom of God as the preeminent reality in the biblical history of salvation, he must certainly recognize that kingdom is prominent. The Old Testament presents God's Israel as his kingdom and God himself as Israel's king, especially in King David. On the foreground of Old Testament prophecy is the coming of the great king, by whom Israel will be saved and who will establish the everlasting kingdom of God with its peace and prosperity, to the glory of God (Deut. 17:14–20; Ps. 72). The history itself of the larger part of the Bible is mainly the history of Israel, the kingdom of God, and its kings. In terms simply of the number and importance of Old Testament references and emphasis, kingdom does not suffer in comparison with covenant.

Kingdom is also prominent in the New Testament. The angel identified Jesus at his birth as Christ the Lord, inasmuch as he is the royal son of King David (Luke 2:11). The ministry of Jesus was the preaching of "the gospel of the kingdom of God." His message was that the Old Testament prophecy of the kingdom "is fulfilled, and the kingdom of God is at hand" (Mark 1:14–15). The issue in Jesus' trial before Pilate was his kingship. To Pilate's question whether he was indeed the "King of the Jews," Jesus answered, "Thou sayest it" (15:2). Regardless of the motives of Pilate, God directed that the placard over the crucified Jesus would read, "THIS IS THE KING OF THE JEWS," and that this explanation of the suffering and death of the cross would call attention to the ecumenicity of the kingship of Jesus inasmuch as it was written in Greek, Latin, and Hebrew (Luke 23:38).

Times without numbering, and in all kinds of ways, the epistles herald the risen Jesus as God's anointed king over his kingdom (see Eph. 1:20–22). Indeed, the title Christ is itself the proclamation of the kingship of Jesus. The fundamental confession of the Christian, indeed a confession that one day every tongue will make, is that "Jesus Christ is Lord" (Phil. 2:11). The eschatological end of all things, according to the last book of the Bible, is the revelation of Jesus Christ as king and, in him, the perfection of the kingdom of God worldwide (Rev. 1:5; 6:2; 14:14, 17:14, 19:11–16). The daily prayer of every believer for this revelation of Jesus as king is, "Come, *Lord* Jesus" (Rev. 22:20; emphasis added). This surprises no believer. Christ taught his disciples to pray, "Thy kingdom come" (Matt. 6:10).

Is then kingdom more important to the Reformed, Christian faith than covenant? Are the Reformed theologians and churches that emphasize covenant, as does this study, mistaken?

The mistake is to emphasize either covenant or kingdom to the minimizing and even exclusion of the other. Covenant and kingdom are two distinct but inseparable aspects of one and the same spiritual reality. The reality is God's salvation of his elect people in Jesus Christ, to the glorifying of himself. Covenant, rightly understood, is the friendship of God with his people. Kingdom is God's reign over his people. The covenant is a *kingly* relation of friendship. It is not friendship between equals, but between sovereign and citizens. Kingship, on the other hand, is covenantal rule. It is not the rule of a distant, terrifying, and cold lord, but the rule of a close friend.

The inseparable, mutually qualifying relation of covenant and kingdom in the Bible is evident in the name of the book. The two sections of the Bible are known as Old and New *Testaments*, "testament" meaning the same as "covenant." At the same time, John Bright proves his assertion that "the Bible is one book...'The Book of the Coming Kingdom of God.'"[1]

---

1   John Bright, *The Kingdom of God* (Nashville, TN: Pierce & Washabaugh, 1953), 197.

The danger in theology is such an emphasis on one or the other of the two fundamental, saving realities as to minimize and even exclude the other. This would be to do injustice to important biblical revelation. God is not only king; he is also friend. It is not only important that the church know God as friend; it is equally important that the church know him as sovereign. Jesus the savior is not only in intimate communion with the believer; he is also exalted high above the believer on the throne of his awesome glory.

The danger of so emphasizing the one as to minimize the other carries with it serious practical consequences in the teaching of the church and in the life of the Reformed Christian. The proper response to kingship is awe and, in this awe, obedience. The response to covenant is love and, in this love, a drawing near to the savior. Emphasis on kingship that ignores or minimizes covenant will produce a fear that borders on terror and an obedience that does not arise out of love. Emphasis on covenant that virtually ignores kingship is liable to lose the awe that is basic to the Christian faith and to overlook the calling to obey the sovereign. The one evil is a "Christian life" lacking love; the other is a "Christian life" without reverence.

The institution of kingship in 1 Samuel 8–16, finding its fulfillment as it does in the coming of the great king, Jesus Christ the Lord, insists that the covenant of God established with father Abraham and Israel is a kingly covenant with a royal friendship and that the life of the covenant is obedience to the sovereign will of the king. To put it differently, in 1 Samuel 8–16 the covenant takes form in kingdom. And the first king of the kingdom is Saul.

CHOICE OF THE PEOPLE

Saul was the king chosen by Israel in disobedience to God. Israel's request for a king was wicked. It represented Israel's rejection of the kingship of Jehovah (1 Sam. 8:7; 10:19; 12:12). This rejection of the kingship of Jehovah was a climax of the overall nature of Israel's walk from the time of the deliverance from Egypt. Israel rejected the theocracy. Motivating this rejection was a carnal desire to be like the other nations. This was the very evil that Moses had warned against, indeed prophesied, in Deuter-onomy 17:14–20, his great prophecy of the coming kingship in Israel: "Thou...shalt say, I will set a king over me, like as all the nations that are about me" (v. 14). This desire for a king like the other nations was a great wickedness, according to 1 Samuel 12:17, which Israel confessed, according to verse 19.

In keeping with Israel's rebellious, God-dishonoring desire for a king like the other nations, the qualifications of the king they receive were mere natural, man-pleasing attributes: stature, physical appearance, and charisma (1 Sam. 9:2). Saul exhibited bravery, leadership qualities, and modesty (10:21–27; 9:21; 15:17). In explanation of Saul's bravery, he was of the tribe of Benjamin, the most warlike of all the tribes. This was the blessing of dying Jacob: "Benjamin shall ravin as a wolf: in the morn-ing he shall devour the prey, and at night he shall divide the spoil" (Gen. 49:27). This bravery would commend itself to carnal Israel.

Saul was likeable. Even Samuel had great affection for Saul (1 Sam. 15:11, 35). Saul was the king after Israel's heart, as David would be the king after the heart of Jehovah.

In keeping with Israel's rebellious request, there is, second, the warn-ing that Saul will burden Israel with the typical burdens of earthly rulers: high taxes and impressment of Israel into his service. That is, the king will make the nation serve him, rather than that he serves the nation (1 Sam. 8:10–18). Samuel's warning to Israel was, at the same time, the divine admonition to the people to repent of their sinful request for a king like the nations: "Nevertheless the people refused to obey the voice of Samuel" (v. 19).

Also in keeping with Israel's rebellious request for a king was the wickedness of the king whom they chose and whom God gave them: Saul was rebellious against Jehovah. Already very early in his reign Saul disobeyed the command of God that he wait for Samuel to offer the necessary sacrifice unto Jehovah (1 Sam. 13). In his disobedience, Saul represented the people who chose him. Like people, like king.

The fulfillment of Israel's wicked choice of a king will be the nation's choice of Caesar rather than Jesus the Christ (see John 19:15).

Ultimately, the choice of Saul finds its fulfillment in the false church's choice of antichrist as its ruler. The son of perdition will sit in the temple of God (2 Thess. 2:3–4).

Jehovah's appointment of Saul therefore is nothing more than to give the people what they want, indeed what they demand. Jehovah does appoint Saul. He chooses Saul (1 Sam. 10:24). He qualifies him for office (v. 1). This is the significance of the election of Saul by lot (vv. 17–27). Hence, afterward David regards Saul as the Lord's anointed (2 Sam. 1:14).

Nevertheless, the nature of the appointment, in the judgment of God, is that expressed in Hosea 13:11: "I gave thee [Israel] a king in mine anger, and took him away in my wrath."

The manner of God's appointment of Saul to be king is noteworthy. He brings Saul to the attention of Samuel, so that Samuel anoints Saul as "captain over his inheritance" (1 Sam. 10:1) by means of the lost donkeys and Saul's seeking for them (chap. 9). The day before Saul came to Samuel, Jehovah announced to Samuel that the man he had chosen to be king would come to Samuel (vv. 15–16). When Saul arrived, God identified Saul to the prophet as Israel's king by his appointment (v. 17). Jehovah "sent" Saul into the kingship by means of straying asses, an ignoble route to royalty.

Samuel announces Saul's kingship to him (1 Sam. 9:20; see also v. 25). The prophet anoints Saul with oil, symbolic of the Holy Spirit, in a solemn, official ceremony, which was, however, private (10:1). In his description of Saul's office, Samuel instructs Saul how to behave as king: "captain over his [Jehovah's] inheritance" (v. 1). Israel is Jehovah's inheritance, to be governed for Jehovah. It is not Saul's inheritance, to be ruled as he pleases and for his advantage.

Samuel foretells three signs that will honor Saul as the anointed king, thus confirming his appointment and assuring him of God's help in his kingship (1 Sam. 10:2–7). Two men will inform him that the asses are found (v. 2). Three men going to Bethel will give Saul a salutation and two loaves of bread (vv. 3–4). Most significantly, Saul will receive the Spirit of Jehovah when he meets a company of prophets, who prophesy. Under the influence of the Spirit, Saul will prophesy with the school of prophets. This will seal to Saul his anointing to be king. By prophesying here is to be understood "an ecstatic utterance of religious feelings to the praise of God."[2] It was not for Saul the utterance of the word of God from a heart that was zealous for the glory of God in the salvation of the people of God. The recording of this last sign indicates that the purpose of it was to bring Saul to the attention of the people, as anointed by God to his special office among them (vv. 10–12).

THE CRUCIAL TEST

On the occasion of Samuel's anointing of Saul as king, the prophet charges Saul with a certain duty that he must fulfill later, after becoming king, when there will be a battle against the Philistines (1 Sam. 10:8). This is the command that Saul will disobey (13:8–14), thus showing himself rebellious against the authority of God over him and the nation and disqualifying himself as fathering the line of kings in Israel. With the honor of office comes a calling by which Saul must show himself a faithful, godly king. The command is a test, as Saul knows. The test is fitting: wait on the prophet of God and depend on the sacrifice properly offered by the priest of God. The command is similar to the command to Adam in paradise and to the calling of Christ to wait on God in the wilderness, when he was tempted by Satan.

Obedience to God is crucial to kingship in the kingdom of God, as the time of the issuing of the command shows. On the occasion of the appointment to the office of king, Saul receives the command that will prove him: "Thou shalt go down before me [Samuel] to Gilgal; and, behold, I will come down unto thee, to offer burnt offerings, and to sacrifice sacrifices of peace offerings: seven days shalt thou tarry, till I come to thee, and shew thee what thou shalt do" (1 Sam. 10:8).

Figuring largely in the appointment of Saul as king was the threat to Israel of the Philistines. God himself made this clear in his announcement to Samuel that he must anoint Saul to be king: "that he may save

---

2 Keil and Delitzsch, *Biblical Commentary on Samuel*, 100. On this kind of prophesying, see also Numbers 11:25.

my people out of the hand of the Philistines" (1 Sam. 9:16). Deliverance of Israel from the Philistines would be the immediate, urgent duty of the king. In fulfilling this duty, he must rely on God and obey.

Upon leaving Samuel, having been anointed, Saul receives "another heart" from God (1 Sam. 10:9). This is the fulfillment of Samuel's promise to Saul in verse 6: "The Spirit of the LORD will come upon thee, and thou…shalt be turned into another man." Receiving another heart and being turned into another man take place when the Spirit comes upon Saul and refer to an extraordinary, non-saving empowerment of Saul to carry out the office of king. This change certainly affected his mind and will and was experienced by the king. He felt himself qualified to be king of the nation, except of course for the fundamental qualification of genuine spirituality. He had access now to supernatural power. The change that overcame Saul was not, however, a spiritual change. It was not regeneration, as his immediate behavior demonstrated. Of this anointing, Saul tells no one. This phase of the appointment of Saul to the kingly office is strictly private.

The response of the people to Saul's prophesying among the prophets consists of two questions: "Is Saul also among the prophets?" and "But who is their father?" (1 Sam. 10:11–12). The first question is readily understandable. The people are surprised to find Saul, who has had no training, who has not hitherto been included in the company of prophets, and who is, in the judgment of those who have known him, altogether an unlikely candidate for the prophetic office. "Is Saul also among the prophets?" became a proverb. It is still a proverb today.

But the second question is more difficult. The question, "Who is their father?" is the response of one to the question about Saul's prophesying, "What is this that is come unto the son of Kish?" The point of the response is that if the company of prophets prophesied, even though their fathers were not prophets, why should it surprise that Saul should prophesy, contrary to his former behavior? That is, if prophesying is not by family tradition or pedigree for the company of prophets, why should it be for Saul?

PHASES OF APPOINTMENT

The first phase of the appointment of Saul to the kingship over Israel was the private anointing by Samuel. The second phase was his public selection by lot (1 Sam. 10:17–27). This occurred at the historic place Mizpeh. Among other significant events, it was there that Israel in a national repentance confessed its sin of idolatry and experienced a miraculous deliverance from the Philistines (chap. 7).

In his office of prophet, Samuel conducted the selection of Saul. It is significant that the prophet inaugurates the kingship in Israel. Israel as a kingdom derives from, depends upon, and is to be governed by the word of God. This implies that the king is always accountable to the word of God as brought by a prophet. His sovereignty is not absolute. Time and again in Israel, a prophet rebukes a king and calls him to repentance.

The selection of Saul is preceded by a repetition of the rebuke of Israel for the nation's sin in desiring a king like the nations. The rebuke is sharp: "Ye have this day rejected your God" (1 Sam. 10:19). Israel showed itself unthankful and unfaithful to its divine king, who had "brought up Israel out of Egypt, and delivered you out of the hand of the Egyptians, and out of the hand of all kingdoms, and of them that oppressed you" (v. 18). In light of the rebuke, the gift of the king does not bode well for the nation. God gives the king in his anger (Hos. 13:11).

It is God who gives Saul to Israel. The selection of Saul is God's doing, evidently by lot. One meaning of the Hebrew word translated "taken" in 1 Samuel 10:20–21 is "taken by lot." This was the manner of the "taking" of Achan in Joshua 7:14–18, where the text states that it was the Lord who took the sinner, that is, identified him. The use of the lot was the common way in the time of the old covenant that God decided matters and made known his will: "The lot is cast into the lap; but the whole disposing thereof is of the LORD" (Prov. 16:33).

As the selection of himself takes place, Saul, who knows the outcome beforehand, hides among the baggage. This is not to evade the appointment. Neither is it due to timidity. Rather, it is the expression of an appropriate modesty. Keil quotes one Seb. Schmidt, who is usually right:

"In order that he might not appear to have either the hope or desire for anything of the kind, he preferred to be absent when the lots were cast."[3]

If Israel inquires of the Lord for Saul by means of the Urim and Thummim, as is likely, the presence of the high priest is implied. This means that all three offices in Israel are present and functioning on the occasion of the selection of Israel's first king. The occasion of the historical formation of Israel as the kingdom of God is momentous.

Saul's selection is not by democratic election, because Israel is a theocracy, not a democracy. Samuel presents King Saul to the people as the man whom the Lord has chosen (1 Sam. 10:24). Even though they have not elected the king, Israel's reception of their king is required. God does not simply impose officebearers upon his kingdom, then or now. The citizens are called actively to receive them.

This applies to the appointment of officebearers in the New Testament church. Not only does God give them by means of their being chosen by the confessing male members of the congregation, but also upon their election the entire congregation is admonished to "receive these men as the servants of God."[4] In its own way, this is true also regarding the divine appointment of Christ Jesus as prophet, priest, and king in the reality of the kingdom of God. God not only gives Jesus to the kingdom/church as its great officebearer, but he also works in the citizens of the kingdom the reception of Christ by faith. Faith acknowledges Christ as the king, confesses him as the anointed one, and bows to him in willing submission.

The refusal of some in Israel thus to receive Saul showed them to be children of Belial (1 Sam. 10:7). Israel received Saul with the shout, "God save the king," or more literally, May the king live (v. 24).

On the occasion of the institution of the kingly office in Israel, and

3 Keil and Delitzsch, *Biblical Commentary on Samuel*, 108. Alfred Edersheim, in contrast, sees Saul's hiding as his fear of the office to which he is being selected and therefore as indicative of his lack of spirituality (Alfred Edersheim, *Old Testament Bible History* [Grand Rapids, MI: William B. Eerdmans, repr. 1990], 4:49).

4 Form for Ordination of Elders and Deacons, in *The Confessions and the Church Order of the Protestant Reformed Churches* (Grandville, MI: Protestant Reformed Churches in America, 2005), 293.

thus the formation of Israel as a kingdom, Samuel instructs the people—and Saul!—concerning "the manner of the kingdom" (1 Sam. 10:25). Such is the importance of this instruction that Samuel writes it in a book, which he then lays up before the Lord (v. 25). This is the constitution of the kingdom of God. No doubt, this book becomes part of the precious contents of the tabernacle, if not of the ark of the covenant. The "manner of the kingdom" of Israel is the unique nature of Israel and its life, particularly with reference to the rule of the king over the nation as the kingdom of God. The manner is that the king rules and the citizens live in submission according to the will of God, so that God is glorified. This manner of the kingdom was described in the prophecy of the king in Deuteronomy 17:14–20. By means of the king, Israel is ruled by God and for God.

The manner of the kingdom is not learned from or patterned after the manner of the kingdoms of the surrounding nations. God prescribes and reveals the manner of his kingdom. Likewise today the kingdom of God, which is the church, does not take its marching orders or derive its way of life from the kingdoms of the world of the ungodly among which it lives. The church has its own, unique, God-given "manner of the kingdom." This manner is written in a book. The book is the Bible, which as to essentials is the book that Samuel once laid up before the Lord.

Some in Israel rejected the king, doubting that he would save Israel (1 Sam. 10:27). This opposition to Saul verged on revolution and treason (11:12). As rebellion against the authority of God, who had chosen the king, it was worthy of death, although Saul shows a clemency that undoubtedly commends him to the people and spares the life of the rebels (vv. 12–13).

Here some biographical data about Saul are in order. He was of the tribe of Benjamin. He was the son of Kish, a prominent, wealthy member of the tribe. Saul was about forty when he became king, since he had a son, Jonathan, who was at least twenty years old at his father's accession to the throne. Jonathan was old enough to command men in battle (1 Sam. 13). Saul's home was Gibeah. As figured prominently in Israel's attraction to him, Saul was exceptionally tall for an Israelite and likely well-built. He had natural qualities of a winsome modesty and of bravery.

In short, Saul came from a prominent family and had the personal, natural characteristics that impress people. He would have been a successful politician in twenty-first-century America. He was the man of the people. Like most politicians, he was not the man of God.

The third phase of the appointment of Saul to the kingship followed Saul's brave deliverance of Jabesh-gilead from Nahash, cruel king of Ammon. It consisted of the public installation of Saul into the office of king (1 Sam. 11:14–15). Samuel again presided, as the testimony to the necessity of the word of God in the prophetic office for the legitimate rule of the covenantal people. Saul's installation occurred at Gilgal. It was a renewal of the kingdom, with reference to the public selection of Saul at Mizpeh. On this occasion, the people caused Saul to be king before the Lord (v. 15), that is, they acknowledged God's selection of Saul by honoring Saul as their king in a formal, official, public way.

The significance of this third phase of the installation of Saul as king is that his kingship is fully established, or confirmed, by means of his kingly behavior in delivering Israel from Ammon. Saul became king *de facto* as he had been *de jure*. It belonged to his final phase of his installation into the royal office that he silenced his critics. There was no longer any challenge to his kingship.

This understanding of Saul's becoming king in three distinct phases is that of faith that receives the biblical narrative as inspired. It conflicts with the higher-critical dismissal of the biblical account as contradictory explanations that have been patched together. These contradictory stories, reflecting different sources, are supposed to express different attitudes toward the monarchy. John Bright is representative of this unbelief:

> The account of Saul's election comes to us in two (probably originally three) parallel narratives, one tacitly favorable to the monarchy, the other bitterly hostile...In view of these varying accounts, we cannot undertake to reconstruct the sequence of events.[5]

---

5   John Bright, *A History of Israel*, 2nd ed. (Philadelphia, PA: Westminster Press, 1952), 166–67.

The real difficulty in the history of the election of Saul as king is the affirmation of Jehovah's appointment of him in spite of God's condemnation both of Israel's demand for a king and of Israel's selection of Saul. The explanation is that Jehovah appoints Saul to be the reprobate (rejected) king, in sharp contrast with his choice of David as the elect king. God is sovereign over the wicked choice of Saul by unthankful Israel. In Saul's disobedient kingship will be manifested the unapproved kingship. The end of Saul will be that he is rejected of Jehovah regarding both the kingship of his house and his own personal reign. As the divinely determined but unapproved king, Saul will be the dark background and counterpart of David.

The kingship of Saul and the kingship of David appear in the nature of the kingdom of Israel as antithetical. The antithesis—the spiritual difference and opposition of the godly and the ungodly—is fundamental within the sphere of the covenant and kingdom of God, as it is fundamental to the separation of the covenantal community from the world of the ungodly. Although both are physical Israelites, Saul and David are spiritual opposites. Between them is the opposition of the kingdom of spiritual darkness to the kingdom of spiritual light. Saul hates David with a murderous hatred, is determined to destroy him, and exerts himself to kill David at the expense of all else, including the welfare of the nation and the life (at the hands of Saul, according to Saul's intention) of his own son Jonathan. They were not all Israel who were of Israel already in the earliest days of the kingdom of God in the world (see Rom. 9:6–8). The reality of election and reprobation, which is the ultimate origin of the antithesis, is basic to the history of the kingdom of God in the world.

MERCIFUL PURPOSES WITH A SINFUL REQUEST

Implied by the truth that the unapproved Saul is nevertheless, in his own peculiar way, also the choice of God is that God determines and uses Israel's wicked choice and Saul's rebellious kingship for his own good purposes. One such good purpose is the deliverance of Israel from the marauding Philistines. God announced this use of Saul in his word to Samuel concerning his selection of Saul as the king that Israel desired:

"Thou shalt anoint him to be captain over my people Israel, that he may save my people out of the hand of the Philistines" (1 Sam. 9:16). Another purpose is the immediate deliverance of Jabesh-gilead from Nahash the Ammonite and his shaming of God's inheritance. Chapter 12:12 discloses that the threat posed by Nahash was the occasion for Israel's request for a king. Looking back upon this request, Samuel reminded Israel, "When ye saw that Nahash the king of the children of Ammon came against you, ye said unto me, Nay; but a king shall reign over us: when the LORD your God was your king." Still another purpose of God with the choice of Saul as king was simply to introduce kingship and kingdom in Israel, ultimately with a view to the establishment of the reality of the kingdom in Jesus Christ.

Saul's deliverance of Israel from Nahash and Ammon was of special importance for the kingship of Saul, for the royal office in Israel, and therefore for Israel as the kingdom of God. Nahash had invaded Israel in the territory east of the Jordan River prior to Israel's request for a king. It was the pressing threat from Nahash that was the immediate occasion for the request. Nahash had not as yet attacked Jabesh-gilead and laid down the cruel condition for peace consisting of the thrusting out of the right eyes of all the men of Jabesh-gilead. The fact that Israel's request for a king to deliver them from Nahash was her response to the invasion by Ammon exposed the unbelief of Israel's request. Israel did not respond to the threat by seeking help from Jehovah, as Israel had often done during the time of the judges, with the result that Israel had received the help she needed. It was this that made Israel's request for a king rejection of Jehovah as king (see 1 Sam. 8:7).

For this reason also, Israel's request for a king in the face of the Ammonite invasion was her rejection of Samuel, as Samuel recognized (1 Sam. 8:6–7). Samuel was a judge, provided by God exactly for such work as the deliverance that Israel now needed. But Israel did not seek deliverance from Samuel. Rejection of God's judge, however, serious as this was, was at bottom rejection of God, who gave the judge and saved Israel by him.

The barbarous condition for peace laid down by the heathen king, namely "that I may thrust out all your right eyes," and the purpose of the condition, "lay it for a reproach upon all Israel" (1 Sam. 11:2), indicate that more is involved than mere national aggression and desire for expansion of national boundaries. Nahash is intent on settling the old score from the time of Judge Jephthah (see Judges 10–12). He insists on pressing Ammon's claim to the land of Israel east of the Jordan. And Nahash desires to shame "all Israel," not only Jabesh-gilead, to avenge the shame of Ammon inflicted by Jephthah's defeat of Ammon many years before.

Israel at this time is in a sorry state. She is attacked by the Philistines from the west and by Ammon from the east. In addition, she is so dispirited that likely she will not rise to Jabesh-gilead's defense or even to the warding off of national disgrace by the blinding of the eyes of the men of Jabesh-gilead. Nahash gives Jabesh-gilead the seven days respite it asks for in the confidence that no help will be forthcoming.

The desperate plight of Israel evokes the pity of God, the pity that has already given Israel the king who is to be Israel's deliverer (see 1 Sam. 9:16). The divine pity is all the more wonderful in that Israel seeks a king like the nations, thus rejecting God as her king.

In the pity of God for his people, the Spirit of God comes upon Saul, to stir him up to undertake the deliverance of Jabesh-gilead and all Israel. The Spirit works in Saul a kingly courage (see 1 Sam. 11:6). Although Saul has been anointed king and publicly acknowledged as king, he is not yet functioning as king. The news of Jabesh-gilead's plight finds him plowing with oxen as a farmer.

Saul cuts up his yoke of oxen, sends the pieces throughout Israel, and threatens to kill the oxen of those who refuse to assemble for battle against Ammon. The killing of their oxen is not a minor matter to the Israelite farmers, but the inspiration to enlist for war is mainly the heroic and resolute spirit of their king. The Spirit of the Lord who emboldens King Saul now goes out from him to the citizenry of the kingdom. The Spirit goes out to the nation in the fear of the Lord (1 Sam. 11:7), that is, a reverence that Jehovah causes. The result is that the entire nation sends men to defend Jabesh-gilead against Ammon. Three hundred and thirty thousand men gather for battle.

It is significant regarding the office of king now being instituted in

Israel that all the nation unites. During the time of the judges, only some of the tribes cooperated in the defense of Israel. The judges did not command or unite the entire nation. Saul does command the entire nation. The entire nation unites around him in the battle against Ammon.

Kingship is necessary for the union of the covenant. Covenantal history unfolds here in the revelation that the covenant of grace is one in the person and work of the Messiah, King Jesus, and that the covenantal people of God, whether in the old and new dispensations or among all nations, are united in their common king, Jesus the Messiah. One purpose of this unity is the defense of the members of the covenant and citizens of the kingdom against their enemy, who would shame them.

Nevertheless, even in this, one of the finest moments of Israel's history, there is the hint of a serious rift that will break out in division. There is an ominous distinction between Israel and Judah: "The children of Israel were three hundred thousand, and the men of Judah thirty thousand" (1 Sam. 11:8). Always in the history of the covenantal community there are fault lines beneath the surface, threatening schism. The unity of the church in the world is both a precious gift of her king and a blessing carefully to be guarded.

In his preparation of Israel for battle, Saul wisely allies Samuel with himself. Samuel is still functioning as judge in Israel, as well as being the embodiment of the word of God (see 1 Sam. 11:7).

The host of Israel—hastily assembled, untrained in the military arts, it is hardly an army—defeats and destroys Ammon. God gives the militant farmers and shepherds victory, as Saul confesses (see 1 Sam. 11:13). Israel keeps the land that God gave her east of the Jordan. Jabesh-gilead is spared cruel suffering. Israel escapes the reproach of Nahash. And rather than Israel, it is the enemies of the covenantal people of God who are put to shame.

As is usually the case, God's working out the salvation of his people employs wise means: a courageous leader; a large host; and shrewd battle tactics—attacking Ammon from three directions and in the "morning watch," that is, between three and six in the morning, when an overconfident Ammon sleeps. The grace that accomplishes and decides the victory of the kingdom of God in history by no means implies inaction, folly, or lack of wise human leadership on the part of the citizens of the kingdom.

It was no small part of the Spirit's qualifying of Saul to be king that Saul displayed a royal spirit after the victory. He gave Jehovah the glory of the victory. With magnanimity toward his personal detractors, motivated by his recognition of God's grace to Israel, Saul spared those who had challenged his kingship earlier (1 Sam. 11:12–13). This made a good impression on the nation. At the very outset of his reign, Saul conducted himself wisely and well.

Yet another use that God made of Israel's wicked choice and of Saul's rebellious kingship was his preparation of Israel for the king after God's heart, David. Now kingship is established. Presently the rightful king, whom God elects, will function in the office. And Israel will have learned by bitter experience to appreciate the king who views himself as Jehovah's and their servant and who does the will of Jehovah on their behalf. All of this will find its fulfillment in David's great Son, Jesus the Christ.

Jehovah God certainly decreed and governed Israel's request for a king, for he foretold it in Deuteronomy 17:14: "When thou art come unto the land...and shalt say, I will set a king over me, like as all the nations that are about me." He accomplished his purpose in the way of Israel's wicked request. In Jehovah's yielding to Israel's desire for a king and even making the evil request turn out for their profit, both by delivering them from their enemies and by causing the kingship to terminate in David, Jehovah's unswerving covenantal faithfulness and mercy are evident. In the context of his vigorous charge against Israel of their great sin in their request for a king, Samuel equally vigorously proclaims the faithfulness and mercy of God toward them in his covenant: "For the LORD will not forsake his people for his great name's sake: because it hath pleased the LORD to make you his people" (1 Sam. 12:22).

The covenantal faithfulness of God to Israel is the message of Samuel in 1 Samuel 12, immediately after the final phase of the installation of Saul into the office of king, as recorded in chapter 11:14–15. In this address, Samuel retires as judge (chap. 12:1–5), although not as prophet (v. 23). Upon the institution of the office of king, the office of judge necessarily ceases. God now will rule Israel by means of the former. Retiring from the office of judge in the kingdom of God, Samuel can challenge the people to charge him with any injustice or other malfeasance in office. He is confident that he has exercised his office honorably before God and his people (vv. 3–5). Such ought to be the confident claim of every officebearer in the New Testament kingdom of God at his emeritation, or retirement.

Again Samuel charges Israel with sin in asking for a king. He calls on God to severely chastise Israel for the sin by the miracle of a heavy storm during this time of the wheat harvest, which must have done great damage to the crop (1 Sam. 12:17–18). Israel repents (v. 19). It is then that Samuel proclaims to Israel the gospel of God's merciful faithfulness to them in the covenant (v. 22). Completing the salvation order of misery (repentance), mercy (forgiveness), and holiness of life, Samuel then calls Israel to reverence and obey God in the covenant: "Turn not aside from following the LORD, but serve the LORD with all your heart; and turn ye not aside" (vv. 20–21). To the exhortation to serve the Lord, the prophet adds a sharp warning: "But if ye shall still do wickedly, ye shall be consumed, both ye and your king" (v. 25). "Grace is conferred by means of admonitions."[6]

Puzzling in the address of Samuel is the mention of Bedan evidently as one of the judges (1 Sam. 12:11). The history of the judges knows no Bedan. Bedan is either a copyist's mistake for Barak or another spelling of Judge Abdon. Some versions of scripture in various languages have these other names.

Looking back over the determination of Israel to have a king, it is evident that the occasion was Israel's need as the nation perceived it. The immediate need was the threat of the Philistines and of the Ammonites (see 1 Sam. 9:16). In this connection, Israel was seduced by the example of the heathen nations about them. Always Israel, like the churches today, allowed itself to be influenced by the world. More remotely, the lessons learned, or thought to be learned, from the history of the judges played a

---

6 Canons of Dordt 3–4.17, in Schaff, *Creeds of Christendom*, 3:592.

role. Only when there was a strong leader did Israel enjoy deliverance, a measure of peace, prosperity, and some power to resist the nations about it. Even then, the limited sphere of the power of the judge failed to unite the tribes and thus give national deliverance and power.

Then there was the old age of Samuel, the one national figure on the scene, and the miserable failure of his sons, whom Samuel had appointed to succeed him as judges in Israel (1 Sam. 8:1–5). Great men in the church often have unworthy sons. Leadership in the kingdom of God in the world is not a matter of natural generation but of divine appointment and spiritual qualification. Here it may be noted that Joel in 1 Samuel 8:2 is Vashni in 1 Chronicles 6:28.

Analysis of the occasion of Israel's requesting a king acknowledges Israel's real need. Nevertheless, Israel ought to have sought and relied on the kingship of Jehovah for its help. Whatever lack of help there was at this time and throughout the time of the old covenant was due to Israel's unfaithfulness in the covenant and to the will of God to give full deliverance to his people by himself as come in the flesh, that is, in Jesus Christ.

Chapter Seven

—

Saul:
Unapproved for Office

(1 Samuel 13–15)

*I*n 1 Samuel 13–15, King Saul shows himself to be reprobate in the sense of being unapproved by God. The meaning here is not that of being eternally appointed to damnation, as is the sense of the word in Reformed theology. Rather, the meaning is that God does not approve of Saul's conduct in his kingly office but condemns it as not fitting for one who occupies high office in the kingdom of God. The word *reprobate* has this sense in 2 Corinthians 13:5–6 and in 2 Timothy 3:8. In the Greek original of the New Testament the word is *adokimos*, which expresses that someone fails a test, so as to show himself unfit for the task to which he is called. This was the case with Saul at the very beginning of his reign.

Saul failed the first and fundamental test, namely, obedience to the command of God's prophet to wait for God's priest to offer sacrifices at Gilgal prior to the conflict with the Philistines. Edersheim puts it well: "What they [Israel] had asked, they obtained; and what they obtained, must fail; and what failed would prepare for what God intended."[1] Samuel gave this order to Saul from God at the time that

---

1 Edersheim, *Old Testament Bible*, 4:47.

Samuel anointed Saul as king (see 1 Sam. 10:8; 13:8). This order was the basic test of Saul's kingship, whether it would be in the service of Jehovah or a kingship of self-will. This test Saul promptly and inexcusably failed (chap. 13).

The history recorded in 1 Samuel 13, the impending war with the Philistines, is confusing in the AV on account of a textual problem in verse 1. This verse dates the event in the chapter some two years after the full, public installation of Saul into the office of king and after the charge to Saul to wait for Samuel at Gilgal seven days for sacrifices to be made (see 1 Sam. 10:8). In fact, Saul's disobedience happened immediately after Samuel gave the command and after the renewal of the kingdom as recorded in chapter 11:14–15.

The confusion in the AV regarding the timing of Saul's disobedience is a textual error in verse 1. The first part of verse 1 in the Hebrew Masoretic text intends to give Saul's age at becoming king. The second part intends to give the length of Saul's reign, as is customary at the beginning of the history of a king's reign. Both parts are missing numbers due to the error of a copyist. Saul was about forty when he began to reign. He reigned forty years (see Acts 13:21). What is important in all this for an understanding of 1 Samuel 13 is that the history of the chapter, and especially the disobedience of Saul, happened at once after Saul became king and after Samuel had charged him with waiting for Samuel to come to offer sacrifices.

Saul's son Jonathan, who is met here for the first time in the history, takes the initiative against the Philistines. He takes the Philistine garrison at Geba. Saul calls all Israel to war. The Philistines attack in great force. The Hebrews desert and hide. Those who remain are terrified ("trembling," 1 Sam. 13:7). Saul waits for Samuel for seven days, as he had been commanded. When Samuel does not appear, Saul has the sacrifices offered. Samuel then appears within the allotted time. He rebukes Saul and announces that in judgment upon the king's disobedience his descendants will not succeed to the kingship (v. 14: "But now thy kingdom shall not continue").

The grievous sin on the part of the king of Israel is disobedience.

This is the charge against Saul by Samuel: "Thou hast not kept the commandment of the LORD thy God, which he commanded thee… thou hast not kept that which the LORD commanded thee" (1 Sam. 13:13–14). The disobedience rises out of and reveals a heart that is not set on doing the will of Jehovah, because it does not love Jehovah nor seek his glory in Israel. Saul does not regard the government of Israel as a theocracy. Neither does he regard Israel as the "inheritance of Jehovah," as Samuel described the nation when he appointed Saul as king in chapter 10:1 (see also Deut. 4:20; 9:26, 29). Instruction in precisely this truth must have been the content of Samuel's book of "the manner of the kingdom" (1 Sam. 10:25), where the Hebrew original has the sense of the judgment, or that which is right, of the kingdom. Obedience to God is not only the manner of the *king*, as though setting forth royal prerogatives, but rather the manner of the *kingdom*, setting forth the right, the constitution, of the *kingdom*. By his disobedience to the command of God, Saul reveals that he occupies his office without regard for the kingdom on behalf of which the office is to be exercised, indeed for which the office exists.

That the sin is disobedience to the command of God must not be weakened by finding Saul's sin in his offering sacrifice himself personally, whereas he is not a priest. It would be a mistake to understand 1 Samuel 13:9, 10, and 12 so. The verses only charge Saul with the responsibility of conducting the sacrificial service. Saul has priests in attendance who actually offer the sacrifices. Samuel does not accuse Saul of trespassing on the priestly office. He accuses Saul of disobedience.

Saul's disobedience betrays contempt as well for the content of Samuel's command. The command was not arbitrary. The king of Israel must conduct the warfare of the nation in dependency upon the favor of God. This favor is shown and received by means of the sacrifice and the sacrificing priest. The battle then must be waged and won in reliance upon the word of God, which is brought by the prophet. Saul must wait for the prophet so that the word of God by the prophet will "shew thee what thou shalt do" (1 Sam. 10:8). Disregard of the sacrifice and ignoring of the word of the prophet are unbelief.

Such is the importance of obedience to the will of God in the matter of the establishment of God's kingdom and the salvation of its citizens that the entire ministry of the messianic king is described as obedience: "Then said I, Lo, I come (in the volume of the book it is written of me,) to do thy will, O God" (Heb. 10:7). Doing God's will is obedience. The volume of the book is the reality of Samuel's book setting forth the manner of the kingdom. In Deuteronomy 17, it is required of the kings of Israel that they have a copy of the law, that they read it daily, and that they keep it without turning aside to the right or left.

There is application of this fundamental importance of the law to all officebearers in the church always. They must themselves be, and be seen by the people to be, obedient—obedient in the work of their office and obedient in their personal life.

It is no mitigation of Saul's guilt that he is sorely tried by Samuel's apparent delay, by the desertion of his men, and by the looming threat of the Philistines. (Regarding the thinning of Saul's army, only six hundred men remained to Saul, whereas he had three thousand when he called all Israel to battle [see 1 Sam. 13:2, 15]). First, Samuel did come within the specified time of seven days. Second, the prophet of Jehovah explicitly commanded him to wait as a direct order from Jehovah God: "Seven days shalt thou tarry, till I come to thee" (10:8). Third, it is always the nature of a test that hardship brings out the reality of obedience rooted in nothing else than the fear of Jehovah. Even the unbeliever can obey God (outwardly) when the circumstances are favorable to obedience. Faith manifests itself by obeying when obedience is opposed by all earthly circumstances and by everything that is seen and felt, indeed when obedience appears as folly.

Saul himself admits his inexcusable sin when, in defense of his disobedience, he states that he "forced" himself to disobey (1 Sam. 13:12). Literally, the text has Saul saying that he restrained himself from obeying the word of God. Thus he forced himself to disobey. Such was the weight of the divine command that only with difficulty did he disregard it. The excuse is ironic. The force that he ought to have exerted upon himself to obey he rather exerted to disobey.

UNAPPROVED WITH REGARD TO HIS HOUSE

For Saul's offense of disobedience, the judgment is God's rejection of
Saul's house as the royal house of Israel (1 Sam. 13:13–14). This is not
yet the judgment that Saul himself is stripped of the kingship. Rather,
"thy kingdom shall not *continue*" (v. 14, emphasis added; see also v. 13).
In pronouncing this judgment, severe in itself, Samuel speaks of the man
whose house *will* be the dynasty as "a man after his [Jehovah's] own heart"
(v. 14). This is an accomplished reality in the purpose of Jehovah. The
Lord "hath commanded him to be captain over his people" (v. 14) already
while Saul still reigns, indeed before Saul became king.

The judgment upon Saul and the sin that brings the judgment down
are in accordance with God's counsel. Long before the events concerning
the kingship of Saul, Jacob had prophesied that the scepter would not
depart from *Judah*, not Benjamin, until Shiloh come (Gen. 49:8–12).
The ruling house in Israel is to come from Judah, in David, not from
Benjamin, the tribe of Saul.

Saul shows himself reprobate, that is, unapproved of God in his royal
office in Israel, in another way by his taking of the name of Jehovah in
vain in the battle with the Philistines. He cursed in the name of Jehovah
anyone who ate food during the day of the battle. This is the "adjured"
in 1 Samuel 14:24: "Saul had adjured the people, saying, Cursed be the
man that eateth any food until evening." This is the oath in verse 28:
"Charged the people with an oath, saying, Cursed be the man that eateth
any food this day." Saul's was a foolish, rash oath and therefore the violation of the third commandment of the law: "Thou shalt not take the
name of the LORD thy God in vain" (Ex. 20:7). It was an instance of the
"false swearing" and "unnecessary oaths" condemned by the Heidelberg
Catechism as a form of the profaning and abusing of the name of God
forbidden by the third commandment.[2]

The motivation of the rash swearing was Saul's carnal desire for personal revenge on the Philistines: "that I may be avenged on mine enemies"

---

2 Heidelberg Catechism A 99, in Schaff, *Creeds of Christendom*, 3:343.

(1 Sam. 14:24). By his oath, Saul troubles God's people: Israel and his own son Jonathan. The effect of the oath is that Saul allows Jehovah's enemies—the Philistines—to escape to some extent their deserved punishment: "Had there not been now a much greater slaughter among the Philistines?" (v. 30).

Again Saul disobeys one of Jehovah's commandments. He manifests that he does not regard his kingship as that of a vicegerent of God but rather as his own possession. His office does not serve God but himself.

Also in the church today there is a self-seeking zeal on the part of officebearers. It manifests itself in injury to the people of God and harshness toward other officebearers. As was true of the zeal of Saul regarding the destruction of the Philistines, this zeal also can have the appearance of a zeal for God.

Saul's disregard for the name of God came to expression also in his slaying of the Gibeonites in violation of the oath sworn by Joshua and Israel to them, to let them live. The history of this oath is recorded in Joshua 9:3–27, especially verses 15, 18, and 21. The record of Saul's violation of this oath is found in 2 Samuel 21:1–14. Years after Israel's making of the oath to spare the Gibeonites, who were Canaanites and therefore otherwise subject to the decree of God that the Canaanites be destroyed, God chastised Israel with a famine. When David, who by that time was king of Israel, inquired of God the reason for the famine, God answered, "It is for Saul, and for his bloody house, because he slew the Gibeonites" (v. 1). Verse 2 informs us that "Saul sought to slay them [the Gibeonites] in his zeal to the children of Israel and Judah."

The sin of Saul was his contempt for the name of God, which was at stake in the violation of the oath to spare the Gibeonites. God highly esteems his name. The king of his kingdom is called similarly to esteem the name of the king whose kingdom Israel is and on whose behalf he rules. Strikingly, in the history of Saul's taking the name of God in vain and of the judgment of God upon this sin in Israel, it is noted that David, the king after God's heart, honored a solemn oath and thus the name of God. The judgment upon Saul's sin was the killing of seven descendants of Saul. But David spared Mephibosheth, the son of Jonathan, "because of the LORD's oath that was between them, between David and Jonathan the son of Saul" (2 Sam. 21:7). Even though Jonathan had been the closest of friends to David, it is not so much this friendship that accounted for the sparing of Jonathan's son. It is rather the oath that David swore in the name of God that explains it. To David, the name of God was precious above all else.

The reality in the kingdom of God will be the ministry of Jesus Christ. All of his ministry, culminating in his death, will be the honoring of the name of God in the establishment of the kingdom of God by the salvation of the elect citizens of the kingdom out of all nations. Christ's lifelong obedience, including the lifelong suffering that culminates in the cross, was not so much due to his love of the citizens of the kingdom as it was zeal for God's name. God had sworn by himself that he would establish a kingdom of righteousness, peace, and eternal life, a kingdom that would be inhabited and enjoyed by a multitude of elect humans. To Jesus Christ it fell to realize this oath and thus honor the name of God. In all the difficulty of his way and against all the temptation to depart from the way, zeal for the name of God more than anything else, including love for his people, motivated the messianic king of the kingdom of God to carry out his calling. The doxological conclusion of the great psalm of the messianic king and, as it were, the explanation and goal of himself and all his kingly ministry is: "Blessed be the LORD God, the God of Israel, who only doeth wondrous things. And blessed be his glorious name for ever: and let the whole earth be filled with his glory; Amen, and Amen" (Ps. 72:18–19).

The third and conclusive manifestation of himself as reprobate, that is, unapproved of God, is Saul's disobedience to Jehovah's command to destroy Amalek utterly (1 Sam. 15). Saul's sin is disobedience to a clear command from Jehovah. The command is described as the "voice of the words of the LORD" (v. 1). His sin is also rebellion against the sovereign decree of the Lord putting Amalek under the ban as the enemy of his beloved people. God grounds the command and motivates Saul to obey the command by reminding the king of the wickedness of Amalek in attacking Israel during its exodus from Egypt to Canaan: "I remember that which Amalek did to Israel, how he laid wait for him in the way, when he came up from Egypt" (v. 2).

The account of Amalek's attack on Israel, soon after the people had left Egypt, is found in Exodus 17:8–16. Saul and all Israel are well aware of God's determination utterly to destroy Amalek. God had had his decree written in a book: "And the LORD said unto Moses, Write this for a memorial in a book, and rehearse it in the ears of Joshua: for I will utterly put out the remembrance of Amalek from under heaven" (v. 14). Moses had impressed all Israel with the reality and solemnity of God's decree that Amalek be destroyed by a public ceremony at which he had said, "The LORD hath sworn that the LORD will have war with Amalek from generation to generation" (v. 16).

Also in the matter of his disobedience to the command of God regarding Amalek, Saul profanes the name of God. Exodus 17:16 states that Amalek's destruction is decreed and therefore commanded by an oath of God: "The LORD hath sworn." Since God swears only by himself, his name is profaned by Saul's disobedience to the command to destroy Amalek utterly.

The Hebrew verb that is translated as utterly destroy in 1 Samuel 15:3 and 9 has the literal meaning of consecrating to God by laying one under a curse that dooms one (in this case, the nation of Amalek) to utter destruction. The destruction of Amalek, unto which Saul was commanded, is more than the punishing of an especially wicked nation, a nation that intended the destruction of the people of God and thus the Messiah and his kingdom that are in this people. But it is, by this destruction, the consecration of Amalek to God. We commonly think of consecration to God as the devotion to God of those who are saved. There is also a consecration to God of those who are lost, by their punishment. God is glorified in the damnation of his enemies. Their very punishment is their devotion to him, that is, their being consecrated to him. Every human will be consecrated to God, some in the way of their holiness, others by means of their punishment.[3]

---

3 On the consecration to God of the wicked in the way of their destruction, see also Joshua 6:17, where "accursed" is the same Hebrew word translated "utterly destroy"

The just judicial ground of the divine consignment of Amalek to destruction is the nation's hatred of and attack upon Israel during Israel's trek through the wilderness on its way to Canaan. This destruction is eternally determined by God's decree of reprobation, appointing the members of the nation of Amalek to damnation in the way of their wicked attack on Israel and the punishment of death due that iniquity. Amalek is the nation that descends from Esau, the reprobate brother of elect Jacob (see Mal. 1 and Rom. 9). Like its father, Amalek is the object of God's eternal hatred. In accordance with this eternal hatred appointing Amalek to damnation, God consecrates Amalek to the destruction of being the object of his curse, which curse serves the safety of Israel and the glory of God.

This sovereignty of God in determining the destruction of reprobate Esau in his reprobate descendants—Amalek—in no wise rules out or detracts in the slightest from the responsibility of Amalek for its destruction. As clearly as the biblical text declares the sovereignty of God in the destruction of Esau's descendants, so emphatically does it insist on the responsibility of Amalek for its punishment by God. When God commanded Saul to destroy the Amalekites, he declared that the ground of the destruction was their wickedness: "Go and utterly destroy the sinners the Amalekites, and fight against them until they be consumed"—"the *sinners* the Amalekites" (1 Sam. 15:18).

In saving King Agag and the best of the animals of Amalek, Saul therefore goes so far as deliberately to oppose Jehovah's sovereignty: Saul is the rebel against heaven. Such is the judgment of Saul in the word of God in 1 Samuel 15:22–23: "Rebellion is as the sin of witchcraft, and stubbornness is as iniquity and idolatry." Saul is a rebel. His rebellion is an assault upon the majesty of God. It is a violation of the first commandment of the law of God, for witchcraft and idolatry are transgressions of the first commandment.

---

in 1 Samuel 15:3. In Joshua 6, the wicked inhabitants of Jericho are consecrated to God by their death. Rahab the harlot is consecrated to God by the salvation of sanctification: she hides the spies.

The sparing of the king of Amalek and the best of the animals was Saul's decision, not merely his acquiescence to the people, as Saul excused himself. Saul the rebel is also a liar. First Samuel 15:9 ascribes the sin to "Saul and the people." Verse 19 accuses *Saul* of "fly[ing] upon the spoil."

Saul disregards Jehovah's prerogatives in the ban because he has regard to his own advantages as king. The good animals will promote Saul's prosperity. Parading Agag about in Israel as a royal captive in Saul's train will enhance Saul's glory. Saul's glorifying of himself in the victory over Amalek is evident in his immediate erection of a monument to himself in Carmel, according to 1 Samuel 15:12: "It was told Samuel, saying, Saul came to Carmel, and, behold, he set him up a place, and is gone about, and passed on, and gone down to Gilgal." "Place" in the AV refers to a memorial or monument. At once after the defeat of Amalek, Saul takes measures to assure that the glory of the victory redounds to himself. Simply put, the king of the kingdom of God seeks his own glory, rather than Jehovah's.

At the root of Saul's rebellion is pride. Samuel implies as much in his rebuke of the king: "When thou wast little in thine own sight, wast thou not made the head of the tribes of Israel, and the LORD anointed thee king over Israel?" (1 Sam. 15:17).

Saul's guilt is not a whit lessened even were it the case that he had given in to the people, for the king must lead the people of God to obey him, not permit himself to *be* influenced to disobey Jehovah.

Nor is the motive of sacrifice an excuse or justification for disobedience to God's command. Saul gives this excuse: "The people spared the best of the sheep and of the oxen, to sacrifice unto the LORD thy God" (1 Sam. 15:15; see also v. 21). In response to this defense by the king, Samuel condemns all ceremonies of worship that are at the expense of obedience. God has delight in obedience: "Samuel said, Hath the LORD as great delight in burnt offerings and sacrifices, as in obeying the voice of the LORD? Behold, to obey is better than sacrifice, and to hearken than the fat of rams" (v. 22). God does not reject sacrifices, but he prefers obedience. And sacrifices at the expense of obedience are obnoxious. Calvin explains:

It was as much as to say that the sum and substance of divine worship consisted in obedience, with which it should always begin, and that sacrifices were, so to speak, simple appendices, the force and worth of which were not so great as of obedience to the precepts of God.[4]

The warning inherent in this incident in the history of the covenant and kingdom of God in the Old Testament has urgent application to the thinking and practice of the church of the New Testament. First, what is of primary importance for the manner of right worship is obedience. Jehovah has "delight" in it. Second, obedience is preferred to elaborate liturgy. When the worship of the church conflicts with obedience, the worship is not acceptable to God but abominable. Third, God-pleasing worship will express obedience to the will of God for worship. Specifically, the church must worship God as he wills. This is the regulative principle of worship, implied by the condemnation of "will worship" in Colossians 2:23 and required by the Heidelberg Catechism in question 96.

Apostate churches and carnal Christians, like Saul, are enamored of elaborate ritual and ceremony—the modern equivalent of the showy sacrificing of multitudes of animals. The true church of Christ and genuine believers are marked by the simple, to unbelief unimpressive, "obeying [of] the voice of the LORD" (1 Sam. 15:22)—the all-important voice of the Lord, that is, God's word.

It belongs to the manifestation at this time of Saul as unapproved, now in the sense of his being a reprobate personally in God's decree, that he is impenitent. His profession of penitence and his confession of sin are insincere: "I have sinned: for I have transgressed the commandment of the LORD, and thy words" (1 Sam. 15:24). This is evident in the subsequent history. Samuel refuses to pronounce the pardon of Saul's sin, even though the king begs for pardon. This refusal stands in sharp contrast with the prophet Nathan's ready forgiveness of David when David besought it in the same words with which Saul sought pardon (see 2

---

4 John Calvin, quoted in Keil and Delitzsch, *Biblical Commentary on Samuel*, 156.

Sam. 12:13). The passage itself in which Saul professes penitence suggests that Saul's motivation in seeking Samuel's public forgiveness of the king is to retain the allegiance of the people: "Honour me now, I pray thee, before the elders of my people, and before Israel" (1 Sam. 15:30). Saul's subsequent behavior is that of a man who is impenitent. This includes his readiness to kill the prophet of God, as Samuel states in chapter 16:2: "If Saul hear it, he will kill me."

Saul's confession itself shows the insincerity of his confession of sin in disobeying the voice of the Lord. For in the confession he continues to mitigate his own guilt and to blame the people: "I have transgressed the commandment of the LORD, and thy words: *because I feared the people, and I obeyed their voice*" (1 Sam. 15:24, emphasis added).

UNAPPROVED (REPROBATE) REGARDING THE KINGSHIP PERSONALLY

In 1 Samuel 15, Jehovah rejects Saul as unapproved for kingship in Israel regarding Saul himself personally. Jehovah's rejection of Saul regarding kingship is twofold. The first aspect has to do with Saul's dynasty: his house will not reign in Israel forever (1 Sam. 13:13–14). Saul is rejected regarding his sons being kings after him. This rejection Samuel pronounces upon Saul on account of Saul's failing the first and basic test of a king over God's kingdom in the matter of waiting for Samuel to offer sacrifices at Gilgal. On this occasion, Samuel prophesies another man as Saul's successor, rather than one of Saul's sons: "a man after his [Jehovah's] own heart" (v. 14). This rejection of Saul regarding a dynastic succession is decisive: God has commanded this other to be captain over the people of God, even though this other man as yet knew nothing of his succeeding to the throne.

The second aspect of the rejection of Saul consists of the fact that Saul himself personally is virtually deposed from office: "The LORD hath rent the kingdom of Israel from thee this day, and hath given it to a neighbor of thine, that is better than thou" (1 Sam. 15:28; see also vv. 23, 26). Samuel announces this deposition to Saul upon the occasion of Saul's rebellion in the matter of executing the ban against Amalek. There are two aspects to this personal rejection of Saul as king. The first will be the

violent, apparently premature removal of Saul from office later in the battle with the Philistines, to be replaced at once by David (see 1 Sam. 28).

Second, there is a realization of the personal rejection of Saul at once
upon Samuel's announcement of it to the king: this day, as 1 Samuel
15:28 plainly declares ("rent the kingdom of Israel from thee this day").
This aspect of the personal rejection consists of the departure of the Spirit
of Jehovah from Saul to rest instead upon David, who is anointed to be
king in the place of Saul almost at once. This departure of the Spirit of
God does not refer to the saving presence of the Spirit but to the presence
of the Spirit qualifying Saul to function more or less ably in his office in
the kingdom of God. The departure of the Spirit from Saul is recorded in
chapter 16:14: "But the Spirit of the LORD departed from Saul."

Three things about this departure of the Spirit of God from Saul are
noteworthy. First, it is simultaneous with the coming of the Spirit upon
David at his anointing: "The Spirit of the LORD came upon David from
that day forward" (1 Sam. 16:13). The very next verse declares the departure of the Spirit from Saul. Second, the departure from Saul of the Spirit
of Jehovah is at once accompanied by the presence in Saul of an evil spirit:
"An evil spirit from the LORD troubled him" (v. 14). When an officebearer
in the church does not function by the Spirit of Jesus Christ, his work and
he himself in his work are troubled by a devil. Thus by bad officebearers
the kingdom of God in the world is troubled. Third, the Spirit departs
from Saul at the same time that the prophet Samuel departs from the king:
"Samuel came no more to see Saul until the day of his death" (15:35).
Spirit and word function in union, even regarding the function in his
office of the unapproved man in the church. Where the word of God is
no longer present, even regarding the external carrying out of the duties of
the office, the Spirit of God is wholly departed as well.

Even though Saul does rule yet for some years, and David does not
ascend to the throne, Saul rules *as deposed*, and David does not rule *as
elected*. That Saul is deposed even though still ruling and that David is
king before he actually takes the throne are expressed by Samuel to Saul
(who is still king in fact) in 1 Samuel 28:17: "The LORD hath rent the
kingdom out of thine hand, and given it to thy neighbor, even to David."

From the moment that Samuel pronounces this second phase of Saul's rejection as king, Saul is a "lame duck." As Saul's relentless hatred and pursuit thereafter of king-elect David demonstrates, Saul is fully aware of his status as deposed and of David's status as appointed king.

Jehovah carries out his rejection of Saul in strict and perfect justice. The rule, particularly in the sphere of the kingdom of God in the world, is simply this: one who rejects Jehovah, Jehovah rejects. "For thou hast rejected the word of the LORD, and the LORD hath rejected thee from being king over Israel" (1 Sam. 15:26). Still, this rejection accords with God's eternal, sovereign purpose. Not Benjamin (Saul's tribe) but Judah (the tribe of David) must bring forth the king of the kingdom of God, according to the prophecy of Jacob (Gen. 49:8–10).

That it is God's eternal purpose that David and his sons, rather than Saul and his descendants, reign over Israel bears strongly also upon the right understanding of scripture's statement that "the LORD repented that he had made Saul king over Israel" (1 Sam. 15:35; see also v. 11). This strong statement of God's displeasure at Saul's disobedience does not in fact teach that God actually changed his mind and went back on his act of enthroning Saul, because Saul's wicked kingship took him by surprise. That this is not the meaning of the statement, verse 29 in the immediately preceding context makes plain: "Also the Strength of Israel will not lie nor repent: for he is not a man, that he should repent."

The statement that God repented of making Saul king is a linguistic device that in biblical literature, as in secular literature, is known as an anthropomorphism. A certain reality in God is presented in a form that characterizes humans, even though the form itself does not describe God. In this case, the reality in God is that he is strongly displeased with the kingship of Saul, which kingship he himself effected (at the sinful urging of Israel). When humans are displeased with some action of theirs, they repent what they did, that is, in sorrow they wish that they had not done it and go about to change what they have done. This feature of humanity is ascribed to God so that the reader will be impressed with the divine displeasure with Saul's kingship, as well as with God's determination radically to change the kingship of Israel.

Chapter Eight

Saul:
The Reprobate Personally

(1 Samuel 28, 31)

$\mathcal{G}$od's rejection of Saul as king of the theocracy of Israel raises the question as to Saul's personal, spiritual state. Rejected as to office, is Saul also personally a reprobate? In this connection, how is the gift to Saul and then the withdrawal from him of the Spirit to be understood?

Personally, Saul is an ungodly man whose end is damnation, according to the eternal decree of reprobation. In this respect too, Saul contrasts sharply with David, who is not only chosen to kingship in the kingdom of God, but also personally eternally elected to salvation.

The evidence of Saul's reprobation personally is his lifelong walk of ungodliness: disobedient, rebellious, self-seeking, ruthless murderer, and that of the priests of Jehovah (1 Sam. 22); and most convincing, his ongoing persecution of David, whom he knew to be the Lord's anointed. Because David is the type of Christ Jesus, Saul showed himself to be the antichristian enemy of King Jesus. The death of Saul, then, was in keeping with his wicked life: suicide (31:4)—a final act of rebellion and despair. To the very end, Saul's concern is himself personally: "lest these uncircumcised come and thrust me through, and abuse me" (v. 4). Not the kingdom of God as was the supreme concern of David, which he expressed on more than one occasion by refusing to kill Saul when this was in his power, but himself and his interests were the governing motive of reprobate Saul.

When in one of the stranger events in the Bible Samuel is brought back from the dead by a woman with a familiar spirit, he tells Saul that Saul will soon be with him. This is not the promise of heaven but the warning that Saul will be with Samuel in the state of death (1 Sam. 28:3–25). In whatever form Samuel appeared to Saul, Samuel did not descend from heaven but ascended "out of the earth" (v. 13). Saul did not bring Samuel down but brought the prophet up (v. 15). Saul would die, as Samuel had died.

Both C. F. Keil and S. G. De Graaf are seriously in error regarding the spiritual condition of King Saul personally, especially at the beginning of his reign. Keil finds in Saul not only natural qualifications for kingship, but also a pious heart.[1] De Graaf too contends that Saul was originally a pious man, indeed a believer, although lacking a completely victorious faith. Saul had been called in his [God's] covenant. Presumably, from the covenant Saul had fallen away. Because of Saul's disobedience, God had let him go from the covenant, although not easily.[2] Having taken note of Saul's suicidal death, De Graaf observes: "That was the end of Saul… How close he had come to the kingdom of God! The Lord had drawn near to him, but he had not surrendered to his grace in faith; instead he had glorified himself over against that grace."[3] Here De Graaf's theology of the conditionality of the covenant and its salvation betrays him.

Apart from all else, the explanation of both Keil and De Graaf is guilty of the false doctrine of the falling away of saints from the covenant and its salvation, contrary to the testimony of the Reformed creed the Canons of Dordt.[4]

---

1 Keil and Delitzsch, *Biblical Commentary on Samuel*, 79.

2 S. G. De Graaf, *Promise and Deliverance: The Failure of Israel's Theocracy*, vol. 2, trans. H. Evan Runner and Elisabeth Wichers Runner (St. Catherines, ON: Paideia Press, 1978), 91, 121.

3 De Graaf, *Promise and Deliverance*, 143.

4 Canons of Dordt 5.1–15, in Schaff, *Creeds of Christendom*, 3:592–95.

In the sphere of the covenant, that is, in the instituted church, are those (especially officebearers—ministers, elders, deacons, and professors of theology) who are gifted with the Spirit of God for their work on behalf of the covenantal people of God. They have and exercise gifts of leadership, teaching, and preaching even though they are devoid of saving, sanctifying grace. It is not unusual that they occupy a prominent place among the church's officebearers. Often they come to a sorry end. They are exposed as unsaved men whose labor was motivated by self-seeking.

Judas Iscariot was such a gifted but unsaved man. For a while, as a member of the intimate band of Jesus' special disciples, he enjoyed closest earthly fellowship with the Lord, heard all the teaching, saw all the miracles, himself taught the gospel of Jesus, performed miracles, and even held the responsible position of treasurer in the band of future apostles. His was the Spirit of office in the manifestation of the kingdom of God, but not the Spirit of regeneration and covenantal communion with the Savior. Despite obtaining "part of this ministry" and holding the office of bishop in the church institute (Acts 1:15–20), he was a reprobate, unbelieving, ungodly man whose end, like Saul's, was damnation by suicide.

The Spirit gifted Saul with qualifications for the office of king in Israel. Again and again the Spirit enabled Saul to perform the work of a king, delivering Israel from its enemies. An outstanding instance was Saul's deliverance of Jabesh-gilead from Nahash and the Ammonites. To this deliverance belonged Saul's discretion in not punishing those Israelites who had objected to his kingship (1 Sam. 11).

By the power of the Spirit of God equipping him for office, Saul delivered Israel from many of its foes throughout much of his kingship, according to 1 Samuel 14:47–48. The Spirit of office did not save Saul, but he saved Israel by means of the king. That God gave Saul "another heart" when Samuel anointed him to be king concerns not a spiritually renewed heart but the wisdom, bravery, and other qualifications for kingship (10:9). It was a heart for office—kingship—in the kingdom of God.

This endowment with the Spirit for office in the kingdom of God increased Saul's guilt. Not only was he born into the sphere of the covenant, marked with the sign of the covenant, but also he was privileged to receive the Spirit of the Lord for high office in the kingdom. So closely did he come into external contact with the covenant itself. This closeness took special expression in the fact that more than once Saul was seized by the Spirit to prophesy (1 Sam. 10:9–13; 19:23–24). In spite of himself, he spoke the word of God concerning the God whom he disobeyed and concerning the Messiah against whom he was rebelling.

So far is it from being true that Saul was a pious member of the covenant that he is the outstanding reprobate in the Old Testament especially with reference to office, as Esau is the outstanding reprobate personally. In striking contrast is Saul's neighbor, elect David.

JUDGMENT AND GOSPEL AT THE END

Earlier, reference was made to the difficult, indeed puzzling, account of the strange appearance to Saul of the prophet Samuel after Samuel's death (1 Sam. 28). Regardless of all the difficulties in understanding the appearance, it must be understood as genuine. That is, it was a real appearance of the prophet in some form or other. Samuel returned from the realm of the dead, conversed with Israel's king, and pronounced upon Saul the message of condemnation, impending death, and damnation. The account does not describe merely what went on in Saul's and the woman's heads. It is not the description of hallucination, not even divinely realized hallucination. Nor is it merely a vision, whether of the woman or of Saul.

Everything in the biblical account insists upon a genuine, if mysterious, appearance of Samuel. The woman saw Samuel "ascending out of the earth," that is, coming back to earth from the realm of the dead (1 Sam. 28:12–13). Samuel spoke to Saul, rebuking the king for disquieting the prophet by bringing him back into the tumultuous history of the kingdom of God in the world with its warfare, seeming defeats, and especially sinfulness (v. 15). The words of rebuke and condemnation were "the words of Samuel" (v. 20). Saul perceived that the unearthly form ("gods," v. 13) confronting him was Samuel (v. 14).

Man being body and soul, and Samuel's body having not yet been resurrected, the explanation of the appearance of Samuel must be that God sent Samuel back to earth in his soul. His soul was temporarily clothed with the appearance of Samuel's earthly body so that Samuel could be objectified and recognized by the woman and, by means of the woman's description, recognized by the king himself ("an old man…covered with a mantle," 1 Sam. 28:14).[5]

Such a return to earth from the dead by saints for important purposes is not unheard of elsewhere in the Bible. Moses and Elijah appeared with Christ on the mount of transfiguration (Matt. 17:1–8).

Samuel appeared to Saul for important purposes. His appearance was a final condemnation of the rebellious king of the kingdom of God, justifying God in his awful ways of punishing the king and apparently allowing the defeat of the kingdom of God by its heathen enemies on the morrow.

Nor was the prophet's message only one of judgment. It was also the gospel of the preservation and salvation of the kingdom of God by him who was the type of the Messiah in his kingship in the Old Testament: "The Lord hath…given [the kingdom]…to David" (1 Sam. 28:17). Such an extraordinary and mysterious act of God as was the return of the prophet from the dead—the disquieting of him, as it were—had to serve a grander purpose than only a repetition of the denouncing of judgment. It had to be nothing less than the proclamation of the glorious gospel of the Messiah, who typically was David.

Indeed, the *purpose* of the awful judgment upon Saul and Israel by the prophet was the announcement of the glory of the messianic king, the establishment of the kingdom of God, and the salvation of the citizens of the kingdom. The judgment upon Saul would be the accession of David to the throne of Israel. For the announcement of such a glorious message, it is fitting that the outstanding prophet of the Old Testament come back from the dead, just as it would be fitting in the future that Moses and Elijah return from the dead to strengthen the Messiah himself to suffer the judgment of God upon himself as the substitute of his people in order to establish the kingdom of God.

---

5 The text states that the medium saw Samuel. It does not state that Saul saw Samuel, only that Samuel spoke to Saul and that Saul spoke to Samuel.

Not only must Saul know the truth about his impending death and dethronement, but also all Israel must know this, as they would later when they read and heard of it as part of the inspired Old Testament scripture. Likewise, the church of the New Testament benefits from the account of this strange event in the history of the kingdom of God in the world. The church takes comfort from the truth that in all her seeming inglorious defeats in history, often on account of foolish, even evil, office-bearers, God is working her good.

As for the role of the demonic woman in all this, the passage does not state that she brought Samuel up from the dead, nor even that God *used* her to send Samuel to Saul. The witch of Endor was surprised, indeed shocked, to see Samuel: "When the woman saw Samuel, she cried with a loud voice" (1 Sam. 28:12). If any human played a role in Samuel's return from the dead, it was Saul, whom Samuel blamed: "Why hast thou disquieted me, to bring me up?" (v. 15). God accomplished the wonder. The significance of the woman in all this was that she accentuated the wickedness of Saul in resorting to her when God righteously would have no communication with the king (vv. 6–7). It was as though when God would give no help, Saul sought deliverance from the devil. In every way, Saul showed himself worthy of the dreadful punishment that would befall him the next day.

That Saul's recourse to the necromancer was gross disobedience and offensive to God, who reveals by his word what his people need to know, is emphasized in the explanation of Saul's death in 1 Chronicles 10:13–14:

13. So Saul died for his transgression which he committed against the LORD, even against the word of the LORD, which he kept not, and also for asking counsel of one that had a familiar spirit, to enquire of it;
14. And enquired not of the LORD: therefore he slew him, and turned the kingdom unto David the son of Jesse.

Thus the contrast between Saul and the king who comes to the throne of Israel by means of the judgment upon Saul, namely David, is stark.

David:
Man after God's
Own Heart

Chapter Nine

The Election of David

(1 Samuel 16–2 Samuel 1)

*D*avid was the eighth and youngest son of Jesse, of Bethlehem, Judah. Jesse was in the family line of Boaz, the husband of Ruth (Ruth 4:17–22). David became the great king of Old Testament Israel; the founding father, by divine promise, of the ruling house of Israel; and most importantly the progenitor of the Messiah, Jesus, the everlasting king of the kingdom of God and the head of the everlasting covenant of God with his chosen people. David is the outstanding type in the Old Testament of the Messiah, or Christ, as the king of the kingdom of God.

David is anointed as king by the prophet Samuel. Here is the climax of the very fruitful ministry of the old prophet. Having been instrumental in the institution of the office of kingship in Israel, he now appoints to the office the man who will be Israel's great, glorious, and beneficent king. Indeed, King David will be the man who, to a large extent, creates the kingdom of Israel, the kingdom of God in the Old Testament. And he will be the man from whom will come the real king, Jesus the Messiah.

Soon after his anointing of David as king, having provided some protection of the king-elect from the murderous intentions of Saul (1 Sam. 19:18–24), Samuel dies (25:1). The founder of the permanent prophetic office in Israel has completed his ministry and may pass from the scene.

The anointing of David signified that Jehovah had chosen him to the office of king and that the Spirit of Jehovah would qualify him for the office. David is the man elected by Jehovah. Israel had chosen Saul; Jehovah chose David. That Jehovah chose David is expressed in 1 Samuel 16:1: "I have provided me a king among his [Jesse's] sons." The same is taught in verse 12: "The LORD said, Arise, anoint him: for this is he." The election of David is implied by the statement concerning Jesse's other sons, "The LORD hath not chosen these" (v. 10).

The Hebrew word translated "chosen" carries the idea that the choice is made in love for the one who is chosen. Jehovah chose David in love for him. David's name indicates that he has been chosen in divine love for him. The name means "beloved." Also in his being loved of God, David was the type of Jesus, of whom God himself said in his voice from heaven, "This is my beloved Son, in whom I am well pleased" (Matt. 3:17).

David lived in the consciousness of his election. Again and again the psalms, many of which were written by David, refer to David as the one whom God had chosen. Even though the word "chose" or "elect" does not occur in Psalm 2, the idea of election unto kingship is certainly expressed in verses 6 and 7: "Yet have I set my king upon my holy hill of Zion. I will declare the decree: the LORD hath said unto me, Thou art my Son; this day have I begotten thee." The verses that follow make this clear. Upon this election David falls back when the heathen rise up against him as king of the kingdom of God.

Other psalms are explicit. Psalm 89:3 has Jehovah saying, "I have made a covenant with my chosen." The choice concerns David's office of kingship in Israel: "I have sworn unto David *my servant*" (vs. 4; emphasis added). Verse 20 goes on to speak of God's anointing David "with my holy oil." This anointing of David as king assures that David's many enemies will not triumph over him, but that God "will beat down his foes before his face" (vv. 22–23).

The election of David to the office of king is typical. The reality is the anointing of Jesus the Christ. Jesus is "the chosen of God," according to Luke 23:35. God appointed Jesus king of his kingdom in the eternal decree, as Psalm 2:7 teaches. Election to office implies God's qualifying of the man who is chosen. God qualified Jesus for the work of the office by anointing him with the Holy Spirit at his baptism (Matt. 3:13–17). Similarly, David's election is immediately followed by the necessary qualifying for the work of the office by the coming upon David of the Spirit of Jehovah: "The Spirit of the Lord came upon David from that day forward" (1 Sam. 16:13).

This election of David contrasts sharply with the rejection of Saul. The Lord rejects Saul: "I have rejected him from reigning over Israel" (1 Sam. 16:1). The Spirit of the Lord, which up to now has qualified Saul for his office, now leaves him (v. 14). There cannot be two men who are qualified for, and by implication chosen to, the kingship in the kingdom of God. When the Spirit of the Lord forsakes Saul, an evil spirit troubles him. This evil spirit troubles Saul exactly regarding his conduct in his office. He behaves himself badly as king, with dire consequences for Israel. When the covenantal people of God choose their rulers—ministers and elders—foolishly, they thereby reject the good rule of God over themselves. The result, under the judgment of God, is not only that they forfeit the good rule of God in Jesus Christ, but also that they bring upon themselves an injurious rule by evil spirits. And this miserable reality is the doing of God in judgment: the evil spirit that troubled Saul and rendered his rule over Israel distressing to the nation was "from the Lord" (1 Sam. 16:14).

The election of David to office symbolized by the prophet's anointing of him was closely related to David's personal election unto salvation. Indeed, fundamental to God's choice of David as king was God's election of David unto salvation. This is indicated in 1 Samuel 16:7. When Samuel was inclined to choose a king among Jesse's stalwart sons, Jehovah said to Samuel that, whereas man looks on the outward appearance, "the Lord looketh on the heart." David has a godly heart. But he has such a heart only because the Lord gave him the godly heart, according to divine election—election unto *salvation*. Jehovah has appointed David unto salvation in the eternal decree of election, and the Spirit qualifies David to live the life of holiness unto the Lord.

This personal election unto salvation and the holiness that is the certain fruit of election are fundamental to the office of kingship in the kingdom of God. They are basic qualifications for service of God and his people in the office. How important David's personal holiness was for his functioning in his office became apparent after his sin with Bathsheba. His wickedness drastically weakened his kingship, indeed came close to rendering his kingship impotent.

The eventual impossibility of a wicked man's serving well in office in the kingdom of God has been demonstrated in Saul. Although office and person can be distinguished, they are intimately related. A godly king in the Old Testament must first of all be a godly person. The same is true of officebearers in the church today. For this reason, 1 Timothy 3 and Titus 1 emphasize the spiritual qualifications of pastors, elders, and deacons in the church. Churches ignore this to their own peril in the election of their officebearers.

The nature of David's election to the kingly office in Israel is noteworthy. First, it is sovereign. It is the will or decree of God that is due exclusively to his own unconditional good pleasure. Saul is rejected; David is elected. Also the rejection of David's older brothers, of whom at least some showed physical attributes that qualified for kingship, while the youngest brother, a mere shepherd boy, is chosen, calls attention to the sovereignty of God's choice of the king of Israel. In this respect, God's election is always contrary to man's choice. God himself called attention to this aspect of his election of David. Of his "refusal" of the impressive oldest brother, Eliab, Jehovah said in explanation that he does not see, in choosing, as man sees, in choosing (1 Sam. 16:7).

Because God's election of David was a gracious act regarding both David and the Israel of whom David will be a savior in his lordship, God's sovereignty in the election of David was the sovereignty of grace. This will find its fulfillment in the election of the man Jesus as messianic king. Although God's choice of Jesus was not gracious in respect of sin, for Jesus was conceived and born sinless, it was gracious with respect to Jesus' lowliness, his humble estate. The child born in a stable, the man without form or comeliness, without any beauty that we should desire him (Isa. 53), was not Israel's choice of their king, as he is not ours or the choice of the human race. As the king of the shameful cross, he is rejected by all without exception. But he is God's choice in the sovereignty of his good pleasure.

David's election serves the covenant of God with Israel. God elects David with the purpose that David will realize the covenant as king. He will unite the nation under one head; he will deliver Israel from their foes, especially the Philistines; he will enlarge the kingdom and make it glorious; he will make ready in important respects the worship of God around the ark of God in Jerusalem, even though he himself may not erect the temple.

The reality of all this covenantal work will be the accomplishment of David's son, the Messiah, Jesus. This will be the inspired prophecy of Zacharias concerning the as-yet unborn child of the virgin Mary. In Jesus, God "raised up an horn of salvation for us in the house of his servant David…that we should be saved from our enemies, and from the hand of all that hate us." All of this salvation would be God's remembrance of "his holy covenant" (Luke 1:67–75).

That David's and the Christ's election serves the covenant means that the covenant depends upon election and therefore that the covenant depends upon the sovereign grace of God.

Concerning the election of David, Jehovah richly endows and equips the elect head of the covenant with abilities and graces for his office. David is a marvelously gifted individual. There are the spiritual graces that issue from his godly heart: zeal for Jehovah and his kingdom; wisdom to rule the people of God; humility before God; obedience to the will of God; and more. David also has many natural gifts and abilities that enhance his kingship: handsomeness in face and body; skill as a musician, with the sensitive temperament that accompanies this gift; a poetic soul, as many of the psalms testify; intelligence; courage; obviously a winning personality and a commanding presence (see 1 Sam. 16:12, 18).

Often overlooked among David's attributes is that of eloquence. The gift of apt, skillful, moving speech is important, if not invaluable, to the ruler. As the psalms abundantly testify, David had this gift in extraordinary measure. On a possible, indeed preferable, translation of 1 Samuel

16:18, this gift is expressly attributed to David. Where the AV has "prudent in matters," the Hebrew has "skillful of speech."

Varied, numerous, and glorious as these gifts are, they are limited. He of whom David is the type regarding gifts for a great kingship in the kingdom of God will receive the Spirit and therefore all the gifts for a glorious kingship without measure (John 3:34).

The election of David also assures his accession to the throne, despite all the powerful opposition of the enemy withstanding this accession. Once enthroned, David cannot be overthrown, numerous, determined, strong, and even crafty as his foes will be. The security of his kingship in the face of opposition is the theme of Psalm 2: "Why do the heathen rage, and the people imagine a vain thing?" (v. 1). By his election of David, God has set his king upon his holy hill of Zion. Still today, all the efforts of the ungodly to dislodge Jesus the Messiah from his throne in and over his kingdom, the church, whether by heresy or by persecution, must fail. God has chosen him, and divine election renders certain.

Having chosen David, Jehovah prepares him for the throne.

PREPARATION FOR KINGSHIP

David does not immediately ascend to the throne, nor is the way to the throne smooth and easy. There is a long period of waiting and training between the time of David's anointing and his accession to the throne. Scripture suggests that ten years intervened. David is thirty when he becomes king (2 Sam. 5:4). If he was about twenty when he was anointed by Samuel, he waited no fewer than ten years to become king. If he was anointed at a younger age, the period of waiting was even longer. During this period, with all its disappointment, hardships, and danger, Jehovah was preparing David not merely to become king, but to become the kind of king who would serve God acceptably in God's kingdom.

For one thing, Jehovah brought David to the attention of all Israel as the man elected by Jehovah to be Israel's king. At the same time, Jehovah made Israel know that Saul was rejected by him. By the time that David becomes king of all Israel, all Israel will be able to say, "Also in time past, when Saul was king over us, thou wast he that leddest out and broughtest in Israel: and the LORD said to thee, Thou shalt feed my people Israel, and thou shalt be a captain over Israel" (2 Sam. 5:2). As this acknowledgment of David by Israel indicates, God was preparing David for the throne already before David's anointing. David grew up tending his father's sheep (1 Sam. 16:11). The king of God's kingdom must be a spiritual shepherd of God's spiritual flock. Tender care of such weak, vulnerable persons, prone always to stray, could be learned by oversight of physical sheep. The authority and might of a king are tempered by the tenderness and compassion of a shepherd. What Israel needs is a shepherd-king. This is what Israel would receive in King David, even as the real Israel of God, the church, is ruled and saved by King Jesus, who is also the great shepherd (see John 10:11–30).

It is no insignificant aspect of herding sheep that the shepherd, at considerable risk to his own life, protects the sheep from those that would devour them. In his calling as a shepherd, David defended his flock from both a lion and a bear, killing both. David himself recognized these acts of a shepherd as fitting him to deliver Israel from Goliath (1 Sam. 17:34–37).

After David's anointing, Jehovah brought him to the court of Saul, where David can display his gifts and show himself to Israel as the Lord's anointed by his striking behavior. God did this by having David the harpist brought to Saul to refresh him when Saul was troubled by the evil spirit from Jehovah (1 Sam. 16:14–23). In this activity also, David foreshadowed his great son, the Lord Jesus. As Jesus had the power to cast out devils, so also David cast out the evil spirit that troubled Saul, if only temporarily (v. 23).

David also manifested himself to all Israel as the king-elect by his courageous taking up the challenge of the giant Goliath and by his defeat of that monstrous foe of Israel, which led to a rout of the Philistines (1 Sam. 17). In this deliverance of Israel, David displayed not only personal bravery and skill in fighting, but also, and especially, zeal for Jehovah and Jehovah's covenant with Israel. When he defied the armies of Israel, the giant of Gath defied Jehovah (v. 10). So David analyzed Goliath's defiance in verse 26: "Who is this uncircumcised Philistine, that he should defy the armies of the living God?" This was also the reply of David to Saul when Saul attempted to dissuade David from fighting the Philistine: "seeing he hath defied the armies of the living God" (v. 36).

In the battle with Goliath, David is not merely a daring, heroic fellow. But he is a man moved with zeal for Jehovah's name and covenant. He reveals this in his response to Goliath's contemptuous challenge to him: "I come to thee in the name of the LORD of hosts, the God of the armies of Israel, whom thou hast defied" (1 Sam. 17:45). He added, "that all the earth may know that there is a God in Israel" (v. 46). It is this that accounts for David's confidence regarding the outcome of the confrontation (vv. 46–47): "The battle is the LORD's, and he will give you into our hands."

This is not to minimize David's courage. By his enormous size of something over nine feet, with his armor and weaponry, and in view of his experience in warfare, Goliath was the human "tank" of his day. On his part, David was indeed a mere youth as 1 Samuel 17:42 describes him, having only a sling for his weapon. God does not look kindly on cowards in the warfare of his kingdom in history, regardless of the daunting power of the enemy; he creates men and women of courage.

In a striking way, the battle of David against Goliath represented Jesus' personal warfare with the devil, the personal adversary of God, his covenant, and his covenantal people. Goliath was a monster, a monstrosity, as is Satan, the great dragon. Jesus began his ministry with a battle against Satan (Matt. 4:1–11). Hebrews 2:14 describes the entire ministry of Jesus as warfare against the devil. Revelation 20 has history ending with an all-out assault on the kingdom of God by Satan. The outcome is the full and final defeat of the devil, who is then cast into the lake of fire. This will be the reality of David's beheading the fallen giant.

It was David's glorious deed of killing Goliath that catapulted David at once to national prominence as the likely "heir apparent" to the throne of Israel. The deed exalted David especially in contrast to the cowardice of Saul and, under his depressing influence, all the other warriors in Israel. In addition, the defeat of the Philistine champion was immediately followed by a resounding victory over the Philistines (1 Sam. 17:51–54). The response of all Israel was expressed by the women in their song of victory: "Saul hath slain his thousands, and David his ten thousands" (18:6–7). Even the Philistines drew the right conclusion from David's defeat of Goliath: "Is not this David the king of the land? did they not sing one to another of him in dances, saying, Saul hath slain his thousands, and David his ten thousands?" (1 Sam. 21:10–11).

In addition to his fame as the victor over Goliath, David came to be held in high repute throughout Israel by his wisdom, his success in warfare against the Philistines, and his general prospering as a captain in Israel's army (1 Sam. 18). All Israel not only esteemed David, but also loved him (v. 16). This is important preparation for one who has been appointed to be king. The king over the kingdom of God does not rule by terror. Rather, he rules by such goodness as commands the affection of the people. The citizens of the kingdom of God love King Jesus. They esteem him for all that he is. But they also love him for all that he has done on their behalf, particularly for his sacrifice of himself on behalf of their redemption from sin, death, and damnation. Theirs is a willing submission and obedience.

Scripture sums up all in David that brought him the esteem of Israel as Jehovah's being with him: "The LORD was with him" (1 Sam. 18:14). This was God's blessing of David with the covenant personally. As the covenant is God's fellowship with his people, God's being *with* them, so David enjoyed the covenant personally, with special application to his position in the covenant as elected king. Everyone saw this covenantal blessing of the future king. The people saw it. Saul saw it.

Among all the gifts and attributes that commended David to Israel during the time between his anointing and his accession to the throne, scripture stresses his wisdom. David "behaved himself wisely," indeed "very wisely" (1 Sam. 18:5, 14–15, 30). Wisdom is commonly associated with David's son Solomon, who made wisdom his choice. But this important qualification of a king of the kingdom of God was exceptional also in David. This is to be expected of the one who is an outstanding type of Jesus the Messiah. As the book of Proverbs teaches, Jesus is personally the divine wisdom. It is by this personal wisdom that kings reign, among whom surely is David (see Prov. 8).

As King Jesus irresistibly draws to himself the love and willing honor of his people by his deliverance of them from all their foes, so also David gained renown and affection by his deliverance of Israel even when he himself was suffering persecution at the hands of Saul (see 1 Sam. 23:1–5; 27:8–12). When finally all Israel received David as their king, they acknowledged David's deliverance of them even when Saul was the king: "Also in time past, when Saul was king over us, thou wast he that leddest out and broughtest in Israel" (2 Sam. 5:2). Like the Anointed of whom he was the type, David had a heart for the people of God, even though they, under Saul's direction, were rejecting and even persecuting him. David served Jehovah, not himself. He was the *servant of God* and therefore the servant of the people of God.

Yet another way in which David gained a certain prominence in the time between his anointing and his taking the throne was by becoming Saul's son-in-law. He married Saul's daughter Michal. Unhappy as the marriage proved to be, with Michal showing herself to be the daughter of Saul spiritually, particularly in the matter of David's dancing in joy at the coming into Jerusalem of the ark (2 Sam. 6), the marriage gained some stature for David in the nation (see 1 Sam. 18:18, 23, 26–27; 22:14).

All of this preparation of David for the throne finds its fulfillment in the increasingly clear manifestation to Israel of Jesus as the Messiah-king by means of his ministry of mighty deeds, which included delivering the people from their bondage to devils, sickness, and even death, and of the teaching of the gospel of grace. In light of this preparatory ministry, Israel acknowledged him, at least outwardly, to be the Christ at his triumphant entry into Jerusalem (Matt. 21:1–11). Today the true church confesses that Jesus is the Christ, the king of the kingdom of God, on the basis in part of the ministry that led up to his ascension into heaven and his sitting at the right hand of God. Even when all were denying him at his crucifixion, he was serving and saving the citizens of the kingdom.

Chapter Ten

———

Preparation
by Persecution

(1 Samuel 18–28)

*O*ne way by which God prepared David for his kingship over Israel was his bringing David to the attention of Israel by various deeds of valor and deliverance. A second way in which David was prepared was the persecution and other forms of suffering that David endured between the time of his anointing and the time that he began to reign. Jehovah disciplined and trained David during a long period of trial. The trial was "with fire," in the words of 1 Peter 1:7. In this aspect of his preparation for the throne, David was the type of Jesus Christ in a striking, unmistakable manner. According to Hebrews 5:8, with reference to Jesus the Christ, "though he were a Son, yet learned he obedience by the things which he suffered." The purpose of this suffering was that "being made perfect, he became the author of eternal salvation unto all them that obey him" (v. 9). The suffering of Jesus was preparation of him to be the savior of the people of God.

David himself gave expression to the preparatory nature of his suffering, especially during the time immediately following his anointing, in many of the psalms, including 52, 55, 56, 57, 59, and others. Reflecting in old age on his many trials and sorrows, in Psalm 71, David confesses not only God's deliverance of him from his enemies and troubles, but also that these foes and their persecution of him were means of his spiritual growth. By means of the "great and sore troubles," which *God* showed him, God increased David's "greatness" (vv. 20–21).

In Christ, this is also the experience of the God-fearing: they suffer with Christ in order that they may reign with him in glory hereafter (Rom. 8:17).

The chief persecutor and therefore the main agent of this aspect of David's preparation for the throne is Saul. The main persecution comes from within the sphere of the covenant and then from the most prominent member in that sphere: the king himself. The reprobate within the sphere of the covenant and within the boundaries of the manifestation of the kingdom of God hates and is determined to destroy God's elect. This was a deliberate attempt to destroy the one whom Saul knew to be the Lord's anointed. The reason for the attempt was exactly that David was appointed by God to replace Saul, both personally and as the founder of the royal house of Israel. Saul feared David because Jehovah was with David (1 Sam. 18:12, 28–29).

Saul made two confessions to David himself about David's being God's ordained king. Both were prompted by David's sparing Saul when he could have killed his enemy. The one was made in the wilderness of Engedi: "Behold, I know well that thou shalt surely be king, and that the kingdom of Israel shall be established in thine hand" (1 Sam. 24:20). The other was made in the wilderness of Ziph: "Blessed be thou, my son David: thou shalt both do great things, and also shalt still prevail" (26:25). This knowledge did not deter Saul but was the provocation itself of the persecution.

The fact that the persecution is enmity against David and the determination to kill him on the part of the king, who has all the resources of the kingdom in his power, made that persecution extremely sore for David. A number of incidents stand out. The persecution began very early in the contact of Saul with David, almost as soon as David was honored at court for his killing of Goliath. Aroused to jealousy by the women's praise of David above himself, Saul tried to kill David with his javelin (1 Sam. 18:10–11; see also 19:8–10). Saul then tried to kill David by means of David's marriage to Saul's daughter Michal (18:17–30). He demanded of David a dowry of a hundred dead Philistines, hoping that David would be killed in the execution of this demand. Then he tried to capture David with the cooperation of Michal. On more than one occasion, Saul attempted to enlist the help of his son Jonathan to capture David. When Jonathan, who was a godly son of the ungodly king and who loved David, refused, Saul tried to kill his own son (19:1–7; 20:27–34).

In Jonathan, an altogether admirable citizen of the kingdom of Christ, is reflected something of the spirit of John the Baptist. Although himself a prominent figure in Israel as heir apparent to the throne upon the death of Saul, Jonathan willingly gave way to David, whom he loved not only as a friend, but also as the anointed of God. Both Jonathan and the John Baptist had advocates who urged them to challenge in the one case David, in the other instance Jesus, thus contending for their own glory at the expense of the glory of David and of Jesus. John's response spoke also for Jonathan:

28. I am not the Christ, but that I am sent before him.
29. He that hath the bride is the bridegroom: but the friend of the bridegroom, which standeth and heareth him, rejoiceth greatly because of the bridegroom's voice: this my joy therefore is fulfilled.
30. He must increase, but I must decrease. (John 3:28–30)

Saul marshaled the army of Israel in a campaign against the Lord's anointed. He sent his troops to capture David when David was finding refuge with Samuel at Ramah among the school of the prophets (1 Sam. 19:18–24). Frustrating this effort and demonstrating in a remarkable manner God's protection of David was God's miraculous causing of Saul's soldiers to prophesy. When Saul himself went to Ramah to discover the whereabouts of Samuel and David, the Spirit of God caused Saul himself to prophesy, naked. This seizure and unlikely behavior of Saul occasioned a proverb that is still in vogue today, "Is Saul also among the prophets?" (v. 24). Not even this dramatic, undeniable evidence that God was with David and against his enemies dissuaded Saul from his murderous campaign against God's son and servant. But it left him without excuse.

By his persecution of David, Saul harried David out of the society of Israel. David sought refuge in the wilderness area of southern Judah. Occasionally he fled outside the boundaries of Israel altogether, with the Philistines. This may suggest a weakness on the part of David, in that he did not trust in God to protect him within the land of promise. It certainly indicates that enemies of the saints are guilty at times of excommunicating them out of the instituted church. Not every instance of excommunication will be confirmed at the final judgment.

In the intensity of his enmity toward David, Saul chased David also in David's wilderness hideout. Saul devoted himself to this pursuit at the expense of all his kingly responsibilities, specifically the defense of Israel from the threatening Philistines. He was ready to pursue David in Keilah (1 Sam. 23:7–13). He hunted David in the wilderness of Ziph and in the wilderness of Maon (vv. 14–29). With three thousand men he sought David in the wilderness of Engedi (chap. 24). On this occasion David spared Saul's life when he might have taken it. The explanation brought out the godliness of David in contrast to the ungodliness of Saul: David had respect to the fact that God had appointed Saul as king. "The LORD forbid that I should do this thing unto my master, the LORD's anointed, to stretch forth mine hand against him, seeing he is the anointed of the LORD" (v. 6). Regardless of the wickedness of his enemy and of the evil of the measures taken against him, the child of God may never take matters into his own hands. He must conduct himself lawfully, today according to the church order. If this means that he must suffer wrong, so be it. In the meanwhile, he submits his righteous cause and his unrighteous suffering unto God, who sees all, is sovereign over all, and will in the end rise to his defense. So sensitive was David's conscience that it smote him because he had merely cut off a piece of Saul's clothes (v. 5). Yet once again Saul pursued David in the wilds of Ziph (chap. 26).

Scripture indicates the determination of Saul in this pursuit of

David, and thus his hatred of David, in a number of ways. First Samuel 23:14 states that "Saul sought him every day." Only when David sought refuge outside of Israel in Gath of the Philistines did Saul cease. Saul was willing to try to seize David from his personal protection by Samuel and in spite of God's protection of David by the overpowering of Saul's men and of Saul himself by the Spirit of Jehovah (chap. 19:18–24). Saul was willing to kill his own son Jonathan, the crown prince, when he showed love for David (chap. 20). Saul had the high priest and the entire priestly company brutally murdered for their unwitting help of David. He then devoted the whole city of the priests to destruction, under the ban (chap. 22:6–23). Willingly functioning as Saul's executioner, Doeg the Edomite, reprobate son of his reprobate grandfather Esau, killed the high priest and eighty-five priests. Among all the wicked deeds of Saul, the enormity of this evil stands out, crying for divine vengeance, which cry was answered in the terror and despair of Saul at the very end of his life and then in the eternal torment of hell.

First Samuel 18:29 declares that "Saul became David's enemy continually." Saul's enmity against David, taking form in persistent effort to destroy him, was the opposition of Satan ("adversary") to God in his Christ ("Anointed One") both typically and actually—actually, because the Christ of God was in David.

To one act of David in the extremity of his suffering as he was relentlessly pursued by Saul, Jesus himself called attention in his own ministry. This had to do with David's eating the showbread of the tabernacle. Hardly beset as they fled Saul and his army, David and his men had no food. David therefore requested and with his men ate the hallowed bread of the tabernacle, which, as Jesus later observed, it was not "lawful to eat but for the priests." Jesus appealed to this event in order to justify his approval of his disciples plucking and eating ears of corn on the sabbath, thus showing himself "Lord also of the sabbath" (Mark 2:23–28). As David showed himself lordly in requiring the showbread for himself and his men, so Jesus revealed himself to be Lord of the sabbath. Christ's awesome lordship shone back faintly into the Old Testament as the lordship of David.

Chapter Eleven

Hardening and Preservation

(1 Samuel 16–30)

*H*ere may briefly be noted the awful hardening of Saul by Jehovah, culminating in his death by suicide. The hardening began with Saul's envy of David, coupled, as is always the case, with fear of the one envied (1 Sam. 18:8–15, 29). This ought not to be overlooked or minimized in the account of Saul's enmity against David. Envy played a powerful role in the opposition to Jesus on the part of the Jewish leaders. "He [Pilate] knew that the chief priests had delivered him for envy" (Mark 15:10). Still today, Christ Jesus is opposed especially in his orthodox, godly officebearers by attacks on them from within the church by their envious colleagues.

Saul's hardening continued with the clever attempt to destroy David by means of the Philistines (1 Sam. 18:8–15, 29). It advanced to the open hostility that ordered all Israel, including David's wife and his dear friend, to destroy David (19:1–17). It culminated in open war with Jehovah himself. This is what Saul's antagonism to David was from the very beginning. Saul warred against Jehovah's deposition of him from office and his election of David in his stead. But this disguised opposition became open war. Saul resisted the Spirit of God in the Ramah incident

(vv. 18–24). Saul persisted in seeking David's life even after he himself had been compelled to acknowledge God's appointment of David as king and not only to declare the certainty of David's eventual kingship, but also himself to pray that God will bless David with the kingship: "The LORD reward thee good" (24:16–22).

The end of this awful hardening was Saul's terror at the attacking Philistines, his seeking a favorable word from Jehovah by means of a woman with a familiar spirit—the "witch of Endor"—and then his committing suicide (1 Sam. 28). Although the text does not explicitly state that this development in sin was God's hardening of Saul, in its account of his steady, increasingly dreadful wickedness the history itself demands that it be explained in light of Romans 9:18: "whom he will he hardeneth." The text suggests divine hardening in its statement that an evil spirit from God troubled Saul (1 Sam. 16:14).

There were other aspects of suffering for David during this time besides the persecution by Saul. A great sorrow for David was his forced separation from the company of the people of God and from the public worship of God. This separation was enforced upon him all the while that he was an outlaw. David lamented this exclusion from the public worship of the church of the Old Testament in 1 Samuel 26:19: "They have driven me out this day from abiding in the inheritance of the LORD, saying, Go, serve other gods." Psalm 42 bewails the sorrow of this separation: "As the hart panteth after the water brooks, so panteth my soul after thee, O God…when shall I come and appear before God?" (vv. 1–2). The separation from friends forced upon David by Saul included estrangement from his intimate friend, Jonathan, and his wife, Michal. In fact, Saul gave David's wife to another man (1 Sam. 25:44), no small grief to a husband.

David was, although unwittingly and innocently, the occasion of the death of the priests of God. He felt this: "I have occasioned the death of all the persons of thy [the sole surviving priest, Abiathar] father's house" (1 Sam. 22:22).

David was betrayed by his own people, the people of Judah (1 Sam. 23).

By all of this almost incredible suffering, David was trained for the kingship, even as his great son will be trained by suffering for his kingship over the church. David learned by this suffering. He learned obedience to God. Throughout all the ten years that David suffered at the hands of Saul, he sought the will of God for his life and obeyed. He obeyed even when the will of God seemed to go contrary to his interests and even contrary to his ever coming to the kingship. This is the lesson learned from suffering by the Christ according to Hebrews 5:8.

By his suffering, David learned to trust in God, to trust in God with all his heart, and to trust in God alone. This was exemplified in his encouraging himself in God when he reached the low point in his life of flight from Saul (1 Sam. 30). Even his own band of soldiers and supporters spoke of stoning him as though he were responsible for the burning of their city and homes and for the abduction of their wives and children. David himself was "greatly distressed" by the event (v. 6). He joined his men in weeping "until they had no more power to weep" (v. 4). This was the deepest darkness for David before the dawning of the day. "But David encouraged himself in the LORD his God" (v. 6).

The mention of David's men finally giving up on him and his cause calls attention to the band of men who followed David in his exile and to some extent shared his sufferings. David had his "disciples." They were at first about four hundred and later about six hundred in number. John Bright does not much exaggerate in his description of them: "malcontents, fugitives, and distressed persons of all sorts…this flotsam, ruffians and desperadoes all."[1] Scripture's description is "every one that was in distress, and every one that was in debt, and every one that was discontented" (1 Sam. 22:2). Nevertheless, as Bright also observes, they were "a tough fighting force."[2]

In this too, David was typical of King Jesus. His original disciples were a "David's band": publicans, sinners, and lowly fishers of no standing in the society of that day. Such also for the most part are the followers of Jesus throughout history:

---

1 Bright, *History of Israel*, 172.
2 Bright, *History of Israel*, 172.

26. Not many wise men after the flesh, not many mighty, not many noble, are called:

27. But God hath chosen the foolish things of the world to confound the wise; and God hath chosen the weak things of the world to confound the things which are mighty;

28. And base things of the world, and things which are despised, hath God chosen, yea and things which are not, to bring to nought things that are:

29. That no flesh should glory in his presence. (1 Cor. 1:26–29)

Nevertheless, like the original, this "David's band" throughout history is "a tough fighting force," the church militant.

Throughout the history of Saul's persecution of David, David displayed and exercised trust in God by seeking the will of God for all his important actions. Usually David sought God's approval of actions he was about to take by means of the priestly ephod (see 1 Sam. 23:9–13). David did not even pursue the Philistines who had destroyed Ziklag and taken the wives and children of himself and his men without obtaining the approval of the Lord (30:7–8).

Humility was yet another grace that suffering developed in David. This comes out in many of the psalms. Often in close relation to cries of distress, David humbled himself before God, expressing his own smallness and God's greatness.

In all this distress leading up to his coronation, David did not remain sinless. In these failures he showed clearly that he was only the type of Israel's great king, not the reality himself. One weakness of faith was his seeking refuge from Saul outside the promised land, among the heathen. Early on, he fled to Gath of the Philistines for safety (1 Sam. 21:10–15). Then he sought refuge in Moab (22:3–5). At the end, when without his knowledge deliverance was near, he succumbed to his fears and fled to Philistia, where he remained for almost a year and a half (chap. 27).

Undoubtedly this was a sinful weakness of the beleaguered David. It was not permitted him to seek refuge outside the sphere of the covenant, outside the land of promise. Understandable as his actions were, they betrayed a lack of confidence in the protection of his God. The prophet Gad explicitly rebuked David for seeking refuge in Moab and commanded him to return to Israel: "Abide not in the hold; depart, and get thee into the land of Judah" (1 Sam. 22:5). David himself expressed both his misery and his guilt in finding himself in the countries of the heathen: "They [David's Israelite enemies] have driven me out this day from abiding in the inheritance of the LORD, saying, Go, serve other gods" (26:19). This text points out that such was the close relation in the Old Testament between the land of promise and the worship of Jehovah that the implication of residing outside Canaan was that worship of God was impossible. To abandon Canaan was to forsake the worship of God.

For this reason, it never went well for David among the Philistines. On his first exile, to Gath, he had to pretend insanity in order to save his life (1 Sam. 21:10–15). Later he had to live in the deceit that he was making raids against Israel (chap. 27). Finally, he was almost forced to fight with the Philistines against Israel. While he was leagued with the Philistine army, Ziklag was burned and his wives and children were taken captive (chap. 29–30). These troubles were divine chastisement. David accepted them as from Jehovah, in this too showing himself spiritually different from Saul, who either excused himself for his sins and troubles, blamed others, or blamed God.

Alfred Edersheim lists eight psalms as dating from the time of the persecution of David by Saul, in the chronological order of the events: Psalms 59, 7, 56, 34, 57, 52, 142, and 54.[3]

In all this persecution and trouble, God preserved David. He kept the anointed king of Israel alive and kept him from being captured by his foe. God did this in wonderful ways; for example, when Saul had David surrounded and about to be taken, news came to Saul of an invasion into Israel by the Philistines, so that Saul was forced to give up his siege of David (1 Sam. 23:19–28). Often God counseled David concerning escape from his enemy by means of Abiathar the priest, who had miraculously escaped Saul's massacre of the priestly household at Nob.

---

3 Edersheim, *Old Testament Bible*, 4:115.

God was with David by means of the priestly ephod. Therefore, Saul's shrewdest attacks upon David were frustrated. This was Old Testament evidence of the truth that "if God be for us," no one "can be against us" (Rom. 8:31).

Jehovah preserved David also by keeping him from a sin that would have spoiled him for the kingship of Israel. This was his prevention of David from executing vengeance against the fool Nabal, when Nabal not only refused to show gratitude to David and his band for their protection of Nabal's shepherds and herds with the food that David needed, but also treated David's men and David himself with contempt. The danger was that David was about to act in such a way as would have unfitted him for kingship in Israel. The means God used to keep David from his intention to kill Nabal was Nabal's own wife, Abigail, an example of what is all too common in the history of the kingdom of God: a wise and lovely woman who finds herself married to a damned fool. The man was well named: Nabal in the Hebrew means "fool." Abigail's concern was the peril to David's standing as king-elect, not at all the life of her husband. By means of her wisdom, David came to see his enraged intention so also. Foolishly refusing David a few sheep, in the end Nabal gave David his wife. Upon Nabal's death, by God's doing and not David's, David married Abigail (1 Sam. 25).

God also wonderfully protected David in the matter of his being virtually compelled to join with the Philistines in fighting against Israel, or even being associated with the Philistines in their battle against Israel, something that obviously endangered David's future kingship. In the nick of time, by the providence of God that promotes his kingdom and its king, the princes of the Philistines demanded of their king that David not accompany them to battle (1 Sam. 29).

Especially in this early history of David is revealed, in the deed, that "many are the afflictions of the righteous: but the LORD delivereth him out of them all" (Ps. 34:19). This psalm is applicable to David, especially regarding his afflictions. The heading of the psalm reads: "A Psalm of David, when he changed his behavior before Abimelech; who drove him away, and he departed." The psalm attributes the security of the righteous to "the angel of the LORD" (v. 7). The Old Testament revelation of Christ Jesus safeguarded his type. Verse 20 makes the application to Jesus plain: "He keepeth all his bones: not one of them is broken" (see John 19:32–36).

Chapter Twelve

—

David Brought to the Throne

(1 Samuel 31; 2 Samuel 5:5;
1 Chronicles 10; 11:1–3)

*A*fter about ten years of preparing him, Jehovah God brought his servant David to the throne of Israel. That this was the act of Jehovah is expressly stated in 1 Chronicles 10:14: "The LORD…turned the kingdom unto David the son of Jesse." Chapter 11:3 adds that the elders of Israel anointed David king "according to the word of the LORD by Samuel."

Jehovah did this first of all by killing Saul (1 Sam. 31). David had nothing to do with the necessary removal of the present king. To the very end, David regarded and treated Saul as the Lord's anointed. To one who claimed to have put Saul out of his misery when Saul was wounded by the Philistines, David put the question, "How wast thou not afraid to stretch forth thine hand to destroy the LORD's anointed?" (2 Sam. 1:14). For this offense, David had the man put to death.

In an extraordinary display of reverence for God, who had placed Saul in office, albeit by means of the wicked choice of Israel, David lamented the death of Saul. David composed an elegy that he taught Judah to sing.

In the elegy, David praised Saul. He said not one evil word about the man who had persecuted him for almost ten years. This is the lovely, moving "Song of the Bow" (2 Sam. 1:17–27; see Appendix).

Upon becoming king of Judah, David praised the men of Jabesh-gilead for rescuing Saul's mutilated body from the wall of Bethshan, where the Philistines had hung it on public display, and then burying the remains in Jabesh (2 Sam. 2:4–7; see also 1 Sam. 31:11–13). Later David had Saul's remains, as well as those of Jonathan, buried in Benjamin, in the family plot of Kish, Saul's father (2 Sam. 21:12–14). In all this, David was honoring the office in the kingdom of God and therefore the authority and majesty of Jehovah as God and King of the kingdom.

Jehovah removes Saul from his office, but he does so by means of the Philistines and by means of Saul's own self-murder. In the providence of God, the destruction of Saul, which effectively removes him from his office, is accompanied by a dreadful defeat of Israel and by the abuse of Saul's body by the Philistines. The Philistines take over much of northern Israel (1 Sam. 31:7–13). This aspect of the history brings out that unfaithfulness on the part of the leader of the covenantal people results in misery and shame for the people and in dishonor of the name of Jehovah. The Philistines used Saul's mutilated body and the armor they stripped from him "to publish it in the house of their idols" (v. 9). The very thing that David was concerned not happen in fact took place: "Tell it not in Gath, publish it not in the streets of Askelon" (2 Sam. 1:20). The evidences of the Philistines' triumph over Israel became grounds for the celebration of the victory of the idols of Philistia over the God of Israel.

First Chronicles 10:13 stresses that God's severe judgment upon Saul was in strictest justice: "for his transgression…even against the word of the LORD, which he kept not." Eternal reprobation and the divine hardening that proceeds from reprobation do not infringe upon, much less rule out, human responsibility. Accordingly, belief of the decree of reprobation does not weaken the preaching of responsibility. Saul was fully responsible for his disobedience and therefore deserving of his punishment.

It was also necessary that Jonathan die. First, this is an aspect of the severe judgment upon Saul. He must see the dead bodies of three of his sons before he himself dies, knowing that the judicial cause of their death is himself, surely an agony even for an unbelieving parent. Second, it is necessary that Jonathan die for the solid establishment of the kingship of David. Jonathan's removal from the scene is divine wisdom. If a nonentity like Ishbosheth could unite the ten tribes for seven and a half years, keeping them from going over to David, what might not the crown prince of Saul's line and noble hero Jonathan have done to disturb David's accession to the throne, even against his will?

After ten long and trouble-filled years of preparation, Jehovah, God of Israel, gave David the kingship to which he had been anointed. Even then, the circumstances of David's taking up the rule of Israel were difficult. David became king in reality only over the tribe of Judah. By the machinations of Abner, a general in Saul's army and a close relative of Saul, all the other tribes of Israel yielded allegiance to one Ishbosheth, a son of Saul who had survived the victory of the Philistines in the recent battle. The power behind Ishbosheth's throne was General Abner. The leading tribe of Israel resisting the kingship of David and adhering to the family of Saul was Ephraim, always jealous of Judah and thus disturbing the unity of the nation. Ephraim is singled out as a tribe that led the resistance of the rest of Israel to the kingship of the son of Judah (2 Sam. 2:1–11).

At the time of his coronation as king of Judah, David was thirty. He reigned over Judah for seven and a half years. His crowning as king of Judah took place at Hebron, which was also David's capital for all the time of his kingship over the tribe of Judah alone. Hebron was a significant city in Israel. It had been the home of Abram (Gen. 13:18; 14:13; 18:1; 23:2). It was also the location of the cave of Machpelah, site of the burials of the covenantal family (23:19).

It was Jehovah who exalted David to the throne at this time. David went to Hebron, to make himself available for the throne, only by inquiring of Jehovah and after receiving Jehovah's command, "to go up" (2 Sam. 2:1–2). This command specified Hebron as the place where David should be anointed by the men of Judah. That David waited upon God for the realizing of his kingship even after the death of Saul and when it was obvious to all that David should become king in Saul's stead is significant.

David does not take the crown on his own initiative. Jehovah must call to office in his kingdom, which call includes the actual installation into office. The principle is that "no man taketh this honour unto himself, but he that is called of God" (Heb. 5:4). Reformed church polity honors this principle. Article 3 of the Church Order of Dordt admonishes that "no one, though he be a professor of theology, elder, or deacon, shall be permitted to enter upon the ministry of the word and the sacraments without having been lawfully called thereunto."[1] Subsequent articles describe the lawful call in detail.

After seven and a half years of David's reign over Judah, Jehovah raises up David to the kingship over all Israel (2 Sam. 2:4–5:5). First Chronicles, which also gives much of the history that is found in 2 Samuel, ignores the history of David's reign for seven and a half years over Judah alone and proceeds at once to the history of David's rule over all Israel, after recounting the history of the death of Saul (1 Chron. 10–11).

The seven and a half years of David's reign over Judah alone, while the rest of Israel opposes David's kingship and allows itself to be governed by Abner and Ishbosheth, who have not been anointed kings over God's inheritance, are worthy of note regarding the history of the church. Always there are setbacks and struggles—struggles within the church herself. Never do things go smoothly and easily, not even when the way is plain and when the will of God is clearly revealed, as the will of God concerning David and the unity of Israel was clear to Israel at this time. Particularly, there is often the miserable fact of division within the kingdom of God itself. Often there are Abners and Ishbosheths and a number of people willing to be misled by these leaders. The citizens of the kingdom and members of the covenant must not be surprised or disheartened by these realities of church life—saddened, but not disheartened.

But David's struggles during the seven and a half years of his reign over Judah alone took place according to the sovereign good pleasure of Jehovah. They are further trial of David personally. He has waited already

---

1   Church Order of the Protestant Reformed Churches, 3–10, 22, 24, in *Confessions and Church Order*, 378–88.

some ten years. Now he must wait another seven years. The additional wait is a trial of David especially as the anointed king, who loves the covenantal people and desires their good. He must see most of Israel languishing during this time, suffering from their enemies, especially the Philistines, sacrificing the deliverance that he could give. He must see the beloved people of God divided and even standing on the verge of civil war. Worst of all, the failure of most of Israel to recognize and submit to his kingship dims the glory of Jehovah God that might be shining gloriously in the world in a unified, strong, and flourishing nation under one capable king. It can well be imagined that David would ask, "What is the sense of this division?" and would take matters into his own hands.

In fact, Jehovah is working out his purposes in this seven-and-a-half-years' "delay," as it must have seemed to David and to the spiritual Israel of God. There is further testing and preparation of David himself. It is demonstrated to all Israel that the house of Saul is unqualified for rule. There is the removal of the one possible rival for the throne from Saul's family, as well as of the powerful general who might have challenged David. The history sets forth in even bolder relief the truth of him of whom David is the type in that David does not seize the kingship over Israel but patiently waits for God to bestow it. Likewise, Christ Jesus did not yield to the third temptation of him by Satan in the wilderness but waited for God to exalt him in God's time and in God's way.

WAITING ON JEHOVAH

David's patience is remarkable. Again he waits for God to exalt him, with endurance under extreme provocation. He takes no action to seize the throne of all Israel. He merely defends himself and Judah against the aggressive action of the rival kingdom of the other eleven tribes. Rather than take advantage of the assassination of King Ishbosheth by the two captains in Israel's army, Rechab and Baanah, he has the two assassins punished. He treats Abner, the real power in the nation of Israel, in a brotherly manner. David himself points out the secret of his patience in his condemnation of the two assassins in 2 Samuel 4:9: "As the LORD liveth, who hath redeemed my soul out of all adversity." In the matter of his kingship, David trusts not in himself, nor in any other human, but in Jehovah alone, whom David knows as his redeemer. By promise of the coming redeemer, David's great son, and his redemptive work, God has ransomed David from his sin. Thus he has delivered David as well from all the adversities of life that otherwise would be against David. David lived in the confidence of the redemption of himself by the sufferings and death of Jesus Christ.

The patience born of the confidence of redemption is rewarded. Jehovah does exalt David to the kingship over all Israel, of course. But in the way of his patience, David inherits the throne in such a way that all Israel clearly sees that kingship was not David's ambition, but that the will of Jehovah brought David to the throne.

The resistance to his becoming king over all Israel on the part of Saul's house proves to be a failure. After the death of Saul, Abner, the captain of Saul's army and the power behind the throne of Ishbosheth, makes Saul's son Ishbosheth king. This pawn on the chessboard of the military hero Abner is cursed with two unhappy names. His original name, according to 1 Chronicles 8:33, was Eshbaal, which means "Baal exists."[2] However the giving of the name may be explained: naming the heir to the throne of Israel "Baal" gives some indication of the wretched spiritual condition of Israel at this time. The eleven tribes needed the rule of godly king David. The name that Eshbaal received later, and by which he is better known, was Ishbosheth, which means "man of shame." Evidently, Man of Shame was elevated to the throne of Israel about five and a half years after the death of Saul, for he reigned two years before he gave way to King David, who reigned seven and a half years over Judah alone before coming to the throne of all Israel (2 Sam. 2:10).

For five years after the death of Saul, the nation of Israel, with the exception of Judah, had no king. There was strong resistance to the reign of David on the part of most of Israel, even though it was known that

---

2 Bright, *History of Israel*, 175. Edersheim differs, giving as the meaning "Fire of Baal" (*Old Testament Bible*, 4:154). What is of importance is that parents in Israel, here the king himself, should name a child, indeed a possible heir to the throne of the kingdom of Jehovah God, Baal. It is as if a Christian officebearer would name a son Allah.

Jehovah had appointed David king and even though Saul's kingship had failed. Likely, the cause was the ambition of General Abner, although Ephraim's longstanding jealousy of Judah and the resentment of Judah by Benjamin, the tribe of the house of Saul, also played a part. Still today, Jesus Christ's blessed rule of his kingdom is disturbed by such resentments and jealousies among the rulers, especially the ministers. There are always Abners and Benjamin-families.

In the civil war that ensued upon the death of Saul and Man of Shame's accession to the throne of much of Israel, the civil war that David had done his utmost to avoid, David became stronger and stronger and the house of Saul weaker and weaker (2 Sam. 3:1). Finally, Abner saw that his ambitions on behalf of Israel and of himself were doomed. The occasion of his surrender to David was a clash between Man of Shame and himself over Abner's taking a concubine of Saul for himself. The act was revelatory of Abner's ambition himself to become king of Israel, as Man of Shame rightly perceived. To take the wife or concubine of a former king as one's wife was a step toward claiming the throne for oneself.

Abner then brought all the tribes over to David. When he did so, he made plain that all the while that he supported Saul and then promoted the cause of Man of Shame he knew full well that God had anointed David to the throne of Israel. His refusal to unite the nation under David and his promotion of a rival kingdom under Man of Shame were willful rebellion against David and in reality against the Christ and against Jehovah. In his rage against Ishbosheth, Abner acknowledged that "the LORD hath sworn to David…to set up the throne of David over Israel… from Dan even to Beersheba" (2 Sam. 3:9–10). In his exhortation to the elders of all Israel to submit to David as king, Abner reminded the elders that "the LORD hath spoken of David, saying, By the hand of my servant David I will save my people Israel" (vv. 17–19).

Abner was then murdered by David's general, Joab, with the complicity of Joab's brother Abishai, another leader of David's army. Joab, Abishai, and Asahel were three nephews of David, sons of David's sister Zeruiah (see 1 Chron. 2:16). Abner had unwillingly killed Asahel in the first outbreak of hostilities between the house of Saul and David.

Joab then murdered Abner by deceit, under the pretense of friendship. Joab had several strong motives for the killing of General Abner. First, he wanted revenge upon Abner for Abner's killing of Joab's brother Asahel. Second, Abner's alliance with David threatened Joab's position as general of David's fighting forces. Third, Joab regarded Abner with suspicion, as still a threat to the sole, solid kingship of David over all Israel.

Regarding this last, although an unspiritual man, Joab was single-mindedly a zealot for the kingship of David and therefore an utterly determined foe of all and everyone that in any way jeopardized the kingship of David. Joab represented others in the history of the kingdom of Christ who are zealous for the instituted church for a while, out of motives other than love for Jehovah and delight in the spiritual nature of the kingdom. This is what David meant on more than one occasion when he exclaimed, "What have I to do with you, ye sons of Zeruiah?" (2 Sam. 19:22) and, "These men the sons of Zeruiah be too hard for me" (3:39). Christ dissociates himself from such partisans. This means that the Reformed pastor and consistory must as much as possible keep themselves and their congregation free of association with such members, their worldly concerns, and their carnal methods. One thinks today of those who seemingly are zealous on behalf of conservative Christianity but whose real interest is right-wing politics.

David made plain to all the nation that he was guiltless in the murder of Abner. He arranged a public, honorable burial and mourned the death of Abner publicly. In addition, he composed an ode to Abner (2 Sam. 3:33–34). He did not, however, punish Joab. David was powerless to do so. Joab was too prominent and powerful in the kingdom. David gave expression to his helplessness regarding calling Joab to account for his sin: "I am this day weak" (v. 39). But David did curse Joab and his house, giving him over to the punishment of Jehovah (vv. 28–29, 39). At the end of his life, David charged Solomon with the calling to execute Joab, specifically for the crime of killing Abner. The sin of Joab was described as shedding "the blood of war in peace" (1 Kings 2:5). This charge Solomon carried out (vv. 28–34).

With the death of Abner, Ishbosheth is powerless. Two captains in his army, fellow Benjamites, assassinate him. Thus the last challenge to the kingship of David over all Israel, feeble as it has become, is removed. The heir to the throne in the family of Saul would have been Jonathan's son, Mephibosheth. He is disqualified physically by lameness in both his legs. In addition, like his father Jonathan, he willingly renounces all claim to the throne in recognition of God's choice of David. Again David absolves himself of any complicity in the killing of Ishbosheth by having the assassins killed.

KING OVER ALL ISRAEL

In the providence of God, who directs all for the sake of his anointed, the house of Saul for all practical purposes has run dead. Israel is shut up to the only alternative: David. All Israel, that is, the rest of the nation besides Judah, which has already submitted to David as king, anoints David as their king (2 Sam. 5:1–3; 1 Chron. 11:1–3). In this significant event concerning his kingship, David does not force himself upon the eleven tribes by military might. They are willing in the day of David's power. They recognize his credentials. He is a brother; he is one of them. He has proved himself over a long time by his kingly behavior, even while they were refusing to receive him. Most importantly, he is Jehovah's anointed.

Worthy of notice in the realization of David's kingship over all Israel is that "king David made a league with them...before the LORD" (2 Sam. 5:3). "League" here is a translation of the Hebrew word "covenant" (*berith*). The reference is not merely to a political contract or treaty, but to the covenant of God with his people in Jesus Christ. As typical head of the covenant in his kingship, David renewed with and extended to Israel, as now the kingdom of God in its entirety, the one covenant of God with his people. This covenant is an administration of the covenant that God made with Abraham and his seed in Genesis 17.

It is not without significance that David made the covenant with Israel. The making of the covenant is not mutual; much less does Israel make the covenant with David, even though the setting is Israel's reception of David as their king. In fact, Israel does not make David king on this occasion. He *is* king, as the text states: "All the elders of Israel came to the king to Hebron; and king David made a league with them" (2 Sam. 5:3). Israel finally recognizes and receives the king as their king. By their submission to the king of the kingdom of God and by their union with the Old Testament typical head of the covenant of grace, Israel has the covenant extend to them and embrace them in their consciousness.

One of the first acts of David as king over all Israel is his conquest of the stronghold of Zion and thus his making the city of Jerusalem the capital and heart of the nation of Israel. Jerusalem becomes the city of David (2 Sam. 5:6–9; 1 Chron. 11:4–7). This act is evidence of David's wisdom. Jerusalem is on the border of Benjamin and Judah. It was acceptable, therefore, both to the northern tribes and to Judah. The city is naturally secure, built as it is on high hills with deep ravines on the west, south, and east. The security of the city was the reason for the confidence of the Jebusites when David attacked. They boasted that their lame and blind could defend the fortress that dominated the heights of Jerusalem. They were wrong.

The security of Jerusalem is the message of Psalm 48: "Walk about Zion, and go round about her: tell the towers thereof" (v. 12). Not the natural features of the location of the city, however, were the explanation of its security, but the presence of God in the city by virtue of his covenant with the people whose capital it was: "God is known in her palaces for a refuge" (v. 3). The reality of Jerusalem and its security therefore is the church of the New Testament. God dwells with and in the church, so that the members of the church are secure against the attacks upon them by Satan and his hordes.

The main reason, however, for David's choice of Jerusalem was that Jehovah had chosen it as the place of his dwelling with Israel. "For the LORD hath chosen Zion; he hath desired it for his habitation. This is my rest for ever: here will I dwell; for I have desired it" (Ps. 132:13–14).

David actually conquered not the entire city but a fortress on Mount Zion that was held by the Jebusites and that commanded the city of Jerusalem. The city itself had been taken by Israel soon after their entrance into Canaan (Judges 1:8). With the help of Hiram king of Tyre, a lifelong admirer of David, David had his palace built in Jerusalem (2 Sam. 5:11;

1 Kings 5:1). The word itself, "Jerusalem," means "city of peace," derived as it is from the Hebrew word *shalom*. It came to be called "the city of David," "the holy city," and "the city of Jehovah." As the capital of Israel; as the city of David, the "great king," type of Jesus the Christ; as the city where Jehovah dwelt above the ark in the temple, Jerusalem was typical of the church.

So important is this truth for the right understanding of Old Testament history, as for the right understanding of the kingdom of Israel as fulfilled by the New Testament church, that it ought to be demonstrated from scripture itself. Galatians 4:26 speaks of the "Jerusalem which is above" and that is the "mother of us all." This is the church, which is the mother of all believers by the gospel that is entrusted to her. No other entity is the mother of believers. The church is "above," both in that her origin is from heaven, whence comes the Spirit of Christ who creates and preserves her, and in that her head is in heaven at the right hand of God. Verse 25 contrasts this spiritual reality of Jerusalem with the spurious Jerusalem of the earthly nation of the Jews. This Jerusalem is in the bondage of the false doctrine of salvation by works, in contrast to the Jerusalem of the true church, which is free in that she proclaims and believes justification by faith alone. The heresy of dispensationalism, which identifies the earthly nation of Israel and the Jews according to the flesh as the kingdom of Christ and thus refuses to see Old Testament Israel as the type of the church, is blind to the truth that the real Jerusalem is the mother of believers. It is also blind to the meaning of Old Testament history.

Hebrews 12:22 is, if anything, even more clear and compelling that the church is "the city of the living God, the heavenly Jerusalem," indeed the main fortress in Jerusalem, namely "mount Sion." Verse 23 identifies the "heavenly Jerusalem" as the "general assembly and church of the firstborn, which are written in heaven." Coming to this Jerusalem, the believer comes to Jesus the mediator of the new covenant and to the redeeming blood of sprinkling (v. 24). Failure to see that the Jerusalem of the Old Testament was the type of the church of Jesus Christ, so that the reality of Jerusalem is the church of the New Testament, indeed failure to see that the Jerusalem of the Old Testament *was* the church, is to be blind concerning the meaning of the Old Testament altogether.

Revelation 21:2 and 9 call the "holy city, new Jerusalem" the "bride adorned for her husband" and "the bride, the Lamb's wife." The Lamb's bride is the church (see Eph. 5:23–33). The reality of the kingdom of God therefore is the church, not a restored kingdom of Jews in Palestine. This understanding of Israel in the Old Testament is the *sine qua non* of the sound, orthodox interpretation of the history of the Old Testament scripture.

Another early achievement of David upon becoming king of all Israel was his decisive defeats of the Philistines (2 Sam. 5:17–25). The Philistines were the main foes of Israel for many years. Their serious threat to Israel went back to the time of Judge Samson. During the kingship of Saul, they had come to exercise significant power over Israel. Their power climaxed in the recent devastating defeat of Israel when Saul and his sons were killed. So powerful were the Philistines at this time that John Bright asserts that David was made king at Hebron "with the Philistines' consent...for he was their vassal."[3] Hearing of David's accession to the kingship over all Israel, the Philistines recognized at once the great threat to their power. They knew David well, especially as the victor over Goliath.

In two battles, forced upon David by two campaigns of the Philistines, David decisively defeated the Philistines. These victories broke the power of the Philistines over Israel, effectively destroying their threat to Israel. These battles against the Philistines may be regarded as the beginning of the wars of David, the great warring king of the kingdom of God in the world. Scripture expressly states that David fought in strict dependence upon Jehovah—at his bidding and as he directed—and that Jehovah gave David the victory, going out before David to smite the enemy ("then shall the LORD go out before thee, to smite the host of the Philistines," 2 Sam. 5:24). David also gave the glory of his victories to Jehovah. He named the site of his first victory over the Philistines

---

3 Bright, *History of Israel*, 175.

"Baalperazim," because "The LORD hath broken forth upon mine enemies before me, as the breach of waters" (v. 20). That this battle was essentially a battle between the Philistines and Jehovah, God of Israel, was evident in the fact that the Philistines carried their gods to the war. In their defeat and flight, the Philistines abandoned their idols. David burned them (2 Sam. 5:21; 1 Chron. 14:12).

The effect of this war was that the fame of David went out to all lands. By means of the report of David's victories over the Philistines, Jehovah brought the fear of David upon all nations (1 Chron. 14:17).

Chapter Thirteen

─────

Bringing the Ark to Jerusalem

(2 Samuel 6; 1 Chronicles 13; 15–16)

From the outset of his reign, the overriding concern of David was the "fame," or glory, of Jehovah, covenantal God of Israel. To this David gave expression by demanding the building of a house of Jehovah that would be of "fame and of glory throughout all countries" (1 Chron. 22:5). Zeal for the glory of God explained his act of bringing the ark to Jerusalem and his establishment of a well-ordered, impressive, public worship about the ark in Jerusalem. It was this that made David the great king that he was: he was Jehovah's king—king under and for Jehovah. It was this that distinguished his reign from that of Saul. This difference came out in the matter of the ark: Saul had let the ark languish for the forty years of his reign in the private house of Abinadab. This difference appeared sharply in their treatment of the priesthood. Saul had the priests slaughtered for inadvertently crossing his will. David exalted the priesthood in setting up the public worship of Israel before the ark. In this worship, the priests were prominent.

For some seventy years the ark, the fundamental symbol in Israel of the worship of Jehovah, had been out of the sight and away from the attention of the nation of Israel in the house of Abinadab, in Kirjath-jearim. It had been put there at the time that the Philistines had captured the ark in the days of Eli and Samuel (1 Sam. 6:21–7:2).

David's first attempt to bring the ark to Jerusalem, where it could again be central to the public worship of Jehovah, failed because of the "error" of Uzzah (2 Sam. 6:7). Uzzah touched the ark and was punished by Jehovah with instant death. The sin was disobedience to the divine command that none might touch the ark (see Num. 4:15). The sinful carelessness was rooted in a profane attitude toward the holiness of Jehovah that consecrated the box to God in a special way. Jehovah's name was called upon the ark, and this name is holy. By his name, Jehovah himself dwelt between the cherubim on the ark (2 Sam. 6:2), and he is holy, set apart from common handling by humans. The death of Uzzah was a strong warning to all Israel, responsible for the act of their king in carelessly transporting the holy symbol of the holy God, that the mercy of God in the covenant by no means relaxes the calling of awe for his holiness. The awful deed of God upon Uzzah frightened even David, God's well-meaning but careless servant (v. 9).

David shared the guilt of Uzzah. He did not have the ark transported to Jerusalem in the manner prescribed by Jehovah, namely having it carried by the Levites on poles (Num. 4:15; see 1 Chron. 15:2, 13). In 1 Chronicles 15:13, David confessed his and the people's sin as not having proceeded with the moving of the ark "after the due order." The important truth made known in the history of Uzzah is that of the regulative principle of worship. This principle, which is binding upon the church in all ages, is that obedience to the second commandment of the law consists of worshiping God only in the manner that he prescribes. In the words of answer 96 of the Heidelberg Catechism, God may not be worshiped "in any other way than he has commanded in his word."[1]

For the public worship of the church (and the bringing up of the ark was part of public worship), the rule is not that the elements of worship are any and all that are not forbidden. Nor, as is evident in the case of David, Uzzah, and all Israel in moving the ark, are good intentions sufficient.

---

1 Heidelberg Catechism A 96, in Schaff, *Creeds of Christendom*, 3:343.

The holiness of God demands that he himself prescribe the manner of the worship. The history of Uzzah ought to be an encouragement to true churches that are practicing the regulative principle. It is a warning to churches that contemplate forsaking the regulative principle, yielding to the pressure for contemporary worship. It ought to terrify those churches that have abandoned the regulative principle for the religious antics that amuse their carnal membership. Emblazoned on the walls of all church sanctuaries should be the words REMEMBER UZZAH.

The second effort to bring the ark to Jerusalem succeeds wonderfully inasmuch as David has this aspect of public worship done in the pre-scribed manner. "The children of the Levites bare the ark of God upon their shoulders with the staves thereon, as Moses commanded according to the word of the LORD" (1 Chron. 15:15; see also 16:1–6). The ark is placed in a "tabernacle" prepared for the ark by David (2 Sam. 6:17). This tabernacle was merely a "tent" (1 Chron. 15:1). At this time, David establishes an elaborate system of public worship, led by the priests and Levites (1 Chron. 16:4–6). This liturgy later became that of the worship at the temple (2 Chron. 7:6; 8:14).

On the occasion of the bringing up of the ark to Jerusalem, David wrote a fitting psalm of thanks and gave it to Asaph to be sung in celebra-tion of the event ever after, down to the present day (1 Chron. 16:7–36). This psalm is not, in its exact form, one of the psalms in the book of Psalms. But its content and, to some degree, the form it has in 1 Chron-icles is found in Psalms 105 and 96.

The psalm is a song of thanks to God for his covenantal mercies and salvation as evident in the presence of the ark (called the "ark of the covenant of God" in 1 Chron. 16:6) at the center of the life of Israel in Jerusalem. By the ark, God dwells with his people, to protect, bless, and save them. God has kept the promise of the covenant that he made to Abraham, Isaac, and Jacob. Because the covenant is "everlasting," David and elect Israel may be confident of God's presence and blessing forever. The psalm prophesies the extension of the covenant and its blessings to all the nations and peoples of the earth, a prophecy that will be fulfilled in the salvation of the "heathen" when the apostles proclaim the gospel of

Jesus Christ to all the nations. Indeed, the psalm suggests the renewal of the brute creation by the risen Jesus Christ. It calls on Israel to glorify and thank this covenantal Jehovah and concludes with the blessing of Jehovah, to which blessing all the people of Israel said "Amen, and praised the LORD" (v. 36).

One result of the bringing of the ark to Jerusalem is that there are now two "tabernacles" in Israel, two centers of the revelation of God and of public worship. The original tabernacle stands at Gibeon, having removed there from Nob. The ark is in a tent in Jerusalem. There are also two high priests: Ahimelech, son of Abiathar, and Zadok (see 2 Sam. 8:17). This unsatisfactory state of religious affairs will not be rectified until Solomon builds the temple in Jerusalem and deposes Abiathar from his office as priest (1 Kings 2:26–27).

The significance of the bringing up of the ark to Jerusalem is rich. Since by virtue of Jehovah's name being called upon the ark it is sign and symbol of the presence of Jehovah with Israel as their king, the bringing up of the ark signified the ascension of Jehovah to the position in which he is present with Israel at the heart of their national life as covenant-friend and covenant-sovereign. This ascension of Jehovah takes place by means of the anointed king, David, the typical Messiah. Hence, the rich significance of the ascension of the ark is the exaltation of Jesus in his ascension (Eph. 4:8–10). However, this ascension may not be understood as Jesus' departure from his church, but rather as his going up on high exactly so that he may be present with the church in the world by his Spirit. Having instructed his disciples that he was going away in the ascension, Jesus added at once that he would "come to you" (John 14:2–3, 18). In various psalms, including Psalm 24 and Psalm 68, David celebrated the ascension of Jehovah God unto the heights of Jerusalem as typical of the ascension of Jesus. In its description of the ascension of Jesus Christ, Ephesians 4:8 quotes Psalm 68:18: "Thou hast ascended on high, thou hast led captivity captive: thou hast received gifts for men."

Closely related to David's bringing the ark to Jerusalem was his desire to build a grand house for the ark and, by virtue of his covenantal relation to the ark, a grand house for Jehovah himself (2 Sam. 7). This desire was an aspect of David's zeal on behalf of Jehovah's dwelling with Israel in the covenant and for Jehovah's glory in the covenant. The zealous desire was commendable: "The LORD said unto David...Whereas it was in thine heart to build an house unto my name, thou didst well that it was in thine heart" (1 Kings 8:18). David had a burning zeal for the covenantal God of Israel.

1. LORD, remember David, and all his afflictions:
2. How he sware unto the LORD, and vowed unto the mighty God of Jacob;
3. Surely I will not come into the tabernacle of my house, nor go up into my bed;
4. I will not give sleep to mine eyes, or slumber to mine eyelids,
5. Until I find out a place for the LORD, an habitation for the mighty God of Jacob. (Ps. 132:1–5)

In this zeal for the house of God, David was typical of his great son, of whom it is true that the zeal of God's house ate him up (Ps. 69:9).

Nevertheless, in one of the more surprising acts of God—to us as to David—Jehovah forbade David to carry out his desire. The reason was that David was a king of war, who has shed blood, whereas the house of God must be a house of peace. The nature of the temple, and of the covenant that the temple symbolizes, is not well served by having a warrior like David build it (see 1 Chron. 28:3; 1 Kings 5:3). The deeper reason is that Jehovah has decreed that David's son will build the temple (for which he will be well suited as a king of peace), and this is to typify the building of the real house of God—the church—by David's great Son, Jesus the Christ. Jehovah does permit David to prepare for the building of the temple, both by gathering the materials (in abundance) and by drawing the pattern (1 Chron. 28).

This desire of David to build the temple became the historical occasion for the "Davidic covenant"—a revelation by Jehovah concerning the covenant, a revelation of the covenant that constituted a distinct advance in the progressive revelation and development of the covenant in the history of the Old Testament.

THE DAVIDIC COVENANT

David's desire to build a house as the glorious dwelling of Jehovah with Israel and as the site of the worship of which Jehovah is worthy becomes the occasion of Jehovah's revelation to David and Israel that God will make a house for David: "The LORD telleth thee that he will make thee an house" (2 Sam. 7:11). This promise means, first, that David's descendants ("seed") will reign over the kingdom of God forever. Thus there is important difference between the kingship of David and that of Saul (v. 15).

Second, the promise means that the Messiah will come from David, as the eternal king of the kingdom of God: "I will set up thy seed after thee, which shall proceed out of thy bowels...and I will stablish the throne of his kingdom for ever" (2 Sam. 7:12–13). Only of the Messiah is it true that the throne of his kingdom is forever. Luke 1:32–33 and Romans 1:3 declare that the fulfillment of this promise is Jesus the Christ.

By this promise, Jehovah establishes his covenant with David. That 2 Samuel 7:11–17 is covenantal, the covenant promise, is expressed in Psalm 89:3–4: "I have made a covenant with my chosen, I have sworn unto David my servant, thy seed will I establish for ever, and build up thy throne to all generations." This covenant with David is not a private, new covenant alongside the covenant with Abraham and Israel. Rather, the one covenant of grace is revealed more fully. It takes on a new, distinctive phase. It is brought to a higher, fuller stage of development.

What is distinctive about the Davidic covenant includes the following. First, the main stream of the covenant, producing the Messiah, who will fulfill and realize the covenant, runs through David. There is a certain narrowing of the covenant: from Israel, to Judah, to David. Second, the covenant now takes form as a kingship and kingdom: the reign of Jehovah in and over his people in his anointed, and his people's submission to and service of Jehovah as a kingdom people. Thus, third, the covenant is to be realized in and perfected by the "seed" of David as king.

The essential covenantal idea, namely friendship or fellowship, comes out in the Davidic covenant especially in the purpose of the Davidic covenant. This is the building of a house for Jehovah by the promised seed, the Messiah: "He shall build a house for my name" (2 Sam. 7:13). This promise must be understood in terms of type and reality: Solomon and the material temple as type in Old Testament history of the reality in the New Testament consisting of Jesus Christ and the church as the heavenly dwelling place, or temple, of God. The goal that the Davidic covenant has in view is the full, perfect dwelling together of Jehovah with his people, that is, the perfection of the covenant as the fellowship of God with his people in Jesus Christ. The outstanding commentary on the Davidic covenant, by God himself, is Psalm 89.

Chapter Fourteen

David as Battling, Victorious King, or David's Wars

(2 Samuel 8-10; 12:26-31; 21:15-23:38; 1 Chronicles 11:10-12:40; 18:1-20:8)

The distinguishing feature of the kingship of David was his being a warring king. His many battles with their abundant bloodshed was the reason why he might not build the temple. David was a man of war. Regardless that his wars disqualified him from building the house of God, in respect of his being a battling king David was the glorious type of his greater Son, Jesus. Jesus must battle all the foes of God and of God's people and must conquer. Preaching Jesus as the king of peace may not ignore that he accomplishes peace by fulfilling the prophecy of Isaiah 63:3: "I will tread them [the enemies of Jehovah and of his people] in mine anger, and trample them in my fury; and their blood shall be sprinkled upon my garments, and I will stain all my raiment." The end of history will be the bloody battle of King Jesus and his army against the antichrist and his hordes (Rev. 19:11–21). When liberal Protestantism proclaims Jesus as the prince of peace, ignoring the warfare of Jesus against the enemies of himself and of his church, it creates a false Jesus in its own image and caricatures his ministry.

Warfare was not the sole kingly activity of David. At the same time that David fought the battles of Jehovah against Israel's foes, he reigned over Israel in wisdom and justice: "David reigned over all Israel; and David executed judgment and justice unto all his people" (2 Sam. 8:15).

By his wars, David extended the boundaries of Israel to their utmost extent, fulfilling the promises made earlier about the large expanse of Israel (see Gen. 15:18). Thus David made Israel a great nation, to the glory not only of Israel, but also of Jehovah, the true king of Israel.

Among the wars of David, the following were notable: against Philistia (2 Sam. 8:1; see also chap. 21:15–22, where giants related to Goliath, including an extraordinary monster with six fingers on both hands and six toes on each foot, led the Philistine forces); against Zobah (8:3–4, 7–8); against the Syrians when they came to the aid of Zobah (vv. 5–6, 13); against Amalek (v. 12); against Edom (v. 14; see Ps. 60:8); and against Ammon (8:12; 10:1–14; 12:26–31). This was the war that was going on when David sinned with Bathsheba. It was occasioned by the shameful insult to David's ambassadors and therefore to David himself. Allied with Ammon were especially the Syrians, but also Zobah, Maacah, Tob, and Edom—a veritable alliance of the world powers of the day.

The great psalm on the wars of David and on Jehovah's help of David is Psalm 68: "Let God arise, let his enemies be scattered: let them also that hate him flee before him" (v. 1).

Essentially these wars were holy, spiritual battles of the kingdom of God against the foes of Jehovah and Jehovah's anointed king (Ps. 2:1–2). David and Israel are surrounded by plotting foes, as Psalm 2 declares. Further, it is God's will that his kingdom extend over the whole earth and that all the ungodly nations be destroyed before it (2:6–9; 72). Like the battles of Israel during the exodus and wilderness wanderings, these wars of David were "the wars of the LORD" (Num. 21:14). The fulfillment and reality of David's wars are, first, the victory of Christ Jesus over the world, the devil, sin, and death in his cross and resurrection. This victory is now realized by the gospel and Spirit of Christ (Col. 2:15; Rev. 6:2). Second, the reality of the wars of David will be Jesus' destruction of antichrist and his hordes at Jesus' coming (2 Thess. 2:8; Rev. 19:11–21; 20:1–15).

One of the more ridiculous notions of the apostate church is that, whereas David was a man of war, Jesus is a pacifist. The truth is that Jesus is the reality of the wrathful, battling, bloody king, whereas David was merely the faint type. Jesus is the captain of our salvation (Heb. 2:10). "Captain" is a military designation. Jesus presently subdues all his foes (1 Cor. 15:24–28). The world's last day will see him appearing to the world of wicked mankind on a warhorse, heading up armies, with a sharp sword going out of his mouth with which he will "smite the nations," treading "the winepress of the fierceness and wrath of Almighty God" (Rev. 19:11–21).

Perfectly in keeping with this truth about Jesus is the meaning of the imprecatory psalms: God's enemies are justly cursed and damned (Ps. 55; 59:11–15; 69:22–28; 109:1–20; 137:7–9), and God's friends pray for this cursing and damnation as the just reward of God's enemies. Denunciation of the imprecatory psalms as pre- and un-Christian expressions of the evil, vengeful sentiments of insufficiently sanctified Israelites is, in reality, denunciation of inspired scripture; of Jesus Christ, whose zeal on behalf of God these psalms express; and of the church that loyally, if humbly, sings the just punishment of the enemies of the king of the kingdom of God. One who cannot sing the imprecatory psalms shows that he is lacking in fervent love for the holy God and in zeal on behalf of the king of the kingdom of God.

David fought his wars in the name of Jehovah, and Jehovah gave David the victory over his enemies. In the context of the account of David's battles with various nations, 2 Samuel 8:6 explains David's victories: "The Lord preserved David whithersoever he went." The day that David looked back over all his wars was "the day that the Lord had delivered him out of the hand of all his enemies, and out of the hand of Saul" (22:1). That grand psalm in which David both celebrates and gives thanks for his victories over all his foes describes the wars as the wars of God himself against his enemies and attributes the victories to God himself.

> 17. He delivered me from my strong enemy, and from them which hated me: for they were too strong for me.

39. For thou hast girded me with strength unto the battle: thou hast subdued under me those that rose up against me.

40. Thou hast also given me the necks of mine enemies; that I might destroy them that hate me. (Ps. 18:17, 39–40; see also 2 Sam. 22:18, 40–41)

Repeatedly David acknowledged that the wars he fought were the Lord's battles, not his own, and that his victories were accomplished by the power of the Lord, not by his own strength. Even though the immediate object of the wicked counsel of the kings of the earth is the Lord's anointed, that is, the Messiah, their enmity is "against the LORD," and supreme wisdom for them is that they would "serve the LORD" (Ps. 2:2, 11). The ultimate object of the hatred of those who are anti-David, and in him the Christ, is God himself. As God is the object of the enmity of David's foes, so also is it God who conquers in the wars.

4. Thou art my King, O God: command deliverances for Jacob.

5. Through thee will we push down our enemies: through thy name will we tread them under that rise up against us.

6. For I will not trust in my bow, neither shall my sword save me.

7. But thou hast saved us from our enemies, and hast put them to shame that hated us.

8. In God we boast all the day long, and praise thy name for ever. (Ps. 44:4–8)

Because Israel under David was a type of the church, the church must see in this warfare that she is and must be a militant church. Exactly as a militant church the church can and must sing the Psalms, which are full of enemies and warfare.

An important, gripping aspect of David's kingship as battling king was his mighty men and their devotion and loyalty to David, as well as their heroic deeds (2 Sam. 21:15–22; 23; 1 Chron. 11). Among these mighty men were the three sons of Zeruiah, David's sister; Elhanan, who killed a giant brother of Goliath; Jonathan, David's nephew, who killed a giant who was defying Israel; Jashobeam, a Hachmonite, who killed three hundred adversaries of David by himself alone at one time; Eleazer, who with only two others fought with David against the army of the Philistines and gained a great victory; Shammah, who defended an Israelite garden of lentils against a marauding troop of Philistines; Benaiah, whose exploits were many and great; and Uriah the Hittite, husband of Bathsheba.

David, who himself was courageous and mighty, had a large, skilled, brave, and powerful army (1 Chron. 12). The core was the six hundred who gathered about David during the time of his flight from Saul. These are referred to in the Hebrew as the "*gibborim*," that is, "mighty men" (2 Sam. 16:6; 20:7). The Cherethites and Pelethites seem to have been special forces that served as David's bodyguard. Likely they were foreigners who had been converted to Jehovah and who were specially devoted to David (2 Sam. 8:18; 20:7; 1 Kings 1:38, 44).

The significance of these "mighty men" at this stage of the history of the kingdom of God must not be overlooked. The Spirit of Jehovah that was upon David, empowering him to establish the kingdom of Christ in the world, especially by defeating the enemies of the kingdom, went out from David to gather and equip mighty men to fight under David and for David on behalf of the kingdom. It was as if these men shared in the Spirit that was upon David, for the carrying out of David's mission. In them and their deeds is to be seen the reality of the mighty men of Jesus Christ, beginning with the apostles and continuing with the great men of God in New Testament history: Augustine, Luther, Calvin, Gomarus, De Cock, Bavinck, Hoeksema, and others, including some mighty elders and some heroic women—modern Deborahs.

Satan has his Philistine monsters, Goliath and his relatives; Christ has his mighty men.

SPIRITUAL WARFARE

That David's hatreds and wars were not personal is plain from his readiness to forgive and from his kindness to his own personal adversaries. There is his continuing kindness to the house of Saul in the person of

Mephibosheth (2 Sam. 9). This was motivated by David's love for Jonathan. Nevertheless, David desired to show kindness to the house of Saul: "The king said, Is there not yet any of the house of Saul, that I may shew the kindness of God unto him?" (v. 3). David gave to Mephibosheth all the land of Saul and had Saul's grandson eat at the king's table. The significance of this, particularly in light of the prevailing custom of utterly destroying the family of the king whom one replaced, Mephibosheth himself noted: "For all of my father's house were but dead men before my lord the king" (19:28).

David showed kindness to the house of Saul also by burying the bones of Saul and Jonathan when two of Saul's sons and five of his grandsons were executed to satisfy the justice of God in the matter of Saul's sin against Israel's oath to spare the Gibeonites (2 Sam. 21). In David's execution of some of Saul's "bloody house," there was nothing personal on David's part (v. 1). On this occasion, David buried the bones and bodies of Saul's seven sons, of Saul himself, and of Jonathan in their own tribal land and in the tomb of Saul's father. This was kindness and honor to the dead, but also to a house that had persecuted David relentlessly and for whom it might have been expected that David bore such hatred as to leave their carcasses to rot in the field.

The personal kindness of David to his own enemies was evident also in his refusal to execute Shimei the Benjamite, who had cursed David "with a grievous curse" when David was fleeing Absalom (2 Sam. 19:16–23).

In addition, by far most of David's wars were defensive. The enemies of the kingdom of Jehovah God attacked Israel in order to destroy the nation. Often they formed alliances against Israel, as in the instance of the federation of nations formed by Ammon when it had gratuitously insulted Israel and David by its shameful treatment of David's ambassadors of peace (2 Sam. 10). Especially the many wars against the Philistines were defensive. These inveterate enemies of David and Israel constantly invaded the promised land both to attack the people of God and to occupy the territory that God had given Israel. David defended Israel against these invaders. The two wars with the Philistines recorded in 2 Samuel 5:17–25 are representative: "But when the Philistines heard that they had anointed David king over Israel, all the Philistines came up to seek David…And the Philistines came up yet again."

The result of David's victories and conquests is the enlargement of Israel and the great glory of David. Israel is a great nation, both in size and in power. But this redounds to the glory of King David. The kingdom of Israel is the extension and creature of the king. The king has made the kingdom. Simply put, the kingdom is David the king.

Although this was only imperfectly true of Israel, it is perfectly the case with the New Testament kingdom. The kingdom is Christ Jesus. The kingdom derives its greatness, splendor, and very existence from its glorious head. Scripture makes this virtual identification of the kingdom with Christ its king in 1 Corinthians 12:12. Comparing the church with its many members to the human body, the text concludes, "So also is Christ." One would expect, "So also is the *church*." Since the church, or kingdom, is the spiritual extension of its head, the apostle could write instead of "church," "Christ."

As God's exaltation of him was high, so deeply did David fall.

Chapter Fifteen

David Inglorious: His Great Sin

(2 Samuel 11–12)

egarding the occasion of David's sin of adultery and murder, some
suggest that it was David's failure to accompany his army to the
war with Ammon (2 Sam. 11:1). Against this suggestion stands the prohibition of David's going with them to war by David's men in 2 Sam.
21:17: "Then the men of David sware unto him, saying, Thou shalt go
no more out with us to battle, that thou quench not the light of Israel."
Since this prohibition is part of the chronicles of David's wars, it likely
preceded the sin of David with Bathsheba, even though the account of
the prohibition in the Bible follows the account of the sin. There is good
reason to believe that the history in this part of the book of 2 Samuel is
not presented in chronological order. Nor need it be. Arrangement by
subject is perfectly in order.

Even though it is not the case that David's remaining in Jerusalem
while his army was fighting is itself the occasion of David's sin, as though
he ought to have been on the field of battle with his army, it is certainly
the case that he ought not to have been gratifying his lust when the ark
and Israel were in the field, warring a war of Jehovah. Uriah's confession of devotion to the cause of Jehovah that prohibited him from even

sleeping with his own wife while his comrades were fighting the battles of Jehovah had to have stung David to the quick: "The ark, and Israel, and Judah, abide in tents; and my lord Joab, and the servants of my lord, are encamped in the open fields; shall I then go into mine house, to eat and to drink, and to lie with my wife?" (2 Sam. 11:11). A foreigner—the Hittite—put the Israelite to shame.

The circumstances that contributed to David's fall were rather that David is now at the peak of his power over the then-known world and at the height of his worldwide glory. This is the occasion of danger from the worst enemy of all: one's own sinful nature in the form of pride. David allows himself to be lifted up in pride. As a great king, he may indulge himself as he pleases in *his* kingdom—*his* kingdom. He has the right to any citizen of his kingdom, to use as he pleases. There is a pattern in scripture of godly men falling deeply exactly at the moment that God has highly exalted them: Noah; Solomon; Hezekiah; Uzziah; and others. Indeed, this was true of the fall of Adam: highly exalted as the image of God, with dominion over the entire creation. Edersheim expresses the occasion of David's fall well: "It was in the intoxication of hitherto unbroken success, on the dangerous height of absolute and unquestioned power, that the giddiness seized David which brought him to his fall."[1]

One man, and one man only, resisted the temptation to presume on God's exaltation of him and to indulge himself in seizing a fame and pleasure that were not his to enjoy, at least at the time. This was Jesus in the wilderness, immediately upon his having received the Spirit of God by whom he was empowered to establish the kingdom of God. Rather than take to himself lordship over "all the kingdoms of the world, and the glory of them," he humbled himself to the will of God and the way of the cross (Matt. 4:1–11). By the Spirit of this Christ Jesus, the believer, especially the believer who may be prominent in the kingdom of God in the world, will be able to heed the warning of David's fall, namely, that he live and act covenantally in times and positions of spiritual power and

---

1   Edersheim, *Old Testament Bible*, 4:191.

prosperity. To live and act in the way that befits the covenant is to live in the humility that one is a servant of God and his church/kingdom, not a lord over God's heritage (1 Pet. 5:3), and that whatever has been accomplished by him on behalf of the kingdom has been the doing of Christ through him. He remains only a servant, and an unprofitable one at that (Luke 17:10).

On David's part, the sin was grossest violation of the seventh commandment of the law of God: adultery, the seduction of and intercourse with the wife of another man. This was a different category of sexual sin than David's polygamy. Polygamy in the Old Testament was a corruption of the institution of marriage, which God also visited with the chastisements endemic to the weakness. But polygamy was an aspect of the shadowy nature of the Old Testament. The bright light of the truth of marriage did not yet shine in the holy lives of the saints in the Old Testament. This light waited for the shining of the full truth of the gospel of Jesus Christ, who is the husband of one wife. If God did not tolerate polygamy in the lives of some—not all—of his saints (and he did not, for he chastised it), nevertheless he endured it as an imperfect stage in the development of his people in holiness of life. So much was this true that the prophet could say to David that God himself had given Saul's "wives into thy bosom" (2 Sam. 12:8) and that God could bless the (polygamous) marriage of David and Bathsheba.

Even in the Old Testament, adultery was a radically different, wholly unendurable, and gross violation of the seventh commandment. To sleep with the wife of another man was then, as it is today, such vile transgression of the covenantal law as necessarily to bring down upon the adulterer the fierce anger and heaviest judgment of God, even though the transgressor is the beloved David, the man after God's own heart, the outstanding type in the Old Testament of the Messiah. Especially in the twenty-first century, when adultery is nothing thought of and when all the media in Western society allure married persons with the prospects of the exciting pleasures of adultery, an expositor of this history would be remiss did he fail to call attention to the hard and heavy judgments of God upon David for this sin. God made the rest of David's life miserable, *bitterly*, almost unendurably, miserable. And this says nothing yet of the certainty of hell for the impenitent adulterer.

Behind the deed was sexual lust, lust deliberately yielded to and nurtured, as David looked eagerly upon the bathing wife of another man. "Every man is tempted, when he is drawn away of his own lust, and enticed" (James 1:14).

And then there was the murder of Bathsheba's husband, as the fruition of the lust and the culmination of the adultery. "Then when lust hath conceived, it bringeth forth sin: and sin, when it is finished, bringeth forth death" (James 1:15).

This sin of David was the "presumptuous sin" and "great transgression" of Psalm 19:13.

It is necessary also to judge David's sin as God looked upon it: "The thing that David had done displeased the LORD" (2 Sam. 11:27). David's evil was done "in his [Jehovah's] sight" (12:9). God exposed the evil as it appeared to his eyes by means of the prophet Nathan (vv. 7–10, 14). David had despised Jehovah by despising his commandment. The Hebrew translated "commandment" is *davar*, with reference to the law of God as recorded in Exodus 20. The reference is to the entire law, not only the seventh and the sixth commandments. David broke the tenth commandment by coveting a woman who was another's. He broke the eighth commandment, as Nathan indicated in his fable by having the rich man steal the poor man's lamb. The first was violated in that when David despised the law of God, he despised the lawgiver: "Thou hast despised me" (v. 10). He broke the third, concerning the name of God, in that by his sin he gave occasion to the enemies of God to blaspheme (v. 14).

All this transgression of the law of God was ingratitude for the great goodness of God to David (2 Sam. 12:7–8). It was violation of the covenant, regarding both the covenant with David personally as an elect believer and the covenant with David as the typical Messiah. Violating the covenant with Jehovah, David grievously violated the covenant as it extended to David's fellow citizen in the kingdom of the Messiah: Uriah. This wickedness was aggravated in that Uriah was David's subject in the kingdom. David himself gives expression to the gravity of his sin against

Uriah when he declares, "He that ruleth over men must be just, ruling in the fear of God" (23:3). Making his sin against Uriah even worse is that Uriah was one of David's mighty men, devoted to the safety of David at the peril of their own life. Not only did David sleep with Uriah's wife at the time that Uriah was risking his life fighting David's battle, but also David had Uriah himself carry the letter of his own death sentence to General Joab.

David was cruel to Uriah, as he himself condemns himself in his response to Nathan's story: "He had no pity" (2 Sam. 12:6).

Bathsheba is not free from blame, if not in an immodest bathing with perhaps the intention to catch the roving eye of the king, then in yielding to the king's seduction. Nor does she escape chastisement. The child who dies is hers as well as David's. But scripture, unlike twenty-first-century society, does not blame the woman.

REPENTANCE, FORGIVENESS, AND CHASTISEMENT

Although heavy and extremely painful to David, the judgment of Jehovah upon the gross sinner is not punishment but chastisement. There is a radical difference in the reality of the two consequences of sin for the sinner, even though their form, in time, may be identical. The former is the just wrath of God inflicting upon the sinner the wages of his sin, which is death, thus destroying him in time and in eternity. In punishment the sinner pays the debt he owes to the justice of God. The latter is an anger of God that is tempered with mercy. It inflicts painful suffering, not as payment but as the means to impress upon the sinner the seriousness of his wrongdoing; to sanctify him regarding the specific lust and possible future committing of the transgression; and to draw him to the mercy of God in Jesus Christ for forgiveness. Punishment is damning. Chastisement is saving.

Jehovah chastised his erring son. He did not punish. But this does not mitigate the severity of the fatherly strokes or the pain of them in the experience of the now-penitent child. There would be severe trouble in David's family for the rest of David's life, such trouble as incest, rebellion against parental authority, murder, death, and eternal damnation of

David's own children outside the reality of the covenant of grace. There is no pain more severe to a covenantal father than such troubles in his family, especially if he is the cause of them.

David also would suffer the public disgrace of his wives being ravished by another man, indeed David's own son.

The justice of these chastisements is notable. As David troubled another man's family, so God will trouble David's. As David shamed another man with the ultimate marital shame, so God will shame David.

In addition, the infant son of David and Bathsheba would die, not because he was conceived in adultery, but because God was determined to smite the father with a heavy stroke. A beloved child must die in the cradle because of the sin of the father. How this pained the father is evident from the fact that despite the firm prophecy of the child's death, David fasted and prayed for the child's life, lying upon the ground and refusing to eat for seven days, if God might be merciful to him and spare the child (2 Sam. 12:15–23). David had faults as a father. Lack of love for his offspring was not one of them.

Controversial is David's confidence that "I shall go to him," that is, that David will go to be with the child that died in infancy (2 Sam. 12:23). Some contend that this merely speaks of David's joining the child in the grave and in the sphere of the dead. This explanation does not do justice to the note of hope and comfort that sounds in these words. In all the grief of David's experience that the child has died on account of the father's sin and that the child "shall not return to me" (v. 23), there is, even in the relative darkness of the Old Testament concerning an intermediate state (the life with God of the saved in his soul immediately upon death), a ray of light. Long before the Canons of Dordt made the hope part of the Reformed faith's confession of the gospel of the covenant of grace, David comforted himself on the death of his infant son thus:

Since we are to judge of the will of God from his word, which testifies that the children of believers are holy, not by nature, but in virtue of the covenant of grace, in which they together with the parents are comprehended, godly parents have no reason to doubt of the election and salvation of their children whom it pleaseth God to call out of this life in their infancy.[2]

All of this severe judgment is chastisement, not punishment, because Jehovah forgave David. Jehovah brought David to repentance by his word through the prophet Nathan. There must be repentance! There is no pardon except in the way of repentance. God prepared David for the word of rebuke, "Thou art the man," that brought David to repentance by the working of the Spirit that for almost a year made David miserable on account of his sin. Psalm 32:3–4 is the expression of the spiritual misery of the guilty king: "When I kept silence, my bones waxed old through my roaring all the day long. For day and night thy hand was heavy upon me: my moisture is turned into the drought of summer." But the word worked heartfelt repentance including the required confession of sin: "I have sinned against the LORD" (2 Sam. 12:13). The word was necessary for this repentance, and a courageous prophet brought the word.

David's confession is met immediately with forgiveness: "The LORD also hath put away thy sin; thou shalt not die" (2 Sam. 12:13). Indeed, as George M. Ophoff points out, God had already forgiven David before his confession. Nathan's message was that the Lord "*hath* put away thy sin," in the past.[3] Nevertheless, David could know and experience God's forgiveness only in the way of his repentance and confession. This free, gracious pardon of sin—great sin—was the gospel in the Old Testament, which is the same as the gospel proclaimed in the New Testament. The heart of the gospel is forgiveness, which is the deliverance of the believing sinner from the guilt of his sin by the imputation to him of the righteousness of Christ Jesus, upon whom the sin put away from David is put. On the basis of this forgiveness, God spared David (and Bathsheba) the death due them for adultery. "The man that committeth adultery with another man's wife, even he that committeth adultery with his neighbor's wife,

---

2 Canons of Dordt 1.17, in Schaff, *Creeds of Christendom*, 3:585.

3 George M. Ophoff, "Thou Art the Man," *Standard Bearer* 28, no. 15 (May 1, 1952): 356.

the adulterer and the adulteress shall surely be put to death" (Lev. 20:10). He spared David also the penalty for murder.

God's forgiveness of David (and Bathsheba) is sealed by the gift of another son, Solomon. Solomon is designated by the Lord as David's successor and the typical fulfillment of the promise of the seed who will build God's house (2 Sam. 12:24–25). God sent Nathan yet again to David, this time to name the child Jedidiah, which means "beloved of the LORD." The name Solomon, by which name the child is better known, means "peaceful." This name expresses that this is the successor of David whose reign will be peaceful and who will build the house of God that David might not build.

Although David was forgiven, his sin regarding Bathsheba and Uriah had grievous consequences under Jehovah's chastising rod. The sin marked the end of the period of the glorious rule of David and the beginning of the period of shame and strife, both at home and in the nation, that lasted until David's death. Edersheim puts it well:

> Once more, then, the sunshine of God's favour had fallen upon David's household [in the forgiveness of David's sin and in the gift of Solomon]—yet was it, now and ever afterwards, the sunlight of autumn rather than that of summer; a sunlight, not of undimmed brightness, but amidst clouds and storm.[4]

David himself is weakened regarding both his home and his rule of the nation. By this severe affliction of their king, Israel is troubled. David's sin became public knowledge. The carnal in the nation mocked. The spiritual in the nation lost trust in their king. The weakened king can neither command the strength of the nation as formerly, nor hold the kingdom together. Always these are the effects of such a sin on the part of a head of a home or of a ruler in the church.

Gross as was the sin of David, it must not be allowed to dominate the church's view of David and to determine the church's estimation of

---

4   Edersheim, *Old Testament Bible*, 4:196.

the whole of his kingship. One sin marred his reign, one sin that was not typical of his kingship, one sin that was repented of. First Kings 15:5 calls the sin regarding Uriah the only sin that was the exception to his godly reign: "David did that which was right in the eyes of the LORD, and turned not aside from any thing that he commanded him all the days of his life, save only in the matter of Uriah the Hittite."

The thought of 1 Kings 15:5 is not that David had no other sins, or even that he had no other especially grievous sin. Numbering the people was a grievous sin, as the divine judgment upon it indicated. But the sin in the matter of Uriah stood alone in its egregious disobedience on David's part and in its troublous consequences for David's kingship, for the kingdom of God, and for the name of God.

First Kings 15:5 does not mitigate, much less deny, David's other sins. It emphasizes the gravity of the sin regarding Uriah. Thus, it accentuates the mercy of God in freely forgiving this sin.

Scripture's revelation of the history of the sin, repentance, and forgiveness of David has application to all the children of God, and not exclusively to David. This history is the gospel of the mercy of God toward all his sinful children, which mercy includes chastisement as well as forgiveness. Sordid as is the sin that the passage records, the history is precious and moving to every believer who has cried out in anguish of soul, "I have sinned against Jehovah," and has at once heard the blessed word of the gospel, "The LORD also hath put away thy sin; thou shalt not die." Several psalms related to this history are sung lustily, if with tears flowing down their cheeks, by the worshiping congregation: Psalms 32, 38, 51, and more.

Still, the incident is the revelation of God's mercy and faithfulness particularly to David. God is merciful and faithful to David not simply as a member of the covenant, but to David as king of the kingdom of God. God keeps the Davidic covenant and covenantal promise despite the grossest unfaithfulness of David in the covenant. David himself continues as king. His sons will reign after him. The Messiah will come from him. David himself in a special way may sing of the mercies of Jehovah and may make known Jehovah's faithfulness, as experienced by himself (see Ps. 89).

To all appearances, the sin of David represents a setback to the development of the covenant in history. The fortunes of the covenant are not all glorious advance, from victory to victory. The most harmful injuries to the cause of the covenant in the world are done to the covenant by members of the covenant themselves, and then often by men in high places in the kingdom. Either they corrupt the pure gospel of the kingdom and covenant of God, causing schism, or they bring division into the church by their jealousy of their fellows.

In reality, David's sin was no real defeat of the kingdom of God, for by means of the sin Jehovah showed that David was merely the typical Messiah, not the reality. The type failed miserably and that in the sphere that is essential to the covenant, namely holiness; justice; the humble obedience to Jehovah; the honoring of Jehovah's name. The hope of the Old Testament saints, accordingly, is directed to David's seed, that "holy thing" (Luke 1:35) who would do the will of Jehovah even when Jehovah is pouring out the vials of his wrath upon him. David fell so that Christ Jesus would stand alone, prominently.

Chapter Sixteen

David in Decline

(2 Samuel 13–1; Kings 2:11; 1 Chronicles 21–29)

S ince they play a prominent role in the decline of David at the end
of his reign, David's family ought to be introduced here (2 Sam.
3:2–5; 5:13–16; 1 Chron. 3:1–8; 14:4–7; 2 Chron. 11:18). Eight wives
are named: Michal, a daughter of Saul; Ahinoam, the Jezreelitess; Abigail, formerly the wife of Nabal; Maacah, a daughter of Talmai, king
of Geshur; Haggith; Abital; Eglah; and Bathsheba, formerly the wife of
Uriah and the mother of Solomon. David had other wives and concubines besides (2 Sam. 5:13).

The prominent children of David in the history are Amnon, the firstborn, son of Ahinoam; Absalom, the third son, son of Maacah; Adonijah,
the fourth son, son of Haggith; Tamar, daughter of Maacah and full sister of Absalom; Solomon, son of Bathsheba, heir to the throne and the
builder of the temple; and Nathan, son of Bathsheba and the son of
David through whom Christ descended from David (see Luke 3:31).[1]

Common as it was in the Old Testament, when the light of the truth
of marriage did not shine brightly among the covenantal people and

---

1 For the argument that Jesus Christ descended from Nathan, not from Solomon as
is commonly supposed, see my article "The Genealogy of Jesus according to the
Flesh," *Protestant Reformed Theological Journal* 2, no. 2 (May, 1969): 5–16.

when the example of the heathen kings influenced the kings of the kingdom of God, having many wives and concubines was a sinful weakness of David. For this weakness, Jehovah chastised David. He did this by the natural consequences of polygamy: family intrigue, rather than family unity; strife for the crown among the sons; incest; and more. David had little joy in his family life. He had abundant grief.

Much of this grief David brought upon himself by weakness in addition to his polygamy. One such weakness was his failure to punish sin in the family and thus take the sin in hand so as to protect the family from the further consequences of the sin. This was David's sinful weakness in the sordid, sinful matter of Amnon's rape of his half-sister Tamar, who was full sister of Absalom. Although God's covenant is with David and although the covenantal promise is an elect seed, David has reprobate, ungodly children, one of whom is his firstborn, Amnon. The daughter, on the other hand, the woman who is raped, shows herself a godly woman (2 Sam. 13:12–13, 19).

David makes himself complicit in the sin by failing to punish his rapist son, even though he knows of the evil. The law required that Amnon be punished with death (Lev. 20:17). David is very angry (2 Sam. 13:21). But he fails to punish. Nor is this an exception in David's oversight of his family. He shows himself a poor father, failing to discipline his children. Another instance of his weakness in governing his children is his failure to punish his son Absalom with death for Absalom's murder of Amnon. Scripture explicitly accuses David of sinful indulgence regarding his son Adonijah: "His father [David] had not displeased him at any time in saying, Why hast thou done so?" (1 Kings 1:6).

It strikes one as strange that a man so capable at governing the nation was so weak in ruling his own home and family. No doubt, after his sin with Bathsheba David's natural weakness of doting on his children, especially those who were handsome and able, is intensified by his sense of his own gross sin. It is hard for a father who cannot say, "Do as I do," to say, "Do as I say." At the same time, the sinful and undisciplined goings-on in David's family and the sin of David with Bathsheba, all of which became public knowledge, contributed to the weakening of David's kingly hold on the nation. The disunity and even division of the kingdom, culminating in the schism brought about by Absalom, are directly related to David's failure as a father of his own family. There is good reason why 1 Timothy 3:4–5 requires that a qualification of an officebearer in the church is that he rule his own house well, "having his children in subjection with all gravity."

Now begins Jehovah's judgment upon David of strife in his own family for his destruction of another man's family (see 2 Sam. 12:9–11). Trouble in one's family is an especially grievous chastisement for a covenantal father, especially when he is well aware that he himself is the cause of it. David had to trace the incest, the hatred of brother for brother, the disgust of sister with brother, and presently the murder of a son by another son directly to himself as erring father. All of this as the heavy hand of God upon David! Jehovah does not scourge David lightly, even though he loves David greatly. Indeed, his love for David is the reason why he chastises David severely.

At this time, David is at least fifty years old and has reigned over Israel at least twenty years. Amnon and Absalom were born after David became king in Hebron at thirty years of age.

From Amnon's rape of his sister and as a consequence of David's failure to discipline Amnon for his sin comes Absalom's murder of his half-brother Amnon. Even though the sympathies of much of Israel, as also the sympathy of those who read the history today, probably lie with Absalom, Absalom's killing of his brother is murder. The motive of the murder is not justice, nor is Absalom authorized to execute justice upon the rapist. The motive is vengeance. David is to blame for the evil deed, inasmuch as he, who *is* authorized to punish, has been derelict in his office. Similarly today, elders and ministers who fail to condemn heresy and to discipline gross transgressors of the law of God are to blame for the schism in the church that results when laymen publicly call attention to the heresy and expose the sins that are tolerated in the church. It is hypocrisy that the same derelict ministers and elders then loudly condemn the "schismatics."

David adds to his sin of failing to punish Amnon for his rape by failing to punish Absalom for the murder. After five years, three of which Absalom spent as an exile in Geshur, the native land of his mother, Maacah, and during two of which Absalom was banished from court, David allows himself to be reconciled to Absalom. This reconciliation is not virtuous on David's part, as an act of mercy. It is a fault, inasmuch as it compromises justice and bypasses repentance.

Absalom's murder of Amnon is further fulfillment of the judgment earlier threatened upon David. Now the "sword" strikes his family.

All these bizarre, unholy happenings at the center of the covenant, the life of which is "holiness unto Jehovah," could not but weaken the respect for their king and thus loosen the bands of the covenant between ruler and ruled, especially when an attractive rebel raises a challenge to the old and now largely discredited king.

THE REVOLT OF ABSALOM

The revolt of Absalom happened about the thirty-fifth year of David's reign, when David was about sixty-five years old. At the time of the rape of Tamar, Amnon had to be about twenty. David was about fifty at the time of the rape and the subsequent murder of Amnon by Absalom. This event was followed by some five years before Absalom is again received at court. Then there were four years during which Absalom conspired to raise his revolution (2 Sam. 15:7). The "forty years" of the AV is a copyist's error. Scripture itself makes clear that the length of the conspiracy cannot have been "forty years."

The history of Absalom's revolt, as history predestined by God, discloses several important truths of the covenant. First, there is the reality and severity of God's chastisement of his beloved son David and David's remarkable, humble submission to God's heavy hand upon him.

In close connection with this, there are the affliction and seeming abandonment of the messianic king by God. In this history, David is typical of the Messiah, Jesus. There are several outstanding features to the typology. There is David's weeping on Mount Olivet (2 Sam. 15:30). Also, David is betrayed by a trusted counselor and friend, Ahithophel. This betrayal is prophetic and typical of Jesus' betrayal by a member of his intimate band of disciples, Judas Iscariot (see Ps. 41:9; 109:8; John 13:18; Acts 1:20). Obviously, the forsaking of David by the nation of Israel is typical prophecy of the abandonment of King Jesus by Israel. The revolution against David clearly shows that the career of the Messiah, both personally and regarding the history of his kingdom in the world, is not all victory and glory. Rather, there are seeming defeats and humiliations.

Yet another important truth about the covenant that this history proclaims is that there is treachery against the king of the kingdom of God, and faithlessness and disloyalty to him and to the covenant itself, on the part of the covenantal people. His own son, his close friend and trusted counselor, Ahithophel, and others who had served David in close relation to him now attack him and purpose the overthrow of his reign, and indeed his death. Most striking is the widespread falling away from David and going over to the side of the rebel by much of the nation of Israel itself. Indeed, the nation fell away from their king. "Absalom stole the hearts of the men of Israel" (2 Sam. 15:6; see also v. 12). This is simply astounding in light of all that David had done for and meant to Israel. It is more astounding still in light of Israel's knowledge that David was the anointed of Jehovah.

In part, this falling away of Israel demonstrates that there were many who were only nominal citizens of the kingdom of God. Always, "they are not all Israel, which are of Israel" (Rom. 9:6). In part, the depravity of the covenantal people by nature is evident. Also, some who fell away after Absalom repented of their sin and renewed their allegiance to David.

The rejection of David by the nation of Israel foretells the rejection of David's greater son by Israel, which will renounce him in their cry, "We have no king but Caesar" (John 19:15). The rejection is typical of the apostasy of the nominal church in the last days (see 2 Thess. 2:3). In the end, the faithful people of God are only a remnant.

By no means the least important aspect of this history is that Jehovah maintains the covenant with David and with Israel. He preserves David, restoring him to the throne, by virtue of the covenantal promise. He destroys David's and the covenant's foes. He also preserves a band of faithful adherents to David and to the covenant, for instance, David's mighty men, old Barzillai, and others. Always in the hour of crisis for the covenant, there are those who do not forsake, betray, and deny but who abide faithful and confess. These are spiritual heroes, by the grace of God.

The history itself is briefly told. Handsome, youthful, charismatic Absalom, who is next in line for the throne of Israel but who is undoubtedly aware that Jehovah and David have chosen the younger son, Solomon, woos the fickle people, gaining their affection and following, and raises the revolt from historic Hebron.

The most dangerous element of the revolt is the defection to Absalom of the wise counselor Ahithophel—longtime trusted friend and especially brilliant advisor of David (2 Sam. 16:23). David recognizes the threat from Ahithophel and prays that God would turn the counsel of Ahithophel into foolishness (15:31). In answer to David's prayer—for God has never forsaken his son and servant—God uses the counsel of another advisor of David, one Hushai, to thwart Ahithophel's otherwise successful tactic against David. Thereupon Ahithophel commits suicide, recognizing not only that Absalom will fail, but also that Jehovah is against the revolution. Like Ahithophel, there are brilliant men in the church whose commitment is not one of faith but merely of personal aggrandizement. The church to them is merely a stage upon which they may play a leading role to the applause of the spectators and from which they may exercise ecclesiastical power.

In obedience to the counsel of Ahithophel before his death, Absalom shames his father and solidifies his followers by committing fornication publicly with his father's concubines. In doing so, Absalom fulfills the prophecy of Nathan the prophet that God would chastise David in this way. Again the judgment of God is fitting. David cuckolded another man by fornicating with his wife. God shames David by a man's fornicating with his semi-wives.

Adding to the already almost unbearable misery of David is the grievous curse of him as he flees by the Benjamite Shimei. Shimei hates David on account of the replacement of Saul's house, of the tribe of Benjamin, by David and his house of the tribe of Judah. Shimei's curse and treatment of David in the fleeing king's distress are wicked and provocative in the extreme: "Come out, come out, thou bloody man, and thou man of Belial," with Shimei casting stones at and raising dust against David and his men as they flee. Worst of all about the curse is that Shimei attributes David's misery to Jehovah's cursing of the king: "The LORD hath returned upon thee all the blood of the house of Saul, in whose stead thou hast reigned" (2 Sam. 16:5–13).

In response to the otherwise understandable request of the hard-nosed sons of Zeruiah that David permit them to take off the head of "this dead dog," who is cursing their king, David displays the amazing grace of the child of God in submitting to the evil as inflicted upon him not by the reprobate Shimei but by God himself: "Let him curse, because the LORD hath said unto him, Curse David...Let him alone, and let him curse; for the LORD hath bidden him" (2 Sam. 16:9–11).

This response to the indignity wickedly inflicted upon him by one who was himself truly a son of Belial was remarkable in several respects. First, it was a display of the amazing grace of God in David by which he could submit himself to the painful chastisement of God. David traced Shimei's evil up to the righteous hand of Jehovah his God accomplishing his humbling and purifying of David regarding David's sin with Bathsheba and Uriah. Second, David confessed the sovereignty of God over sin. "Jehovah hath said unto him, 'Curse David.'" Denial of God's sovereignty over sin is not only an assault on the Godhead of God and contrary to the explicit testimony of scripture. It is also the stripping of comfort from the children of God when they find themselves in circumstances similar to those of David as he is abused by Shimei. Time and again, the child of God endures evil unjustly inflicted upon him and restrains himself from vengeance by whispering to himself, "Jehovah has said, 'Curse David.'"

Third, exactly in the way of submitting to the suffering caused by the wickedness and not taking vengeance himself, David had the confidence that God himself would look with pity on David's suffering and reward David with good for patiently enduring the evil. "It may be that the LORD will look on mine affliction, and that the LORD will requite me good for his cursing this day" (2 Sam. 16:12). This aspect of the believing response of David to the wickedness of the damnable Shimei made certain the punishment of Shimei in time and in eternity that would be far, far worse than his decapitation by Abishai and Joab.

Later, when God had put down the revolt of Absalom and restored David to the throne of Israel, David declined to punish Shimei with the execution that he well deserved. This did not, however, amount to forgiveness, although it displayed the lack in David of all desire for personal vengeance, which desire when publicly demonstrated would have weakened his standing as once again king over all Israel (2 Sam. 19:16–23). That David did not, in fact, forgive Shimei his grievous sin against the Lord's anointed became evident when the dying old king charged King Solomon to "hold him not guiltless…but his hoar head bring thou down to the grave with blood" (1 Kings 2:8–9). It is one thing to refrain from taking vengeance against a sinner; it is another thing to forgive.

Amidst all this betrayal and revolution, David has loyal adherents and faithful followers. These include the Cherethites and Pelethites; the six hundred mighty men; Ittai the Gittite; the two high priests, Zadok and Abiathar; Hushai; the two sons of Zeruiah, Joab and Abishai; in Transjordan, Shobi the Ammonite, Machir of Lodebar, and old Barzillai the Gileadite; besides other soldiers and people. Even though they are only a remnant, always in the history of the kingdom of Christ there are some who are faithful to Christ. This is evident repeatedly in the several reformations of the church in New Testament history. Noteworthy is that many of those who were faithful to David were Gentiles. The heathen are faithful when Israel rejects the anointed of the Lord. This is prophetic of the saving of the Gentiles when national Israel goes lost.

The end of the revolution is that Jehovah gives the victory over the rebels to David and his band. In the defeat of his rebel army, Absalom suffers an accursed death. He comes to his sorry end hanging from a tree with his head caught in the boughs. Significantly, scripture adds, "taken up between the heaven and the earth" (2 Sam. 18:9). Thus the judgment of God was fulfilled upon him that was pronounced in Deuteronomy

21:22–23: "If a man have committed a sin worthy of death…thou [shalt] hang him on a tree…(for he that is hanged is accursed of God)."

David shows himself weak and foolish in the matter of the death of Absalom and the defeat of the rebel army. He puts his own personal affection for his wicked son above the welfare of the kingdom of God, thus jeopardizing the kingdom. Rather than rejoicing over the victory of the kingdom of God, he weeps publicly over the death of his rebellious son. The blunt charge of Joab to the king's face is correct: "If Absalom had lived, and all we had died this day, then it had pleased thee well" (2 Sam. 19:6). In this reprehensible and foolish behavior of David, carnal general Joab saves the day. He has Absalom killed, and he puts an end to David's public sorrow over his wicked son. For doing so, to the salvation of Israel, Joab earns the disfavor of David, who replaces Joab with one Amasa—Amasa, who was the commander of Absalom's rebel army and a close relative of Joab. This results in Joab's murder of his rival.

Joab's behavior is characteristic of the man. It is David's judgment and behavior that are noticeably different now than before. He is no longer the same monarch that he was before his sin with Bathsheba. He lacks the wisdom to govern that he displayed earlier. He blunders in important matters of kingship. Another instance of such blundering is his handling of the affairs of Jonathan's son, Mephibosheth. Without demanding proof of the false charge of Mephibosheth's servant Ziba that Mephibosheth had gone over to Absalom in the revolt, David accepts the charge and gives all the property of Mephibosheth to the lying servant. Even when he learns the truth, David does not punish Ziba but allows him to keep half the property.

By his lack of wisdom, David loses the esteem of his followers, contributes to the disunity of his kingdom, and compromises the glory of the messianic kingdom of God in the world. Government of the kingdom of God, now as then, is more than a matter of sheer, natural capability or the holding formally of an office. Above all, it is a matter of spirituality, of holiness of life, of the enjoyment of the blessing of God. By his presumptuous sin, David has, if not mortally then severely, injured himself as king of the kingdom of God. And this entails the injury of the kingdom.

The miserable end of Absalom and the defeat of his rebellious forces are the doing of Jehovah. Only this explains the extraordinary seizure of Absalom in a tree and the wood's devouring more of Absalom's army than the sword (2 Sam. 18:8). The history is graphic warning of the certain end of every rebel against the authority of Messiah, indeed the end of every rebel against God-ordained authority of any sort.

The revolt against King David and the restoration of David to his kingship are attended by division in the kingdom between the ten tribes of the north and Judah. Israel is jealous of Judah. Judah responds arrogantly and angrily to Israel (2 Sam. 19:41–43). As relations between the two sections of the kingdom become strained, in the language of scripture "there happened to be there a man of Belial" who availed himself of the tension to produce a full-scale schism (20:1). Always when there are such circumstances in the church, there "happens to be there" a man who will take advantage of the situation to produce schism. Satan sees to it. This man was Sheba, a Benjamite, and therefore another advocate of the house of Saul. By his instigation, the ten tribes broke away from the kingship of David.

How deadly serious are separation from and revolt against the true church of Christ (which the kingdom of Israel of which David was king truly was) is indicated by scripture's calling Sheba "a man of Belial." The truly dreadful rallying cry of Sheba is, "We have no part in David, neither have we inheritance in the son of Jesse" (2 Sam. 20:1). This separation from David and Judah is presage of the future, permanent division of the nation into the same two segments under Jeroboam. The rebel cry of the ten tribes will echo that of Sheba: "What portion have we in David? neither have we inheritance in the son of Jesse: to your tents, O Israel: now see to thine own house, David" (1 Kings 12:16).

Joab seizes the leadership in putting down the revolt, which never got off the ground in Israel. The defeat of the rebel and his forces without further bloodshed takes place by the delightful appearance and common sense of "a wise woman" and "mother in Israel" in the territory of the ten tribes (2 Sam. 20:14–22).

Certain Psalms bear heavily on this history and shed light on it. Psalms

41 and 55 treat Absalom's conspiracy. Psalm 41 indicates that David was sick during the time that Absalom stole the hearts of Israel. This would explain why Absalom could make headway and why David could not prevent the revolution. Psalm 55 expresses David's desire to fly far away into the wilderness to find rest. The old man is weary of the struggles of life, as every old minister or ruling elder understands full well. The psalm speaks of the guile of David's "guide...and acquaintance," of one who "hath broken his covenant" (vv. 11–20). It prophesies the destruction of such enemies before they live out "half their days" (v. 23).

Psalms 3 and 63 refer to David's flight from Absalom. Both confess David's security in these dire circumstances and his confidence that his foes will suffer defeat at the hands of God.

Psalms 39, 61, and 62 give evidence of having been occasioned by David's flight across the Jordan to escape his son. David cries out to God "from the end of the earth" (61:2). Psalm 39 has David humbling himself in the recognition that his misery is God's chastising him for his sin. In his distress, however, David does not despair. Rather, he casts himself by faith upon God, and upon God alone, so that he is confident that God will deliver him: "God is a refuge for us" (62:8).

Chapter Seventeen

Final Acts of David

(2 Samuel 24; 1 Kings 1-2; 1 Chronicles 21-22, 28-29)

NUMBERING OF THE PEOPLE

David's sin of numbering the people occurred after Absalom's revolt and therefore toward the end of David's reign and life. This indicates that the old age of saints is vulnerable to temptation, specifically to the kind of temptation found in this history. The history of the numbering of the people is not only instructive, but also a fascinating aspect of the history of David.

There is the occasion of David's sin in the supernatural world. Here there are differences in the two accounts of the sin in 2 Samuel and in 1 Chronicles. Second Samuel 24:1 has Jehovah moving David against the nation by saying, "Go, number Israel and Judah." First Chronicles 21:1 states that *Satan* provoked David to number the people.

The two versions of the event are not at variance but complement each other. Jehovah was sovereign in the event. By his counsel of providence he determined that David would decide to number Israel; by his power of providence he moved David to issue the royal order, including the king's overruling the objections of Joab, who in this instance had better insight into the sinful and God-provoking act than did his lord. "The king's heart is in the hand of the LORD, as the rivers of water: he turneth it whithersoever he will" (Prov. 21:1).

The purpose of the Lord was the chastisement of Israel: his anger was kindled against Israel (2 Sam. 24:1). Such is the solidarity of king and kingdom that the sin of the king (in numbering the people) rightfully brings judgment upon the kingdom. It is likely that the sin of Israel that angered Jehovah was Israel's unfaithfulness in the covenant by rejecting the head of the covenant, and therefore Jehovah himself, in the revolts of Absalom and of Sheba.

That God moved David to commit the sin of numbering the people reveals as plainly as possible that God is sovereign over sin, is sovereign over sin in the lives of his people. "Moved" in the text is a form of the Hebrew verb *suth*, which elsewhere is translated "stirred up," regarding Jezebel's influence upon Ahab (1 Kings 21:25) and regarding God's power over Saul so that he would pursue David (1 Sam. 26:19). It is the same Hebrew word used in the parallel account of the numbering of the people, where Satan's influence upon David is translated "provoked" (1 Chron. 21:1). In the latter case, the Hebrew verb expresses the sinful influence of Satan tempting David. In the former case, the same Hebrew verb expresses the sovereign but sinless, providential power of God governing sin for his own holy purposes. In this instance, sound theology governs the translation and understanding of the same Hebrew verb. Satan "provoked," whereas God "moved."

God never tempts. Therefore, he moved David to number the people by the instrumentality of Satan. This explains the account of the sin in 1 Chronicles 21:1 in distinction from the account in 2 Samuel 24:1. Needless to say, Satan acts with his own purpose, namely to play the adversary against Israel, the covenantal people of God. Satan too is fully aware of the solidarity of king and kingdom, of David and Israel. Satan attacks Israel, therefore, by provoking David.

Behind the scene of one and the same event in the history of the kingdom of God are two mighty, spiritual, powerful persons, God and Satan. They have two completely different purposes: Jehovah intends to chastise in love; Satan intends to destroy in hatred. They are not co-equal. Jehovah uses Satan as the instrument to accomplish his saving purpose. What was true on the limited vignette of this particular incident is true also on the vast canvas of world history. Mighty and malignant as Satan is, the sovereignty of God compels Satan to serve the saving purposes of God and the welfare of his kingdom.

The human object of the two powers is David. He is the one whom Jehovah moves and whom Satan provokes. Nevertheless, contrary to the thinking of some philosophers, David is not an example of helpless humans tossed to and fro like a ball between God and the devil. He is not, to change the figure, a helpless pawn on the chessboard of these two mighty spirits. Rather, he is fully responsible for his decision and action. Neither God nor Satan forces him to decide and act as he does. He decides and acts freely. He knows full well that his decision to number the people is corrupt, although for the time he hardens himself against this knowledge. That he acts contrary to the knowledge that the Spirit of God has given him is evident from the fact that he repents on his own, that is, without needing any prophet to point out the evil of his deed and to call him to repentance: "David's heart smote him after that he had numbered the people. And David said unto the LORD, I have sinned greatly in that I have done" (2 Sam. 24:10). His responsibility is heightened in that he was warned off from the evil deed by the unspiritual Joab, who despite his lack of spirituality knows what is right and what is wrong in the kingdom of God (v. 3). David's full and real responsibility is implied by God's judgment of him (vv. 11–13). The righteous God does not judge a man for a deed for which he—God—is responsible.

The sin of David consisted of carnal pride in the size and military might of Israel, as though that were due to the work of David and as though that might glorify David. David viewed Israel as *his* people, rather than as Jehovah's people; he surveyed the nation as existing for David's personal glory, rather than for Jehovah's glory. In keeping with these self-aggrandizing notions, David viewed the strength of Israel as its own military might, rather than as the gracious presence of Jehovah God. Exactly this was the thrust of Joab's rebuke of the enterprise of numbering the people: "Now the LORD thy God add unto the people, how many soever they be, an hundredfold, and that the eyes of my lord the king may see it: but why doth my lord the king delight in this thing?" (2 Sam. 24:3).

David's sin is the same as that of the pagan king Nebuchadnezzar: "The king spake, and said, Is not this great Babylon, that I have built for the house of the kingdom by the might of my power, and for the honour of my majesty?" (Dan. 4:30). The analysis of C. F. Keil is correct: "The true kernel of David's sin was to be found, no doubt, in self-exaltation, inasmuch as he sought for the strength and glory of his kingdom in the number of the people and their readiness for war."[1]

Common though the sin may be in the history of the kingdom of God in both administrations of the kingdom—one thinks at once of the similar sin of King Hezekiah in the Old Testament and of the pride of some ministers in their large congregations in the New Testament—David's sin was great. "God was displeased with this thing" (1 Chron. 21:7). When he repented, David confessed the act to have been very foolish and a great sin (v. 8). The greatness of the sin was that it robbed God of his glory in the saving of his church/kingdom and placed the confidence of the church/kingdom in the arm of human flesh. No greater sin is conceivable.

Jehovah's judgment, even though chastisement and not punishment, is severe. Repentance and forgiveness (in this case, on the part of David) do not rule out chastisement, indeed painful chastisement. The judgment falls upon David, but in this way, that David's nation and people suffer. It must be remembered that the event is due to Jehovah's anger "against Israel" and his will to chastise Israel (see 2 Sam. 24:1). Nevertheless, the evil falls upon David: "thee" (v. 12); "unto thee" (v. 13). Again the solidarity of king and people in the covenant is stressed. And David did indeed suffer in the suffering of his people, as his pitiful plea of verse 17 indicates: "Lo, I have sinned, and I have done wickedly: but these sheep, what have they done? let thine hand, I pray thee, be against me, and against my father's house."

As is always the case with God's judgments, this judgment was fitting regarding the sin. In one day, the number of the people (in which David took pride) was reduced by seventy thousand. God executed the judgment

---

1 Keil and Delitzsch, *Biblical Commentary on Samuel*, 502.

by "the angel of the LORD" (2 Sam. 24:16). If, as was true, the angel of the
Lord in the Old Testament was the preincarnate Messiah, or Christ, who
is Jesus, the awful judgment upon Israel and upon David was inflicted by
the Christ. Jesus is not the soppy, harmless savior of theological modernism, tolerant of unrighteousness. On the contrary, he is zealous, *within the
sphere of the covenant and kingdom of God,* on behalf of the glory of God
his Father, and therefore he is severe in chastising his own.

David saw the angel, as did Araunah (Ornan in 1 Chronicles) and his
four sons. That was an awesome sight: the angel standing between heaven
and earth with a drawn sword poised over Jerusalem. It is no wonder that
David and the elders with him fell on their faces and that Araunah and
his sons dived into a hole and hid. The sight of the angel was no mere
vision, as some suggest, but a genuine glimpse of spiritual reality. "David
lifted up his eyes, and saw the angel of the LORD stand between the earth
and the heaven, having a drawn sword in his hand" (1 Chron. 21:16).
Likewise, "Ornan...saw the angel" (v. 20).

Awesome beings are always in the air about the church in the world,
and awesome events are always taking place there. Occasionally, God permits his servants to catch a glimpse of the beings and events. The prophet
Elisha's servant was permitted to see "the mountain was full of horses and
chariots of fire round about Elisha" (2 Kings 6:17). One day the heaven
will open, and all will see the fulfillment of the angel of Jehovah, that is,
Jesus Christ, coming down from heaven with a host of angels to judge
the world (Rev. 19:11–21). Today, if we were enabled, we could see a
tremendous conflict raging between the devils promoting the kingdom
of darkness and the angelic hosts defending the kingdom of Jesus Christ
(Dan. 11:18–21).

David was permitted to choose what was a real offer on God's part,
not a well-meant offer of salvation but a serious offer of three alternatives
of evil. Among these hard options was that of Israel suffering pestilence
for three days. This option David chose, not because it was of shorter
duration than the other two, but because regarding this evil Israel and
David would fall directly into the hand of God himself. David both knew
and trusted in God as merciful: "Let us fall now into the hand of the

LORD; for his mercies are great: and let me not fall into the hand of man" (2 Sam. 24:14).

In his hope of mercy, David was not put to shame.

Jehovah exercised his mercy toward his people already before David pleaded on behalf of them. Before David made his touching plea, "Lo, I have sinned, and I have done wickedly: but these sheep, what have they done? let thine hand, I pray thee, be against me, and against my father's house" (2 Sam. 24:17), "the LORD repented him of the evil, and said to the angel that destroyed the people, It is enough: stay now thine hand" (v. 16). Jerusalem was spared. The time of the pestilence was less than one entire day, instead of the three days that were threatened. So must the phrase translated in the AV as "from the morning even to the time appointed" be understood (v. 15). The source and cause of the salvation of the covenantal people always and in every respect are the great mercies of God, and only the great mercies of God.

These mercies decisively deliver Israel only in the way of a mediatorial plea and an atoning sacrifice. David raises the intercessory prayer on behalf of the people of God: "These sheep, what have they done? let thine hand, I pray thee, be against me [in the stead of Israel]" (2 Sam. 24:17).

At the instruction of Jehovah, David builds an altar and offers sacrifices on the exact site where the angel stood: "the threshingfloor of Araunah" (compare 2 Sam. 24:16 and vv. 18, 24–25). Fire from Jehovah then consumes the sacrifice (1 Chron. 21:26). Only then, when God himself satisfies his justice by the consuming of the substitutionary sacrifice, does the angel of Jehovah sheathe his avenging sword (v. 27). This dramatic event clearly proclaims that the justice of God regarding his guilty people must be satisfied. There can be deliverance only on the basis of the propitiatory sacrifice. There can be no mercy apart from justice, and mercy provides the satisfaction of justice. In the atoning sacrifice of Jesus Christ, typified by the sacrifices of David on this occasion, "righteousness and peace...kissed each other" (Ps. 85:10). God could sheathe the sword of his strict justice only in the soul and body of Jesus Christ as the sacrifice whom he himself provided in the incarnation of the eternal Son.

It is striking in this event, which is rich in typical significance, that the angel of Jehovah is not only the instrument of judgment, but also the very Jehovah who shows mercy in the way of sacrifice. Although he is distinguished from Jehovah—as the *angel* of Jehovah—the angel is at the same time identified with Jehovah. The angel commands the prophet Gad to instruct David to set up an altar, and this instruction is said to have been spoken by Gad to David in the name not of the angel but of "Jehovah" himself (1 Chron. 21:18–19).

It is the angel who commands Gad the prophet to instruct David to set up an altar. Since the angel is the Old Testament manifestation of Jesus Christ, there is in this incident, at the close of David's reign, a brilliantly clear revelation of the salvation of Israel through substitutionary sacrifice, which sacrifice will involve a mediator who is at once king and priest and will be the fulfillment of prophecy.

Contributing to the rich typical and prophetic significance of the event is that the altar raised on this occasion becomes the location of the temple and its altar of burnt offering. "Then Solomon began to build the house of the Lord at Jerusalem in mount Moriah, where the Lord appeared unto David his father, in the place that David had prepared in the threshingfloor of Ornan the Jebusite" (2 Chron. 3:1). This was also the mount where Abraham sacrificed a ram in the stead of Isaac (Gen. 22:2). All this history is wonderfully arranged by Jehovah, whose providence governs all things on behalf of the salvation of the church. He determines not only by whom and when his house shall be built, but also where. Ever after this history of David these associations ought to have lived in the mind of Israel: the sword of their destruction is sheathed only in the body of the sacrifice offered to the justice of Jehovah, and this gives the right to dwell with God in the temple of the covenant.

Incidentally, in the course of this history we learn of the size of Israel by Joab's reluctant numbering of the people. There were some 1,300,000 valiant men available for fighting in David's army (2 Sam. 24:9; 1 Chronicles 21:5 has a higher number). This would indicate a total population of five or six million persons. This number does not include the membership of the tribes of Levi and Benjamin, because in his opposition to the entire project Joab refused to complete the census (1 Chron. 21:6). God had fulfilled his promise to Abraham to multiply his descendants as the dust of the earth (Gen. 13:16). After the day of Pentecost and by the gathering of the seed of Abraham from all nations, the number of Abraham's (spiritual) seed is far greater still (see Gal. 3:16–29).

CROWNING, CHARGE, AND CALLING OF THE COMING KING

Among the final acts of King David, in knowledge of his impending death, was his public crowning of Solomon, his son by Bathsheba, king over Israel as his God-ordained successor (1 Kings 1). The timing of the coronation was precipitated by yet another revolutionary grasp for the throne by one of David's sons, Adonijah. According to the age of the sons, Adonijah was next in line for the crown after Absalom. In this revolt, important persons in Israel were involved, including the powerful general of the army, Joab, and Abiathar, one of the high priests. Adonijah therefore had both strong military and religious backing. At the urging of Bathsheba and Nathan, old David has Solomon publicly anointed king of Israel. He gives his son, the newly crowned king of the kingdom of God, charges as it were from his death bed (1 Kings 2:1–9; 1 Chron. 22:6–16).

First and foremost, he calls on Solomon to obey the law of God, not only as a child of the covenant, but also as king. He assures Solomon of the covenantal promise that God made to David, namely that "there shall not fail thee [David]…a man on the throne of Israel" (1 Kings 2:4). This promise God would fulfill in the way of David's children taking heed to their way, to walk before God in truth. He solemnly charges Solomon to build the temple, as God had foretold that this son of David would do.

He also lays upon Solomon the duty to do justice to two gross sinners in David's reign, whom David had not punished as they deserved. They are Joab and Shimei. Some are critical of David for this parting order to his son. Even Edersheim, although he first explains the order correctly, concludes with criticism of David: "It is impossible to read his parting directions and suggestions to Solomon without disappointment and pain."[2] However, this charge concerning Joab and Shimei was the requirement for the execution of justice, without which justice a kingdom of peace, which Solomon's kingdom was to be, is impossible. At the same time, the execution of Joab was a hard, practical necessity. As the subsequent plot of Adonijah would prove, future revolutions were a real possibility, and Joab would likely be a dangerous, powerful ally of the insurgents.

In the case of Shimei, his sin had been grievous. He had rejoiced in the ouster of David, the Lord's anointed. He had cursed the typical Christ. David had declined to punish him but had not forgiven him. In addition, in some way the public execution of the great sinner was necessary for the establishment of the kingdom of Jehovah: the effect of Shimei's punishment would be that "king Solomon shall be blessed, and the throne of David shall be established before the LORD for ever" (1 Kings 2:45). Also the reprobate brought his doom upon himself by his own fault. The fault was exactly that which he had committed against David, namely violating the third commandment of the law of God. Shimei broke his oath. He had sworn in the name of Jehovah that he would not leave Jerusalem. But he left.

For his complicity in the revolutionary efforts of Adonijah to become king in the stead of Solomon, the priest Abiathar is deposed from office by Solomon. This solves the longstanding problem of there being two high priests (and therefore two centers of public worship) in the nation. This also fulfills the judgment of Jehovah upon the house of Eli that God would cut off his family from the priesthood (see 1 Sam. 2:22–36; 1 Kings 2:26–27). Abiathar was a descendant of Eli; Zadok, the other high priest, was of another family descended from Aaron. The mills of God's justice ground slowly, but they ground surely.

The last words of David were prophecy of the just ruler in the kingdom of God (2 Sam. 23:1–7). The prophecy introduces David as the anointed of the God of Jacob and the sweet psalmist of Israel. It centers on the Davidic covenant: "He ['the God of Israel,' who is 'the Rock of

2 Edersheim, *Old Testament Bible*, 5:58.

Israel'] hath made with me an everlasting covenant, ordered in all things, and sure." These last words of the great king of the Old Testament kingdom of God are prophetic of Jesus Christ. It is Jesus who "shall be as the light of the morning, when the sun riseth, even a morning without clouds." What was bright and beautiful in David and his reign was the shining back into David's reign of the glorious kingship of the Christ who was coming.

26. Thus David the son of Jesse reigned over all Israel.

27. And the time that he reigned over Israel was forty years; seven years reigned he in Hebron, and thirty and three years reigned he in Jerusalem.

28. And he died in a good old age, full of days, riches, and honor: and Solomon his son reigned in his stead.

29. Now the acts of David the king, first and last, behold, they are written in the book of Samuel the seer, and in the book of Nathan the prophet, and in the book of Gad the seer,

30. With all his reign and his might, and the times that went over him, and over Israel, and over all the kingdoms of the countries (1 Chron. 29:26–30).

Solomon:
Philosopher-King

Chapter Eighteen

—

The Reign of Solomon: Kingdom of Peace and Prosperity

(1 Kings 2:12–11:43; 1 Chronicles 23:1; 29:22–25; 2 Chronicles 1–9)

INTRODUCTION

The glorious reign of Solomon represents a high point and the end of one of the distinct periods in the development of the covenant/kingdom of God in the Old Testament. According to the divisions of Old Testament history proposed by Homer C. Hoeksema, following George M. Ophoff, the principle of the division of the period under consideration is that the period represents a victory of the seed of the woman in fulfillment of the promise of Genesis 3:15, although only typically.[1]

The period culminating in the reign of King Solomon began with the inheritance of Canaan under Joshua. The establishment and glory of the kingdom of God under David and Solomon, climaxing in Solomon's

---

1 Homer C. Hoeksema, *From Creation to the Flood*, Unfolding Covenant History: An Exposition of the Old Testament, vol. 1 (Grandville, MI: Reformed Free Publishing Association, 2000), xxix-xxxiii.

glorious reign, constitute the goal of a distinct epoch in the progress of the typical kingdom/covenant of God. The outstanding elements of this distinct period of covenantal history include the inheritance of the promised land; defeat of the enemies of the people of God; enjoyment of peace and prosperity; and the glory of God's covenantal kingdom shining out to the nations of the world of that time. In power, in wealth, in territory, Israel had become one of the greatest, if not the greatest, kingdom in the world. The surrounding nations recognized the greatness of Israel, as the visit to Solomon by the queen of Sheba indicated.

The root and essence of all this bliss and glory was Israel's living with Jehovah as its friend in the covenant and its living obediently under Jehovah as its sovereign in the kingdom.

The progress in this epoch reached its zenith in David's son Solomon. Under Solomon, Israel experiences the possibilities of the blessing of God in the covenant. Scripture indicates that in the reign of Solomon, specifically by the building of the temple, is reached the end of an epoch in Israel's history. Scripture does so by its dating of the temple in relation to the exodus: "It came to pass in the four hundred and eightieth year after the children of Israel were come out of the land of Egypt, in the fourth year of Solomon's reign over Israel…that he began to build the house of the LORD" (1 Kings 6:1).

What characterized Solomon as king was wisdom, and what characterized his reign were peace and prosperity. In answer to Solomon's request at Gibeon, immediately after David's death, Jehovah gave Solomon great wisdom: "Behold, I have done according to thy words: lo, I have given thee a wise and an understanding heart; so that there was none like thee before thee, neither after thee shall any arise like unto thee" (1 Kings 3:12). In distinction from the reign of David, Solomon's reign was peaceful and extremely prosperous. His peaceful kingship was revealed in Solomon's name. It derives from the Hebrew word for peace: *shalom*. The peaceful nature of Solomon's kingship was the reason why he and not his warrior father, David, was to build the temple (see 1 Chron. 28:3; 1 Kings 5:3–4). This earthly peace of the typical kingdom was the revelation in the Old Testament that the coming messianic king, Jesus, would himself be the prince of peace and would win peace for his kingdom and people—peace with God, peace among themselves, and finally peace on earth.

Where is peace, there is also prosperity. Solomon's reign was the enjoyment of fabulous riches. Second Chronicles 9 describes the riches of Solomon in detail, because the type must impress upon the New Testament citizens of the kingdom of him who is greater than Solomon the reality and greatness of the fabulous spiritual riches that are theirs in Jesus Christ, by faith in him. "King Solomon passed all the kings of the earth in riches and wisdom" (v. 22). In the climate of peace, the people of Israel shared in the prosperity of Solomon: "Judah and Israel were many, as the sand which is by the sea in multitude, eating and drinking, and making merry" (1 Kings 4:20). "And Judah and Israel dwelt safely, every man under his vine and under his fig tree...all the days of Solomon" (v. 25).

Basic to this peace and prosperity was the king's wisdom. This wisdom was not, first of all, knowledge about many subjects, but the practical ability to judge Israel as the covenantal people of God, that is, to judge Israel in the fear of Jehovah. This he requested at Gibeon, upon his becoming king: "Give therefore thy servant an understanding heart to judge thy people, that I may discern between good and bad: for who is able to judge this thy so great a people?" (1 Kings 3:9). This he demonstrated at once in his judgment of the dispute between two harlots over genuine motherhood of a child (vv. 16–28). And this wisdom, all Israel recognized in their king: "All Israel heard of the judgment which the king had judged; and they feared the king: for they saw that the wisdom of God was in him, to do judgment" (v. 28).

As the result of his wisdom and of the peace and prosperity of his reign, Solomon was glorious. The glory of Solomon is an outstanding feature of this part of the history of the Old Testament. Solomon is introduced as glorious in scripture: "The LORD magnified Solomon exceedingly in the sight of all Israel, and bestowed upon him such royal majesty as had not been on any king before him in Israel" (1 Chron. 29:25). "Solomon the son of David was strengthened in his kingdom, and the LORD his God was with him, and magnified him exceedingly" (2 Chron. 1:1). Jesus remarked the glory of Solomon: "Even Solomon in all his glory" (Matt. 6:29). His glory included a numerous people (1 Kings 4:20) and a vast expanse of territory (v. 21).

In all the glorious reign of Solomon, Jehovah fulfilled his covenantal promise. He fulfilled the promise in the form in which he gave it to Abraham: the land from the river of Egypt to the river Euphrates (Gen. 15:18). He fulfilled it also in the form in which he gave it to David: "I will set up thy seed after thee, which shall proceed out of thy bowels, and I will establish his kingdom. He shall build an house for my name, and I will stablish the throne of his kingdom for ever" (2 Sam. 7:12–13).

TYPE OF THE CHRIST

In his wisdom and glory, Solomon was type of the Messiah, Jesus, and his kingdom of peace and prosperity was typical of the messianic kingdom of Jesus, that is, the church. This is the gospel of Psalm 72. Obviously the psalm has reference to King Solomon, as the heading expresses: "A Psalm for Solomon." But the description of the reign of this king surpasses by far the merely earthly, limited, and temporary kingship of Solomon. The kingdom of the king of Psalm 72 is worldwide, as Solomon's was not, extensive as it was: "from sea to sea, and from the river unto the ends of the earth" (v. 8); "all nations shall serve him" (v. 11); "all nations shall call him blessed" (v. 17). The reign of the real king of Psalm 72 is everlasting, as the reign of Solomon was not: "so long as the moon endureth" (v. 7); "his name shall endure for ever: his name shall be continued as long as the sun" (v. 17).

Most striking of all concerning the reality of the king of Psalm 72, and most decisive in identifying him as the Son of David who is Jesus, is that his blessings are spiritual, not the mere earthly good of men sitting under their vine and fig tree, eating and drinking and making merry. The king of Psalm 72 blesses his people with righteousness (v. 7); delivers the needy when they cry out for the pardon of sins; and redeems by the sacrifice of his cross the souls of sinful men and women from their sins and all their miseries (vv. 12–14). By his resurrection from the dead, he "shall live" forever, thus becoming the everlasting savior-king, who in the end will also raise the citizens of his kingdom into eternal life, so that prayer can be made for him "continually" (v. 15).

The king of Psalm 72 is Solomon only in type. The reality is Jesus the Messiah. Jesus himself spoke of himself as the "greater than Solomon" in connection with his reference to the queen of Sheba in Matthew 12:42: "She came from the uttermost parts of the earth to hear the wisdom of Solomon; and, behold, a greater than Solomon is here."

That Solomon was merely the type of the messianic king of the kingdom of God was proved by the fact that the type miserably failed at the end of his reign. Solomon was guilty of folly, indeed the worst of all follies. His heart was turned away from Jehovah after idols (1 Kings 11:4–8). As the result of the folly, he and his kingdom came under divine judgment. The peaceful kingdom was disturbed by the threat of war from without and by schism within. Upon his death, the glorious kingdom was ingloriously broken up. In the words of J. J. Stewart Perowne:

> Solomon did not fulfil the hope of this prayer [Psalm 72]. The righteous judge became the oppressor of his people, the wise king the weak, foolish, despicable voluptuary: God brake in pieces, before the eyes of His people, the frail earthly type, that He might lead them to wait for Him who was "higher than the kings of the earth," and who would "not judge after the sight of His eyes, neither decide after the hearing of His ears, but would judge with righteousness the weak, and decide with uprightness for the afflicted of the earth."[2]

The reality of which Solomon was the type is the ascended Jesus Christ reigning in wisdom in his spiritual kingdom, the church, so that she enjoys spiritual peace and prosperity already now. This heavenly reign with its spiritual blessings will be perfected in all the renewed creation upon Jesus' coming.

Regarding the typology of Solomon, it must not be overlooked that the full type of Christ and his reign is *David* and Solomon. David is the

---

2 J. J. Stewart Perowne, *Commentary on the Psalms* (Grand Rapids, MI: Kregel Publications, 1989), 1:566.

battling king who lays the groundwork for the kingdom of peace. The necessary way to peace is war. This is true of the ministry of Christ Jesus. This is true of the history of the church. This is true in the experience of the individual child of God. Solomon is the king of peace who enters into the kingdom prepared by David, his battling father. Jesus Christ combines the realities of both David and Solomon in himself. Thus it is the Davidic/Solomonic kingdom that constitutes the full end or goal of this period of the development of the covenant.

THE GLORIOUS REIGN OF SOLOMON

The coronation of Solomon was twofold. David and leading figures in Israel first crowned Solomon on the occasion of the revolutionary attempt of Adonijah, an older brother of Solomon by another mother, to make himself king in despite of the well-known appointment of Solomon by God (1 Chron. 23:1; 1 Kings 1). Solomon was crowned a second time at a great gathering of all Israel (1 Chron. 29:20–25). "They made Solomon the son of David king the second time" (v. 22). On the second anointing of Solomon, David announced to Israel that Jehovah chose Solomon "to sit upon the throne of the kingdom of the LORD over Israel" (28:5). David charged Solomon to know and serve Jehovah and to build the temple (vv. 9–10). He charged Israel to cooperate with Solomon in the building of the temple (29:1–5). David blessed Jehovah and called on all Israel to bless him (vv. 10–22). Israel worshiped Jehovah with sacrifices and celebrated with a feast.

At his accession to the throne, Solomon was about twenty years old. Since he reigned forty years, he was about sixty when he died.

Outstanding among the qualifications of Solomon for kingship over the kingdom of God was his wisdom (Hebrew: *chokma*). God bestowed this wisdom upon him in answer to Solomon's request, soon after his coronation at Gibeon (1 Kings 3:4–15). This wisdom was chiefly "a wise and understanding heart," to judge the people of God (vv. 9, 12). This is the wisdom of Proverbs 8, which is personal as Jesus Christ, the eternal wisdom of God in human flesh. By him "kings reign, and princes decree justice." By him "princes rule, and nobles, even all the judges of the earth" (Prov. 8:15–16).

The reference of this application of divine wisdom is chiefly to the government of the spiritual kingdom of Christ, namely the church. The princes are the elders of the congregations. The judges are the delegates at the broader assemblies. Rarely, if ever prior to the second coming of Christ and the reign of the saints in the kingdom of Christ in all the world, is there application of Proverbs 8 to earthly kingdoms except to expose the folly of the rulers, because as Luther observed, "A wise prince is a rare bird indeed; still more so a pious prince. They are usually the greatest fools or the worst knaves on earth…If a prince turns out well, so that he is wise, pious, or a Christian, it is one of the great wonders."[3] In addition, none of the earthly kingdoms in the age of the New Testament is or will be the kingdom of Jesus Christ.

Solomon demonstrated his wisdom at once in his judgment in the case of two harlots contending over a living and a dead baby (1 Kings 3:16–28). Little noted about this touching scene and wise judgment is Solomon's willingness to hear the case of two lowly, indeed ignoble, members of the kingdom. Justice in the kingdom of God is blind to the status of the citizens. As Psalm 72 exults, the king delivers the needy when she cries (v. 12). Regarding the disgusting moral character of the woman whom Solomon delivered, one remembers the word of Christ that harlots enter the kingdom before the outwardly moral, self-righteous Pharisee (Matt. 21:31).

Rooted in the fear of Jehovah, the wisdom of Solomon extended more broadly than only to the government of the kingdom of God. It was more, much more, than only right church polity and the holiness of the life lived according to the ten commandments. In his wisdom and as the application of his wisdom, Solomon wrote the books of Proverbs, Ecclesiastes, and the Song of Songs, the subjects of which are as vast as all human life, indeed as broad as the universe. Solomon's wisdom encompassed what we would call the arts and natural science: "His songs were a thousand and five. And he spake of trees, from the cedar tree that is in

---

3   Martin Luther, *What Luther Says: An Anthology*, 3 vols., trans. Ewald M. Plass (St. Louis, MO: Concordia Publishing House, 1959), 2:588–89.

Lebanon even unto the hyssop that springeth out of the wall: he spake also of beasts, and of fowl, and of creeping things, and of fishes" (1 Kings 4:32–33).

He had profound insight into the unique, blissful, marvelous intimacy of the marriage of one male and one female (his practice was quite another thing), with all that this means for all human life, for family, and for society (Song of Songs). To the consternation of the women's liberation movement, which is folly, the wisdom of Solomon pronounces wise the woman who "looketh well to the ways of her household"—not to the ways of society, but "her household" (Prov. 31:27).

Profoundly wise is the haunting theme of the book of Ecclesiastes. Life lived apart from God in Jesus Christ, whether in the university, in the halls of Congress, on Wall Street, or in the gutter, is "vain": empty, senseless, purposeless, worthless. In the words of the secular poet Shakespeare, all is "sound and fury, signifying nothing." In the positive words of the Preacher, "Fear God, and keep his commandments: for this is the whole duty of man" (Eccl. 12:13; "duty" in the AV is an insertion of the translator).

Solomon was the first, and probably only, philosopher-king. He was the earliest advocate of the good Christian school, the school in which trained, competent, *wise* Christian instructors teach all the truths of human life and of the world in which we humans live in light of Jesus Christ as he is revealed in God's word as "the firstborn of every creature" (Col. 1:15).[4]

Solomon's wisdom reveals that Jesus Christ is wisdom, not only for the life of the soul in the sphere of theology and religion, but also for the whole of human life in all spheres of knowledge. It also makes known that the life lived by the Spirit of the wisdom, who is Jesus Christ, does not consist of fleeing the world but of knowing everything of God's creation and living in all the ordinances and spheres in the fear of Jehovah.

---

4 For an explanation, defense, and promotion of the Christian school, see David J. Engelsma, *Reformed Education: The Christian School as Demand of the Covenant*, rev. ed. (Grandville, MI: Reformed Free Publishing Association, 2000).

If Solomon spoke of trees, beasts, and creeping things, we may, indeed ought to, learn of them.

Solomon's wisdom was world-renowned. "Solomon's wisdom excelled the wisdom of all the children of the east country, and all the wisdom of Egypt…and his fame was in all nations round about" (1 Kings 4:30–31). "All the earth sought to Solomon, to hear his wisdom, which God had put in his heart" (10:24).

The renown of Solomon for wisdom is indicated in the history of the seeking out of Solomon and the attending upon his words by the queen of Sheba (1 Kings 10:1–13; 2 Chron. 9:1–12). She came from southern Arabia, some 1,200 miles distance. She came on account of the "fame" of Solomon's wisdom. It was his wisdom that she wanted to "prove." It was his wisdom that impressed her: "The half was not told me" (1 Kings 10:7).

Essentially, the content of his wisdom was the "name of the LORD" (1 Kings 10:1). Whether concerning right worship, or the purpose of a great kingdom, or the classification of "the hyssop that springeth out of the wall" (4:33), the wisdom of Solomon was essentially the name of Jehovah God. This is exactly what Reformed Christian school societies and Reformed parents have in mind by "God-centered education."

The queen put Solomon's wisdom to the test with "hard questions" (1 Kings 10:1), all of which Solomon "solved" (v. 3). "Hard questions" is the plural of the word in the original Hebrew literally meaning "something twisted, or involved," hence "an enigma." In Judges 14:14, the same word is translated "riddle" (of Samson's enigmatic question to the Philistines).

In Matthew 12:42 and Luke 11:31, Jesus appeals to the queen of Sheba as condemnation of the people of his generation, since she came from "the uttermost parts of the earth to hear the wisdom of Solomon," whereas the men of Jesus' generation despised "a greater than Solomon" in wisdom. They despised the very, personal Wisdom of God himself. The queen pronounced them happy who stood before Solomon and heard his wisdom (1 Kings 10:8). Now all the treasures of wisdom and knowledge are hidden in Christ Jesus. We either honor the divine Wisdom among us by believing the gospel and living all of life in the light of it or despise

Wisdom by unbelief and living all of life in its darkness, for in Christ "are hid all the treasures of wisdom and knowledge" (Col. 2:3).

As the witness among the nations of Solomon's wisdom, the queen prefigured all those among the Gentiles to whom the gospel of Jesus Christ would go out with saving power after Pentecost, thus extending the kingdom of Christ in all the world. The queen of Sheba "turned and went to her own country" as a witness in that heathen land to the wisdom of King Solomon (1 Kings 10:13). Similarly, it is the calling and privilege especially of the minister of the gospel in the new dispensation to declare the wisdom who is Christ Jesus. He does not proclaim the wisdom of men. He does not parade his own wisdom. He does not disparage the wisdom of Christ as taught in holy scripture. He counts all things but "dung" and "loss for the excellency of the knowledge of Christ Jesus" (Phil. 3:8).

THE SPLENDOR OF SOLOMON'S KINGDOM

As the blessing of God upon Solomon's wisdom in ruling the kingdom of Israel, the kingdom was splendid in material riches. The riches and the magnificence they effected were not necessarily evidence of obscene luxury, although Deuteronomy 17:17 does warn the king against multiplying riches "to himself." Rather, they were the manifestation of a legitimately prosperous and truly glorious realm. This is proved from the fact that Jehovah gave these riches to Solomon. Since Solomon asked for wisdom when he had the choice of asking for anything at all from God, Jehovah gave him "riches and honor" also. In these riches and the honor that attended them, Solomon would outstrip all the nations in the world: "There shall not be any among the kings like unto thee all thy days" (1 Kings 3:13). The wealth of the world is God's, and it ought to be used and enjoyed in his kingdom. The purpose of the wealth of Solomon was that it picture and typify the abounding spiritual wealth and magnificence of Messiah's reign.

The wealth of the world poured into Jerusalem by levies on subject nations; by gifts (as from the queen of Sheba); and by trade (Solomon had a navy at Eziongeber on the Red Sea, 2 Chron. 8–9). Precious spices, gold, silver, gems, ivory, exotic animals, valuable wood, horses, all of this and more enriched Israel and contributed to the magnificence of the kingdom. This magnificence is described in detail. There were targets and shields of beaten gold. Solomon had a great ivory throne that was overlaid with gold. On the sides of the six steps leading to the throne itself were the likenesses of twelve lions. About this throne, 2 Chronicles 9:19 states that "there was not the like made in any kingdom." The only throne in history that will be more glorious and awesome is the throne that Jesus Christ will ascend on the great day of the final judgment (Matt. 25:31; Rev. 20:11). All the goblets in Solomon's palace were pure gold. Silver in Jerusalem was so common as to be reckoned as mere stones. There were huge building projects.

There was more to the splendor of Solomon's kingdom, however, than only material wealth. It was also a realm of godly culture. There were harps and psalteries for singers, such as "were none such seen before in the land of Judah" (2 Chron. 9:11). Solomon himself was an outstanding composer: "His songs were a thousand and five" (1 Kings 4:32). There was education and learning of many kinds: theology, philosophy, science, and poetry. It was a literary age. Most of the third division of the Hebrew scriptures—the writings (Hebrew: *kethubim*)—came from this golden age of Solomon: Proverbs, Ecclesiastes, and the Song of Songs.[5]

Contributing to the splendor of the kingdom was its status as a world power. It was a kingdom to be reckoned with by the great nations of the day. This is the meaning of the affinity of Solomon with the Pharaoh of Egypt, cemented by Solomon's marriage to Pharaoh's daughter, apart from the question of the lawfulness of such an affinity with a heathen monarch, indeed apart from the question of the lawfulness of the marriage to a heathen princess (1 Kings 3:1). Pharaoh would not have given his daughter to the ruler of a second-rate power. Solomon reigned over all kingdoms from the Euphrates to the border of Egypt (1 Kings 4:21, 24; 2 Chron. 9:26).

---

5   Franz Delitzsch attributes also the book of Job, if not to Solomon's authorship, then to the same philosophical tendency that characterized the development of the kingdom of God under Solomon. Job is a part, therefore, of the Solomonic literature (see Delitzsch, *An Old Testament History*, 96–97).

Much later, Artaxerxes, king of Persia, recalled that "there have been mighty kings also over Jerusalem, which have ruled over all countries beyond the river; and toll, tribute, and custom, was paid to them" (Ezra 4:20).

Basic to this splendor was the peace of the realm. The surrounding nations either were subjugated or were willing to live peacefully with Israel. In any case, God gave peace to King Solomon and his kingdom: "The LORD my God hath given me rest on every side, so that there is neither adversary nor evil occurrent" (1 Kings 5:4). Solomon had fortifications throughout the land (2 Chron. 8:1–6). If, as is the case, Solomon's peaceful kingdom finds an aspect of its typical reality already in the spiritual peace of the church in history, before the full reality in the new creation, this enforcement of peace by sturdy fortifications testifies to the calling of the church in history to guard spiritual peace with the fortifications of creeds, polemics, and discipline.

Like the New Testament church, of which Solomon's kingdom was the type, Israel under Solomon was well organized. There was internal regulation and order (1 Kings 4:1–19). Disorder jeopardizes peace. Besides, disorder detracts from the splendor of a kingdom, casting aspersions on the nation's ruler. Indeed, disorder is a threat to the very existence of the kingdom. By its rampant disorder, the history of the judges had impressed all of this upon the nation of Israel. The New Testament kingdom of God is governed by King Jesus by a church order, drawn from scripture. One such church order is the church order of Dordt.[6]

Glorious as the kingdom of Solomon was by virtue of all these features, the heart—the life center—of the splendid kingdom was Jehovah's dwelling with his covenantal people in the temple. And the building of the temple was Solomon's crowning work.

---

6 For this aspect of Christ Jesus' government of his kingdom, see the Church Order of Dordt in Idzerd Van Dellen and Martin Monsma, *The Church Order Commentary*, 3rd ed. (Grand Rapids, MI: Zondervan Publishing House, 1954), 374–85, and the Church Order in *Confessions and Church Order*, 378–404.

Chapter Nineteen

———

The Building of the Temple

(1 Kings 5–9:9; 2 Chronicles 2–7)

*T*he building of the temple was Solomon's most important service to the covenant and to the name of Jehovah. Jehovah himself appointed Solomon to this work in the Davidic promise of 2 Samuel 7:13: "He [David's son] shall build an house for my name, and I will stablish the throne of his kingdom for ever." This promise is distinctly recalled by Solomon both before he begins building and after the building is completed (1 Kings 5:5; 8:18–20). The building of the temple is the goal or purpose of the Davidic covenant; as such, it is typical of Jesus' building the house of God, the church. The church, "as lively stones, are built up a spiritual house, an holy priesthood, to offer up spiritual sacrifices, acceptable to God by Jesus Christ" (1 Pet. 2:5). Zeal of God's house, which ate Jesus up, motivated his cleansing of the material temple and his building of the spiritual house, the church (see John 2:13–17).

The temple represented, and as much as was possible in the Old Testament *was*, the essence of the covenant of God: Jehovah God dwelling with his people, by means of the sacrifices, in an intimate relationship of friendship. In this covenantal fellowship, the people worshiped God and God blessed the people. The reality of the temple of Solomon will be the spiritual temple of Revelation 21:3: "The tabernacle of God is with men, and he will dwell with them, and they shall be his people, and

181

God himself shall be with them, and be their God." The significance of the temple of Solomon and of Israel, which cannot be emphasized too strongly, is the covenant of God with his people, if only the covenant is understood not as a contract but as living communion, which communion is life for the people.

The temple was constructed according to the pattern revealed by God to David (1 Chron. 28:11–19). Also the tabernacle had been built according to the pattern made known by God himself, in this case to Moses (Ex. 25:9, 40; 26:30). God, and God alone, establishes his covenant, determining its nature, its ground, and the part in it of his people. The temple was God's gracious work, not that of Israel or even of Solomon. God appointed the site of the building on Mount Moriah in Jerusalem. This was the place where David had offered the sacrifice that stayed from Israel the plague in the matter of David's numbering the people (2 Sam. 24). "Then Solomon began to build the house of the LORD at Jerusalem in mount Moriah, where the LORD appeared unto David his father, in the place that David had prepared in the threshingfloor of Ornan the Jebusite" (2 Chron. 3:1). Inasmuch as the temple was the place of the worship of Israel, God's blueprint of the temple expresses the regulative principle of worship: the people of God are to worship him only in the manner that he himself prescribes.[1]

The building of the temple began early in Solomon's reign, the fourth year, according to 1 Kings 6:1. It was seven years in building (vv. 37–38). The temple was rectangular. Taking the Hebrew cubit at one and a half feet, the temple was ninety feet long, plus a porch of thirty feet at the entrance. It was thirty feet wide and forty-five feet high. Its length ran east and west. It faced eastward. The worshiping people approached from the east.

The temple comprised two rooms. The most important was the holy of holies, or "the most holy place" (1 Kings 6:16). It was a cube of twenty

---

1 The regulative principle of worship holds that the church must worship God only in the manner that he himself prescribes in his word. This principle is the regulation of the second commandment of the law: "That we in nowise make any image of God, *nor worship him in any other way than he has commanded in his word*" (Heidelberg Catechism A 96, in Schaff, *Creeds of Christendom*, 3:343; emphasis added).

cubits, or thirty feet. This contained the ark of the covenant, in which were the two stone tablets of the law that God had given Moses on Mount Sinai. Standing over the ark, facing each other on the north and south sides of the ark, were the images of two huge cherubs with outstretched wings. Each was fifteen feet high. The wings of the cherubs extended fifteen feet. Thus "the cherubims spread forth their two wings over the place of the ark, and the cherubims covered the ark and the staves thereof above" (8:7). The cherubs were made of precious wood and were overlaid with gold.[2] Into this holy room only the high priest might enter, and he only once a year, "not without blood, which he offered for himself, and for the errors of the people: the Holy Ghost this signifying, that the way into the holiest of all was not yet made manifest" (Heb. 9:7–8).

Christ has entered into the reality of the holy of holies, that is, "heaven itself, now to appear in the presence of God for us" (Heb. 9:24). There he, the true high priest, remains on our behalf, as the typical high priest might not do. In him the elect and holy people of God have the fellowship with God that is the essence of the covenant, which is the meaning of the temple, particularly regarding the holy of holies. By him this people themselves enter into the presence of God daily by the prayers that arise out of their faith in Jesus Christ. Always this entrance is based upon the sacrificial blood shed by the high priest, who himself was also the sacrifice to the justice of the holy God (see Heb. 9–10).

---

2 On the carved "cherubim," see 1 Kings 6:23–28. The presence in the holy of holies of the likenesses of angels was not merely decorative. Just as the law itself was originally given "by the disposition of angels" (Acts 7:53; see also Gal. 3:19), in witness of the awesome nature of the revealed will of God to his covenantal people, so the same is figured by the images of angels over the stone tables containing the law. Commenting on Acts 7:53, Calvin writes "that the angels were God's intermediaries, and His witnesses in the promulgating of the Law, so that its authority might be firmly established" (John Calvin, *Calvin's Commentaries: The Acts of the Apostles 1–13*, ed. David W. Torrance and Thomas F. Torrance, trans. John W. Fraser and W. J. G. McDonald [Grand Rapids, MI: William B. Eerdmans, 1965], 215). Located as they were at the heart of the building whose significance was the communion of God with his people, which is salvation by the blood of the Sacrifice, the cherubs also symbolized the "ministering spirits, sent forth to minister for them who shall be heirs of salvation" (Heb. 1:14).

In light of this truth of the temple, particularly of the holy of holies, and the activity within it, which were merely "the figures of the true" (Heb. 9:24), the plans of premillennial dispensationalists to rebuild the typical temple and to reestablish the ceremonies that once were fundamental to the temple are nothing short of a blasphemous denial of Jesus Christ and his redemptive work on behalf of the covenant. It is Jewish unbelief.

The second important room of the temple was the holy place, called simply "the house" in 1 Kings 6:17. This was sixty feet in length. This room contained several symbolic pieces of furniture contributing to the worship of God and the enjoyment of salvation under the old covenant. There was a golden altar of incense; ten seven-branched candlesticks; and ten golden tables of shewbread (see 2 Chron. 4:7–8). Separating the holy place from the holy of holies was a thick, heavy, beautifully decorated cloth, or veil. This was the veil of the temple that was rent upon Jesus' death, thus signifying that the way to the presence of God, long closed to the sinful people, was now opened by the mediator, Jesus the Christ (Matt. 27:51).

Before the holy place was the large porch. The porch was thirty feet wide by fifteen feet deep (1 Kings 6:3). In the porch were the two great pillars, Jachin ("he supports") and Boaz ("in him is strength") (7:21). As one entered the temple proper, the pillars would remind him that the support of the covenant and the covenantal people was Jehovah their God, and that this support was sure. The pillars were massive—some forty feet in height and eighteen feet in circumference. They were made of brass.

In front of the porch, still farther to the east, was the inner court, or court of the priests (1 Kings 6:36; 2 Chron. 4:9). This was one hundred fifty feet wide and three hundred feet long—a large expanse. This area was enclosed by a wall consisting of three tiers of hewn stones and a row of cedar beams (1 Kings 6:36). It was paved with great stones. This court of the temple contained two important items used in the worship of Jehovah. One was the huge altar of burnt offering, and the other, a colossal "sea of brass," or basin. The "molten sea" was fifteen feet in diameter; seven and a half feet high; and forty-five feet in circumference (7:23). The altar of burnt offering was thirty feet square and fifteen feet in height.

Before the inner court, still farther to the east, lay the outer court of the people. It was double the size of the inner court. This court too was surrounded by a solid wall in which were four gates.[3]

The temple was massive.

The temple building itself was constructed of stones, which had been carved out away from the site of the temple. Some of these stones were enormous, as much as thirty feet in length and seven and a half feet in height. Each of these weighed tons. The inside of the entire temple was then covered with rare and beautiful wood. All the utensils used in the service of God in the temple were of gold; all of the inside of the temple, as well as the larger objects in the temple, were covered with gold (1 Kings 7:48–50; 6:20–22). In addition, Solomon "garnished the house with precious stones for beauty" (2 Chron. 3:6).

The temple was beautiful.

In all respects, the temple was a great house for a great God: "The house which I build is great: for great is our God above all gods" (2 Chron. 2:5). Indeed, the temple of Solomon was "wonderful great" (v. 9).

But all this wonderful greatness and glorious beauty were not the reality of the house of God. Therefore, all of it could be raped and razed by the Babylonians in a coming day. Nor is the New Testament fulfillment

---

3 For a more detailed description of the temple and its furnishings with some analysis of the typical significance of all of this, see Edersheim, *Old Testament Bible*, 5:70–84, and *The Temple: Its Ministry and Services*, updated ed. (Peabody, MA: Hendrickson Publishers, 1994). The *International Standard Bible Encyclopaedia* also offers a detailed description of the temple and its furnishings, with a sketch of the temple viewed from above (Grand Rapids, MI: William B. Eerdmans, 1960), 5:2930–34. The *Zondervan Pictorial Encyclopedia of the Bible* contains helpful sketches of both the outer appearance and inner layout of the temple (Grand Rapids, MI: Zondervan Publishing House, 1975–76), 5:625. The nature of the limited biblical revelation concerning the temple makes a full, exact, and certain conception and pictorial description of the temple impossible: "With the scanty data at command, all reconstruction of the Solomonic temple leave much to be filled in from conjecture" (*International Encyclopaedia*, 5:2930).

186 / Solomon: Philosopher-King

of the temple large, beautiful church buildings—vast cathedrals decorated with stained glass windows, elaborate carvings, and mighty pillars, in which are gathered huge numbers of people. The truly massive and beautiful fulfillment of Solomon's temple can be, and often is, found in a shabby, wooden, ramshackle building, in which only a handful of believers and their children worship God in spirit and in truth. The reality of Solomon's temple is the true church of Jesus Christ—not a building but the worshiping believers, beautiful with the beauty of holiness, glorious as the dwelling place of the all-glorious God by his gospel of grace, and worthy as the body of Jesus Christ. What makes the New Testament church beautiful is the presence with the congregation of the all-glorious God by the gospel of Jesus Christ. What makes the congregation massive is that it is the manifestation of the universal church among all nations and peoples.

The real temple of Jehovah God, of which Solomon's temple was merely a faint shadow, is identified in 1 Peter 2:5: "Ye [the New Testament congregation]…as lively stones, are built up a spiritual house, an holy priesthood, to offer up spiritual sacrifices, acceptable to God by Jesus Christ."

Evidently, upon the building of the temple as the permanent house of God, the original tabernacle was broken down, transported to Jerusalem, and stored somewhere in the temple, perhaps in the storage rooms that surrounded the temple on three sides. "They brought up the ark of the Lord, and the tabernacle of the congregation, and all the holy vessels that were in the tabernacle, even those did the priests and the Levites bring up" (1 Kings 8:4). It would not have been fitting to destroy the structure that had been the holy dwelling of Jehovah. But neither would it have been right to set it up in Jerusalem as possibly a rival to the temple. The tabernacle was not replaced by the temple. Rather, God enlarged and developed the tabernacle into the temple.

The temple built by Solomon was destroyed by the Babylonians in 586 BC. Evidently, the ark of the covenant perished in the conflagration. It is never again heard of. Herod the Great, the Roman governor of Judea, rebuilt the temple in about 20 BC. It is this rebuilt temple that is referred to in the gospels, for example, in Matthew 24:1, which reference to the glory of the temple became the occasion of Jesus' instruction concerning the last things. In AD 70, Jesus' prophecy in verse 2 of the complete destruction of the (second) temple was fulfilled. The invading Roman army destroyed the temple. There was not left one stone upon another that was not thrown down.

The temple of the visions of Ezekiel in chapters 40–48 neither describes nor prophesies a material temple, whether past, present, or future. It is rather a visionary symbol of the Old Testament temple in its spiritual reality. That it cannot describe a future material building is evident first from the impossible dimensions of the structure and second from the fact that animal sacrifices are offered in Ezekiel's temple. The physical sacrificing of animals after the sacrifice of the Lamb of God would be the blasphemous denial of the cross of Jesus Christ.

The reality of the temple of Ezekiel, as also of the temple of Solomon, is the body of Jesus Christ. In response to the Jews' objection to his cleansing of the temple, Jesus said, "Destroy this temple, and in three days I will raise it up." John explains: "He spake of the temple of his body" (John 2:18–22). The body of Jesus Christ is in itself the communion of God with men. In the body of Jesus is incarnated God the eternal Son. Inasmuch as spiritually he incorporates the elect church into himself as the head, the church is the body of Jesus and therefore the full reality of the temple (Eph. 2:19–22).

DEDICATION OF THE TEMPLE

The year following the completion of the temple, Solomon and all Israel dedicated the temple to Jehovah. The festive ceremony lasted for two weeks. There were seven days of celebrating the completion of the temple, followed by seven days of observing the Feast of Tabernacles. The celebration consisted of a multitude of sacrifices; of song; of an address by Solomon; of Solomon's blessing of Israel; and of a public prayer by the king. The high point of the dedication was the bringing of the ark into the holy of holies.

As soon as the priests had accomplished this, as the priests and Levites were singing praise to the Lord, "For he is good; for his mercy endureth

for ever," to loud musical accompaniment, the cloud of glory—the Shekinah—filled the temple: "The glory of the LORD…filled the house of God"
(2 Chron. 5:14). This descent of the cloud of glory was the dedication of
the temple by God himself. Closely related both in time and in meaning
to this descent of the cloud was the consuming of the sacrificial animals
by fire from heaven (7:1–3). God dwells with his people by his own gracious, glorious act, and he does so by himself offering up to himself the
sacrifice that his justice requires. The fulfillment of all this revelatory Old
Testament typology is God's offering up of himself in the eternal Son in
human flesh to satisfy his justice in the suffering and death of Jesus Christ.
The purpose is to realize his fellowship with the Israel of God.

The reality of the descent upon the temple of the Shekinah cloud of
glory is the outpouring upon the New Testament church of the Spirit of
Jesus Christ on Pentecost (Acts 2:1–36). In the Spirit, God establishes the
richest and most intimate fellowship with the church of Jesus Christ. In
this fellowship, God is the sovereign, who is worshiped and served; the
congregation worships and serves. God is glorified; the church is blessed
with the blessings of salvation.

The significance of bringing the ark into the temple, with its attendant
events of the cloud of glory filling the temple and of the fire consuming
the sacrifices, was the realization in a typical way of the covenant as God's
dwelling with his people. Solomon gave expression to this: "I have surely
built thee an house to dwell in, a settled place for thee to abide in for
ever" (1 Kings 8:13). That particularly the placing of the ark in the temple had covenantal significance, Solomon stated explicitly: "I have set
there [in the temple] a place for the ark, wherein is the covenant of the
LORD, which he made with our fathers, when he brought them out of the
land of Egypt" (v. 21). Although God dwells in heaven, his name is in
the temple: "My name shall be there" (v. 29). The name of God is God
himself in his revelation of himself. Fundamentally, this name is Jesus the
Messiah.

Solomon blessed Jehovah with words of praise that centered on God's
fulfilling the promise of the Davidic covenant: "Blessed be the LORD God
of Israel, which spake with his mouth unto David my father, and hath

with his hand fulfilled it" (1 Kings 8:15). The king then prayed a dedicatory prayer, a prayer that is marvelous in many respects but especially for its profound recognition that the great need of the people of God is the forgiveness of sins, and that expressed the assurance that God is merciful to forgive again and again, and for gross transgressions (vv. 22–54). There simply is no other way to explain the prayer than that the Spirit of God raised it out of the Old Testament hope of the incarnation and death of the Son of God in human flesh. On this momentous occasion, Solomon and the true Israel of God knew the mystery of the cross. They knew their own sin and sinfulness. They knew also their deliverance by the grace of God in Jesus the Christ.

The king praised the Lord as a covenant-keeping God. He besought God's faithfulness to the Davidic promise, that is, the promise to give the Messiah. He raised a sevenfold petition for the mercy of the forgiveness of sins, a mercy to be sought in and by means of the temple and its services. Again and again the urgent but confident petition is: "Then hear thou in heaven, and forgive the sin of thy people" (1 Kings 8:34).

Solomon raised this prayer kneeling on a platform before the altar of burnt offering in the outer court with hands outstretched toward heaven in the presence of the congregation (2 Chron. 6:12–13). The king of the kingdom of God, unlike all secular rulers, is no arrogant semi-deity, demanding the worship of himself by the citizens, but publicly a humble servant and suppliant of the true lord of the kingdom, Jehovah God.

Rising from his knees, Solomon blessed the people (1 Kings 8:54–61). He thanked God for faithfully keeping the promise he had made to Israel by Moses (thus making known that the Mosaic, or Sinaitic, covenant is one with the Abrahamic and Davidic—the one covenant of grace); he besought God's continuing presence; he asked for holiness on the part of the people; and he gave as the purpose of all the prayer the glory of God: "that all the people of the earth may know that the LORD is God, and that there is none else."

Fire from heaven consuming the burnt offerings and sacrifices was God's answer to the prayer of Solomon (2 Chron. 7:1).

It is noteworthy that the one officiating at this service of the dedication of the temple was the king of the kingdom of God. The messianic king, who governs the kingdom of God, represents the kingdom and its citizens before God in the covenant and dedicates the kingdom and its citizens to God. Again, the close relation of crown and covenant appears. In this connection, scripture calls attention to the close proximity of the palace of Solomon to the temple (2 Chron. 9:4). This layout of the two buildings was itself a reminder to the kings of Israel that their office was service of the nation on behalf of the worship of Jehovah and a means of the communion of the covenantal people with him.

After Solomon had finished the building of both the temple and the palace, Jehovah appeared to the king a second time in a special revelation of himself (1 Kings 9:1–9). He assured the king that he had put his name in the temple and that his eyes and heart would remain in the temple "perpetually." In view of the facts that God promised a perpetual dwelling in the temple and that both the temple of Solomon and the second temple of Herod were destroyed, the explanation of this promise is that it referred to the reality of the temple, namely God's covenantal dwelling with the people whom he has chosen in Christ Jesus (see 1 Pet. 2:1–10; Gal. 3:13–29). Only this understanding of the promise that God would dwell in the temple perpetually can be harmonized with the warning that if Solomon or his children turned from following after God, God would devastate Solomon's temple and cut off Israel out of the land. This warning was realized upon the material temple and upon earthly Israel.

The warning specified the forsaking of God by going after other gods and worshiping them (1 Kings 9:9). This warning, concerning the grossest, most heinous, and grievously unthankful wickedness, Solomon disobeyed, bringing upon himself, the nation, and the temple the judgments that God had threatened.

The covenant of grace includes both an unconditional promise of grace (which is repetition, since grace *means* unconditional) and a solemn warning regarding disobedience. The unconditional promise does not rule out the warning, and the warning does not compromise the unconditional promise. This is a truth with which the church of the New Testament struggles to this very day, supposing that doing justice to the warning implies a conditional covenantal promise and that confession of the unconditional promise rules out or weakens the warning. The unconditional promise realizes itself in the elect in Jesus Christ by means of the warning. And the judgment of damnation threatened by the warning is fulfilled. Regarding the elect, the judgment was fulfilled upon the crucified Jesus Christ in their stead. Regarding the reprobate in the sphere of the covenant and kingdom, those who are *of* Israel but are not Israel (Rom. 9:6), the judgment of damnation falls upon them themselves.

Chapter Twenty

─────

Covenantal Infidelity and Kingly Insubordination

(1 Kings 11:1–40)

W hen he was old, Solomon forsook Jehovah for idols. He did not completely abandon the worship of God but began worshiping other gods with God. He frequented both the temple that he had built for Jehovah and the temples that his pagan women had built to the gods. His sin was religious syncretism. Solomon did this despite God's having appeared to him twice and despite God's abundant goodness to him.

This apostasy of old Solomon is astounding and frightening. Old age and longevity of office are not themselves guarantee of covenantal faithfulness on the part of erstwhile sound theologians, ministers, and elders in the church. Inasmuch as to some extent the nation followed the lead of its king, this history is warning to a church that has been faithful in the past that it may not assure itself of present and future faithfulness simply on the basis of past history. Such self-assurance is not trust but presumption.

The occasion of his appalling wickedness was Solomon's love of many heathen women. He amassed seven hundred wives and three hundred concubines. He transgressed his own sharp warnings in the book of Proverbs against the "strange woman" and his warm encomium of the marriage of one man and one woman in the Song of Songs.

The occasion of this sin was not simply lust. Sexual lust can by no means be ruled out. Scripture states that Solomon "*loved* many strange women" and that "he clave unto these *in love*" (1 Kings 11:1–2, emphasis added). But even the most vigorous sexual lust hardly requires one thousand women for its satisfaction. Solomon was intent on fashioning his kingship according to the practices of the heathen nations about Israel. The heads of the nations formed alliances by means of marriages with the princesses of the surrounding kingdoms and advertised their powers by means of an impressive harem. In Solomon's case, this began with his marriage to the heathen daughter of the Pharaoh of Egypt: "Solomon made affinity with Pharaoh king of Egypt, and took Pharaoh's daughter, and brought her into the city of David" (3:1).

Solomon's sin was not so much sexual lust as conformity to the world of the ungodly nations about Israel. He refused to live what Reformed theology calls the antithesis, that is, the separation of the church from the world of the ungodly. Solomon disregarded the implicit warning of Deuteronomy 33:28: "Israel then shall dwell in safety alone."

The result of the king's marital and semi-marital alliances with many heathen women was his own idolatry and most certainly the idolatry of many in Israel, who followed the lead of their king. Solomon built altars for his heathen wives and himself worshiped their idols—Ashtoreth, Milcom, Chemosh, and Molech. When Solomon was old, "his wives turned away his heart after other gods: and his heart was not perfect with the LORD his God, as was the heart of David his father" (1 Kings 11:4). This was the man who built the temple! This was the man to whom God appeared twice in special revelations of himself! This was the king of the kingdom of God in the world! If ever there were a warning against the seductive power of the wicked world and its idolatry upon a child of God, no matter how privileged, and upon the church, no matter how distinguished, the history of Solomon in his old age is this warning. The admonition of Deuteronomy 33:28 ("Israel then shall dwell in safety alone") cannot be given too strongly or too often to the citizens of the kingdom of Christ.

No doctrine that compromises the antithesis, for example the theory of a common grace of God, may be tolerated in the church.

This history of the world conformity of Solomon and of Israel under Solomon's influence is a warning particularly against the theory and subsequent practice in Reformed, evangelical, and conservative churches of a common grace of God. This is supposed to be both a favor of God upon the world of ungodly and idolatrous people and a divine power for good within them that enables them to perform truly good works, especially in the creation of a good culture. Because of this (imaginary) grace of God at work among the ungodly, the church is exhorted to form alliances with the wicked world, especially in order to create a good and godly culture, or way of life, apart from the wisdom that is Jesus Christ.

The effect of this theory with its practice is that the world of the ungodly influences, corrupts, and eventually destroys the churches that embrace the theory. The antithesis is a fundamental aspect of God's salvation of the church and of his people individually. Common-grace alliances of the church with the world never influence the world for good but always influence the church for evil. "Israel shall dwell in safety alone." The calling of the church and her members is expressed in the admonition of 2 Corinthians 6:17: "Come out from among them, and be ye separate, saith the Lord, and touch not the unclean thing; and I will receive you."[1]

The expense of maintaining Solomon's harem and their worship of their gods must have been enormous. Payment came out of the treasury of the nation and ultimately out of the pockets of the Israelites. No doubt, this aggravated the resentment of the ten tribes and contributed to the future schism in the kingdom of Israel.

A similar instance of Solomon's conformity to the world about Israel was his introduction into Israel, particularly its military, of horses and chariots. "Solomon had four thousand stalls for horses and chariots, and

---

1 For a description and refutation of the theory in Reformed churches of a common grace of God, see Herman Hoeksema, *The Protestant Reformed Churches in America*, 2nd ed. (Grand Rapids, MI: Protestant Reformed Churches in America, 1947), 293–410; and David J. Engelsma, *Common Grace Revisited: A Response to Richard J. Mouw's* He Shines in All That's Fair (Grandville, MI: Reformed Free Publishing Association, 2003).

twelve thousand horsemen; whom he bestowed in the chariot cities, and with the king in Jerusalem" (2 Chron. 9:25). These warhorses came "out of Egypt and out of all lands" (v. 28). The prohibition of horses, like the forbidding of many wives to the king of Israel, was an explicit rule of the great constitution of kingship in Israel in Deuteronomy 17:14–20: "He shall not multiply horses to himself, nor cause the people to return to Egypt, to the end that he should multiply horses" (v. 16). The creation of a cavalry of horses would be an aspect of the fundamental evil of world conformity: "like as all the nations that are about me" (v. 14). It would also betray trust in earthly might in the warfare of the kingdom of God, rather than trust in the God of the kingdom. "Some trust in chariots, and some in horses: but we will remember the name of the LORD our God" (Ps. 20:7).

The judgment of God upon Solomon is severe (1 Kings 11:9–40). In his anger on account of Solomon's idolatry, especially in view of God's having appeared twice to Solomon, God rends the kingdom from Solomon and gives it to one Jeroboam of the tribe of Ephraim. Still, in faithfulness to his promise to David, God preserves one tribe, the tribe of Judah, for the descendants of Solomon. The judgment therefore is the division of the kingdom.

In keeping with the warning of 1 Kings 9:1–9, the judgment upon Solomon's unfaithfulness is also that, although the successors to the throne of Judah are for a while the descendants of Solomon, the Messiah himself will not be the descendant of David's son Solomon but the descendant of another son of David, namely Nathan, a son of David by Bathsheba (1 Chron. 3:5). Zechariah 12:12 makes known that the family of Nathan survived the Babylonian captivity. That the royal line from Solomon runs dead in the history of the Old Testament is the word of God concerning King Coniah, or Jeconiah, the link in the chain of the royal line: "Write ye this man childless…for no man of his seed shall prosper, sitting upon the throne of David, and ruling any more in Judah" (Jer. 22:30).

Understanding Jesus to have descended from Nathan explains the difference between the two genealogies concerning Jesus in Matthew 1 and in Luke 3. The genealogy in Matthew 1 is that of Joseph (as the text plainly, indeed incontrovertibly, states), who although in the royal line descending from Solomon, was not the biological father of Jesus. Matthew 1 makes plain that the royal line did not produce Mary's son. The genealogy in Luke 3 is that of Jesus through Mary, whose father was Heli. Luke 3:31 mentions Nathan.[2]

In addition, the judgment upon the idolatry of Solomon will be that God will cut off Israel from the land and will destroy the magnificent material temple that has just been built. Israel will become a "proverb and a byword among all people" (1 Kings 9:7–9). This judgment is more than the prophecy of the Babylonian captivity and of the destruction of the temple at that time. It is the prophecy of the end of the earthly nation of Israel as the kingdom of God and of the formation of the believing church, from David's son Jesus, as the kingdom. Jesus explained Solomon's warning as the prophecy of the cutting off of national Israel when he condemned Jerusalem: "Your house is left unto you desolate" (Matt. 23:38). God's judgment is the declaration also that the earthly temple of Solomon gives way to the building of the spiritual house of the church by the Spirit of the crucified and risen Messiah, of whom the temple-building Solomon was merely the type.

The immediate judgment upon Solomon is the disturbance of his kingdom and kingship of peace by strife, both external and internal. God raises up enemies of Solomon from without, namely Edom and Zobah (1 Kings 11:14–25). What seems to be the natural warmongering among rival nations is in reality God's doing: "The LORD stirred up an adversary unto Solomon, Hadad the Edomite" (v. 14). "God stirred him up another adversary, Rezon" (v. 23).

The internal strife is the schism of the revolution of the ten tribes, led by Ephraim, which has always been jealous of Judah, under the headship of Jeroboam, who is of the tribe of Ephraim. The actual schism does not

---

2   For the full explanation and defense of Jesus' descent from David through Nathan rather than through Solomon, as is commonly supposed, see Engelsma, "The Genealogy of Jesus according to the Flesh," 5–16. Among the issues upon which this understanding of the genealogy of Jesus sheds light, it does justice to the severe judgment of God upon Solomon for his idolatry.

occur during the reign of Solomon. It takes place during the reign of Solomon's son Rehoboam. But it has its beginning during Solomon's reign. This judgment also is determined by God. God sends the prophet Ahijah to Jeroboam to tell the rebel that God will "rend the kingdom out of the hand of Solomon," even as the prophet rips the garment that Jeroboam was wearing into twelve pieces, and will give ten tribes to Jeroboam, even as the prophet gives ten pieces of the garment to Jeroboam (1 Kings 11:26–40).

Although both by the prophecy of Ahijah and in the event, Jeroboam does not become king over the ten tribes until the death of Solomon, yet Jeroboam had been agitating for the rebellion of the ten tribes already before the prophet appeared to him. Ahijah recognized the revolutionary aspirations and activities of Jeroboam: "Thou shalt reign according to all that thy soul desireth" (1 Kings 11:37).

Unlike his father David, Solomon did not die in peace, but with his kingdom under attack and coming apart.

In his judgment, Jehovah God remembered mercy. As he emphasized both in his word to Solomon and in his word to Jeroboam, he would reserve one tribe of Israel, the tribe of Judah, for the seed of David. "Howbeit I will not rend away all the kingdom; but will give one tribe to thy [Solomon's] son for David my servant's sake, and for Jerusalem's sake which I have chosen" (1 Kings 11:13). "He [Solomon] shall have one tribe for my servant David's sake, and for Jerusalem's sake, the city which I have chosen out of all the tribes of Israel" (v. 32). From the tribe of Judah and out of the family of King David will come the one who is the Prince of Peace, realizing the reconciliation of the elect citizens of the heavenly Jerusalem to God.

The type of the kingdom of God of peace and prosperity fails, almost at once. Israel's "golden age" was short-lived, fewer than forty years, the length of the reign of Solomon. But Jehovah is faithful in the covenant. As this epoch of the history of the covenant and kingdom of God seemingly ends in the utter failure of the apostasy of the king and the schism in the kingdom, God proclaims his keeping of his unconditional promise to David—a keeping that maintains the covenant and preserves the kingdom unto the coming of the true seed of David, who will realize the covenant and perfect the kingdom of God. Everything depends upon the promise. The grievous failure of the typical "Shalom" will not prevent the coming of the real "Shalom": "David my servant [will] have a light always before me in Jerusalem" (1 Kings 11:36). This will be the peace of reconciliation with God by faith in Jesus Christ through the gospel of grace on the part of Jew and Gentile. The victory of the covenant and kingdom is the gracious and sure promise of the covenant-keeping God.

In this peace with God, the citizens of the kingdom of Messiah are glorious. Although in this life they must battle—*victoriously*—against sin and Satan and therefore are already glorious, eternally they will reign with Christ over all creatures.

To the one who cast the shadows that were Israel's greatest kings, David and Solomon, the true Israelite looked forward in hope. His hope was not shattered by the weakness and failure of the earthly types, namely David and Solomon—David's adultery and murder and Solomon's idolatry. Rather, the failure of the types served to concentrate the hope upon the coming reality and to enliven the hope. The merely earthly, no matter how gifted and glorious, could not sustain and fulfill the grand hope. The Israel of God must look further and higher. To David's greater Son and to the greater than Solomon! They did. And by this hope, they were saved.

Appendix

The Song of the Bow

(2 Samuel 1:17–27)

17. And David lamented with this lamentation over Saul and over Jonathan his son:
18. Also he bade them teach the children of Judah the use of the bow: behold, it is written in the book of Jasher.)
19. The beauty of Israel is slain upon thy high places: how are the mighty fallen!
20. Tell it not in Gath, publish it not in the streets of Askelon; lest the daughters of the Philistines rejoice, lest the daughters of the uncircumcised triumph.
21. Ye mountains of Gilboa, let there be no dew, neither let there be rain, upon you, nor fields of offerings: for there the shield of the mighty is vilely cast away, the shield of Saul, as though he had not been anointed with oil.
22. From the blood of the slain, from the fat of the mighty, the bow of Jonathan turned not back, and the sword of Saul returned not empty.
23. Saul and Jonathan were lovely and pleasant in their lives, and in their death they were not divided: they were swifter than eagles, they were stronger than lions.
24. Ye daughters of Israel, weep over Saul, who clothed you in scarlet, with other delights, who put on ornaments of gold upon your apparel.

25. How are the mighty fallen in the midst of the battle! O Jonathan, thou wast slain in thine high places.

26. I am distressed for thee, my brother Jonathan: very pleasant hast thou been unto me: thy love to me was wonderful, passing the love of women.

27. How are the mighty fallen, and the weapons of war perished!

INTRODUCTION

"To every thing there is a season, and a time to every purpose under the heaven: A time to weep, and a time to laugh" (Eccl. 3:1, 4).

The time of the song recorded in 2 Samuel 1 was a time of weeping for David: "David lamented with this lamentation over Saul and over Jonathan" (v. 17). The passage is a song. Poetic, musical David responded to a sad event with a song. But it is a song of sorrow, a funeral dirge, what in literature is called an elegy. It is a song of mourning for the dead.

The occasion of the elegy was a time of weeping also for the nation of Israel. Therefore, David "bade them teach the children of Judah" the song (v. 18). Implied is that there is also a time of weeping for us, the church, a time to sing a song of sorrow.

The background of the composition and singing of the elegy is quickly told. The passage itself tells us that David lamented over Saul and Jonathan. The opening lines are: "The beauty [or glory] of Israel is slain upon thy high places: how are the mighty fallen!" (v. 19). The Philistines, inveterate and fierce foes of Israel, made war again on Israel. Israel is defeated. In the battle, Saul, the king of Israel, and three of his sons, including Jonathan, the crown prince, are killed (see 1 Sam. 31).

News of this calamity is brought to David and his men. The effect of the news is what we read in 2 Samuel 1:11–12 and the song recorded in verses 17–27.

David named his song "The Bow," according to verse 18. The AV is incorrect in its insertion of the words "the use of." The literal translation of the Hebrew original is correct, simply "The Bow." David "bade them teach the children of Judah 'The Bow.'" Later, this "Song of the Bow" was included in a certain book called the "book of Jasher." This book was well-known in Israel at the time. Apparently the book was a collection of songs that had to do with Israel's battles. It is not included in the Bible, except of course for the "Song of the Bow."

The reason for the name of the song is that the bow is mentioned in verse 22: "The bow of Jonathan turned not back." By implication, the bow is mentioned again in verse 27: "The weapons of war perished!" The entire song concerns war. It is a martial song.

One of the main weapons of war at the time was the bow with its arrows. Especially was the bow a weapon of war in the tribe of Benjamin, to which tribe Saul and Jonathan belonged. The men of Benjamin were renowned for their fighting spirit and for their prowess with the bow.

Outstanding scholars of the Old Testament regard the song as "one of the finest odes in the Old Testament."[1] The importance of the elegy for the church is the light it sheds on the defeat of Israel that occasioned the song; on David, for whom the way to the throne of Israel is opened by the death of Saul; and on the response of the New Testament believer to circumstances of the church that are similar to those that occasioned the "Song of the Bow."

THE IDEA

As the title itself points out, the song concerns the warfare of the people of God in the world. It is not merely a song of David's personal grief. That this is not the case is evident from the fact that David commands that the song be taught to the nation: "the children of Judah" (v. 18). In addition, the subject is obviously the sorrow of the whole nation: "The beauty of Israel is slain" (v. 19). The "daughters of Israel" are to weep over Saul (v. 24).

Israel has been engaged in war. The kingdom of Israel has enemies, in this case the Philistines. Two of the main Philistine cities are mentioned: Gath and Askelon. Israel is equipped for fighting with weapons of war, especially the bow, although the song mentions also the sword and the shield. Even in the Old Testament, the war of the people of God was

---

1 Edersheim, *Old Testament Bible*, 4:151.

not earthly, carnal warfare. Essentially, it was spiritual. It was warfare on behalf of Jehovah God. It was warfare for the covenant, for the truth of the gospel, for holiness of life. The Philistines were the "uncircumcised" (v. 20). They were a people outside the covenant. They were enemies of the covenant, of the covenantal people of God, and of the God of the covenant. They were haters of God and therefore haters of his people.

When in the battle Israel defended itself, it did so not merely in self-defense, but chiefly in defense of God's name. The warfare was covenantal warfare. It was the warfare of the circumcised against the uncircumcised. It was the warfare of the kingdom of God against the kingdom of the devil.

Only thus can the praise of the military heroics of Saul and Jonathan be understood. "They were swifter than eagles, they were stronger than lions" (v. 23). The bow of Jonathan drank the blood of many Philistines, and the sword of Saul ate the flesh of many Philistines in the days before the two fell in battle (v. 22). This does not describe a gruesome, bloodthirsty, and evil characteristic of the Old Testament, as unbelieving theological modernism holds. But it was the proper, praiseworthy destruction of the enemies of Jehovah in defense of his kingdom of truth and righteousness. Similar is the reference to the spoils of the victories of Saul and Jonathan in verse 24. The defeats of the foes enrich Israel. The beautiful clothing and ornaments represent the triumph of the people of God.

The church of the New Testament must learn this song. Today too, the church is at war, and the war is essentially the same as it was in the Old Testament time of Saul and Jonathan. It is battle for Jehovah, his covenant, and his truth. This truth about warfare is foreign to the thinking of many who confess to be Christians today. This is why the "Song of the Bow" is strange to them. They are ignorant of the truth that the church of God is surrounded and attacked by Philistines. They have not the foggiest notion that the ungodly world hates the church because the world is idolatrous and God is in the church in Jesus Christ, his Messiah. They repudiate the calling of the church to engage in warfare against the wicked world, asking no quarter and giving none. That the church has a weapon with which to fight, and that this weapon is the bow of the word of God, seems to them un-Christian. They are at peace with the world. The world has "philistinized" them.

The true church is a militant church. In their warfare, there are times when the people of God are defeated. They are not defeated decisively and finally. Never! Nor is it ever the case that the reason for the defeat is the powerlessness of God, although the enemies do make the boast that their gods have triumphed over the God of Israel.

After the defeat lamented in the passage, Israel comes back to power under King David and conquers the Philistines. The reason for the defeat of Israel at the time was that God chastised Israel on account of the wickedness of her king, Saul, and that God willed to punish the wicked king. God's judgment upon Israel by means of the heathen was his chastisement of his people. But exactly in the way of Israel's defeat, God was raising David to the throne, so that Israel could be a mighty people, as she could never be under Saul. Therefore, Israel's temporary defeat was in reality the means to a great victory.

Nevertheless, the victory of the Philistines mourned by David was a defeat for Israel, a temporary triumph of the enemy, and therefore a reason for a song of sorrow by David and by Israel. Israel's army is scattered. Israel's king and princes are slain. The weapons of war, particularly the bow, are perished. The result is that Israel's beauty, or glory, is brought low. And this glory is no mere carnal glory. It is the glory of the kingdom of God in the world. God's name is exposed to dishonor and ridicule. Israel lies helpless before the invading hordes of the enemy. The kingdom of God goes under.

It is a time to weep: "How are the mighty fallen in the midst of the battle!" (v. 25).

The "Song of the Bow" is appropriate at times also for the church of the New Testament. We sing it as we read the book of Galatians. We sing it as we read the church history of the Middle Ages, when the church departed from the pure gospel of grace and adopted the lie of a gospel of works, accompanied as it always is by immorality of life. We sing it as we witness today the apostasy of Protestantism from the glory of the Reformation. We sing the "Song of the Bow" as we see "the shield of the mighty...vilely cast away" by Reformed churches in their departure from the truth of the Reformed and Presbyterian creeds. We sing the song *fortissimo* when we see our own congregations "fallen in the midst of the battle" and our own ministers or elders "slain in thine high places," whether by false doctrine or by immorality of life. Not all our songs are songs of victory and joy. There are also lamentations—songs of the broken and perished bow!

How are the mighty fallen today! How are those who once, historically, stood straight and strong slain on the high places! How does the world laugh at those who deny the fundamentals of the faith and walk now as vilely as the world ever did! How do the Philistines invade Israel! How is the name of Jehovah God reproached on account of the falling in battle of the churches and their officebearers!

We must weep! Do we weep? Can we weep? That is, do we love God's name and covenant? Are we zealous on behalf of the kingdom of God in the Messiah?

A LAMENT OVER THE FALLING OF ISRAEL'S MIGHTY AND THE SLAYING OF ISRAEL'S BEAUTY (GLORY)

The first part of the "Song of the Bow," from verse 19 through verse 24, is a lament over the falling of Israel's mighty and slaying of Israel's beauty. It is the outpouring of grief over the death of Saul and Jonathan, as the God-appointed king over God's people and his son the prince. These were the official representatives of the kingdom of God. Saul's personal wickedness does not come into view here. The personal wickedness of Saul does not nullify his official position. He was the "LORD's anointed" (v. 16). He was the beauty, or glory, of Israel in his official capacity. He was the representative of the kingdom of God as king. Upon him depended the welfare of the kingdom.

Once, Saul functioned properly in his office, at least to outward appearance. He was "mighty." This was when he first became king. David remembers this in verses 22–23: Saul was swift and strong to defend Israel against Ammon, against Amalek, and against the Philistines. This is not a confession of any spiritual good on the part of King Saul. In all his kingly exploits, Saul was not motivated by reverence and love for God, as he clearly demonstrated later in his kingship. The Spirit of God by which he was empowered at the beginning of his reign was not the Spirit of regeneration and salvation, as Saul's life—*and death*—clearly showed. He was rather the Spirit of empowerment in the kingdom of God. He made Saul courageous and strong in his office.

Always Saul functioned in his office on behalf of Israel in close association with his oldest son, Jonathan. This is the meaning of verse 23: "lovely and pleasant in their lives." The meaning is not that Saul personally was lovely and pleasant, as, in fact, Jonathan was. But the two of them, father and son, loved each other, were friends by the natural relation of father and son, and fought and died together. The history of 1 Samuel bears out this testimony to the close relation of the two, especially in war, although Saul spoiled even this natural relationship by his wickedness.

Because of the positions of Saul and Jonathan in the kingdom of God, David utters an anguished curse upon the mountains of Gilboa, the site of the deaths of Israel's mighty ones. So genuine, so deep is David's sorrow! It is as if these mountains share the responsibility of the slaying of Israel's glory. They are tinged with the guilt of that dreadful reality. On their slopes the shield of the king of Israel was thrown away in the ignominious flight of the stricken monarch. On them the kingdom of the uncircumcised put to shame the kingdom of God. Therefore, the heat of the wrath of God must burn up the fields of these slopes. There may be no dew and no rain. No crops may grow on them, to be offered as a sacrifice to God.

Most urgent is that the news of the death of Saul and Jonathan must be kept from the Philistines: "Tell it not in Gath, publish it not in the streets of Askelon" (v. 20). Of course, the Philistines knew. First Samuel 31 records that they did exactly what David feared. They rejoiced over the defeat of the kingdom of God and took action to shame the God of the kingdom. But the song expresses David's desire and fear: "Tell it not…lest the daughters of the Philistines rejoice, lest the daughters of the uncircumcised triumph" (v. 20).

The major cities of the Philistines must not hear. If they hear, they will rejoice and exult. It was the role especially of the women to celebrate the victories of the nations. In their exultation, the heathen will exult over the people of God, the church. The wicked will magnify their idols at the expense of Jehovah, God of Israel. In his song of weeping, David cries out, "Keep the shame of the church from the world, that they not dishonor our God."

What catches and holds our attention is that David laments over and speaks well of Saul, his longtime, hateful, and determined enemy. Saul had persecuted David for years with a cruel, murderous persecution. Saul had caused David great misery. Besides, Saul was a reprobate, evil man, as his end proved. God punished Saul in such a way that Saul took his own life.

Yet not a word of evil does David speak of his adversary. On the contrary, David speaks well of him. He teaches all Israel, and in fact the church of all ages, a song that speaks only good of Saul. David cries over Saul's death with a heartfelt, genuine sorrow: "How are the mighty fallen!" (v. 19). There is no glee that his enemy fell. There is no gladness that the way is now open to the throne of Israel. There is no note of personal revenge in the song.

The explanation is that David puts the kingdom of God first. His own person and his own interests are strictly subordinated to the kingdom. This is what we must learn from the "Song of the Bow." We are tempted to behave differently than David did. We are tempted to take delight in the fall and shame of an enemy. We are tempted to spread the dirty linen of the church before all the world. We are tempted to seize the occasion to revile a fallen foe.

Such must be our love for the kingdom of God, such must be our zeal for the honor of God in the fortunes of his kingdom in the world, that we utterly suppress ourselves and regard events only from the viewpoint of how this affects the kingdom of God and the honor of its king, Jesus the Christ.

Regarding the defection or immorality of a minister or elder, "Tell it not in Gath."

Regarding the shameful advance in apostasy of churches that have injured us, there may be no spreading of the news of the evil in retaliation or self-vindication: "Publish it not in the streets of Askelon."

To us, the kingdom of God is all.

LAMENT OVER THE DEATH OF A FRIEND

A touching verse in David's song of sorrow is David's personal grief over the death of Jonathan. Although David did good to Saul, Saul was no friend. With Jonathan, it was different. This stanza of the "Song of the Bow" consists of verses 25 and 26: "O Jonathan, thou wast slain in thine high places. I am distressed for thee, my brother Jonathan: very pleasant hast thou been unto me: thy love to me was wonderful, passing the love of women."

Such was the close friendship of David and Jonathan that it is the outstanding instance and example of the friendship of humans in all scripture. Theirs was a wonderful love. They loved each other as they loved themselves, indeed more strongly and deeply than they loved themselves. They were one in the bond of the covenant of grace, which binds us not only to God, but also to each other. Their souls were knit. In their love, they were willing to deny self and lose all for the sake of the other. This was true especially of Jonathan, because the will of God was that he yield—yield *much*—to David. Jonathan willingly gave up the crown, the kingship of Israel. He risked the wrath of his father, and even his life, for David.

The love of David and Jonathan surpassed the love of man and woman, including the love of husband and wife, otherwise the strongest love and the most intimate relationship. Their love was rooted in their love of God and nourished by it. It was the outworking of the power of the covenant. It was in them both an especially rich expression of the love of Jesus Christ among his people. It was intensely spiritual. In this respect, on the part of two men it passed the "love of women" (v. 26), considering the love of women as only physical and emotional, powerful and intimate as the love of women is for men.

The explanation of their "wonderful" love is the zeal they shared on behalf of the kingdom of God in Jesus Christ.

Therefore, the death of Jonathan is intense grief to David: "I am distressed for thee, my brother Jonathan" (v. 26). The love of David for his friend and spiritual brother is genuine and deep. There is not a hint of any gratification that with the death of Jonathan is removed the last barrier threatening his accession to the throne of Israel. The death of his friend is loss, and loss only.

Also in this (prominent) aspect of the song there is instruction in the "Song of the Bow" for New Testament Judah, the church. All of the song must be taught to the children of Judah (v. 18). There is place in the church for especially close friendships, the close, holy (spiritual) friendship of a man with a man and of a woman with a woman. Blessed are the men and the women whom the Spirit of Christ graces with such a friendship. And blessed is the church in which such friendships flourish, for in it is zeal on behalf of the kingdom of God.

But oh, the sorrow at the dissolving of these friendships by death!

And how great the sorrow over the defeats of the kingdom in the history of the church militant!

"To every thing there is a season, and a time to every purpose under heaven...a time to weep..."

A time to sing the "Song of the Bow"!